Cultural value in twenty-first-century England

Manchester University Press

Cultural value in twenty-first-century England

The case of Shakespeare

Kate McLuskie and Kate Rumbold

Manchester University Press

Copyright © Kate McLuskie and Kate Rumbold 2014

The right of Kate McLuskie and Kate Rumbold to be identified as the authors of this work has been asserted by them in accordance with the Copyright, Designs and Patents Act 1988.

Published by Manchester University Press
Altrincham Street, Manchester M1 7JA, UK
www.manchesteruniversitypress.co.uk

British Library Cataloguing-in-Publication Data
A catalogue record for this book is available from the British Library

ISBN 978 15261 1690 1 paperback

First published by Manshester University Press in hardback 2014

This edition first published 2017

The publisher has no responsibility for the persistence or accuracy of URLs for any external or third-party internet websites referred to in this book, and does not guarantee that any content on such websites is, or will remain, accurate or appropriate.

Typeset in 10/12pt Sabon by
Servis Filmsetting Ltd, Stockport, Cheshire
Printed in Great Britain by
TJ International Ltd, Padstow

Contents

Acknowledgements	vii
Introduction: culture, value, Shakespeare	1
1 Advocacy and analysis	9
2 The value of value	29
3 Value and Shakespeare	51
4 Value and culture	83
5 Making 'Shakespeare' culture	116
6 Government and the values of culture	144
7 Value in Shakespeare institutions	183
8 Branding Shakespeare	210
Afterword: The continuity of cultural value	241
Bibliography	251
Index	263

Acknowledgements

We are grateful for the support of the Arts and Humanities Research Council, and for the opportunity it afforded us to discover, with doctoral researchers Dr Emily Linnemann and Dr Sarah Olive, that four heads really are better than one. The day-to-day running of the 'Interrogating Cultural Value' project was adeptly supported by Kate Lockhart and, more recently, Natalie Bell; and its development was encouraged by the stimulating company of colleagues and students at the Shakespeare Institute and in the Department of English, University of Birmingham. We are grateful for the generous guidance of a project advisory board that included Paul Yachnin (McGill University), Catherine Bunting (Arts Council England), Diana Owen (Shakespeare Birthplace Trust), Vikki Heywood (Royal Shakespeare Company), John Carman (University of Birmingham) and John Jowett (Shakespeare Institute, University of Birmingham). Mary Butlin and Roger Mortlock from the Royal Shakespeare Company's marketing department have been especially generous in helping us and our PhD students understand the aims and practice of audience development in the company.

We have also been very grateful for opportunities to share and test our ideas with both Shakespeare scholars and cultural policymakers and practitioners. Our warm thanks go to Sharon O'Dair, Robert Hewison, Katherine Rowe, Douglas Lanier and Ronan McDonald, and all the participants in the 'Shakespeare and Cultural Value' seminar at the 2009 annual meeting of the Shakespeare Association of America conference in Washington D.C. as well as to delegates at the 2008 British Shakespeare Association conference, participants in the 2009 London Shakespeare Seminar and the audiences and participants at seminars hosted by Arts Council England, the British Academy and the Institute for English Studies.

We are grateful for permission to include work that has appeared in earlier versions in *Shakespeare Quarterly*, *Shakespeare Survey* and *Cultural Trends*. Dave O'Brien and Roberta Pearson have offered timely and insightful advice on earlier drafts; and it has been a pleasure to collaborate with the whole team at Manchester University Press. Above all, we are grateful to our families and friends for their support and encouragement throughout.

Introduction

Culture, value, Shakespeare

This is a book about 'value', 'culture' and 'Shakespeare'. Each term has been the subject of extended intellectual discussion, as well as being used quite casually in everyday life: so attempts to define any of them at the start are certain to be controversial. We have been intrigued to find that when we combined the words, to create the title for the book, our initial choice, 'The Cultural Value of Shakespeare' resolved rather too easily the ambiguities inherent in the individual concepts. Turning the term 'culture' into the adjective 'cultural' had the effect of limiting the scope of the noun 'value', quarantining it from contamination by other forms of value: the economic, the ethical, even the aesthetic. The adjectival form of 'culture' and its connection to value also limited its potential scope from the full range of human practices all over the world that might or might not be valued or canonical collections of texts and objects whose value was equally a matter for argument. But adding 'of Shakespeare' almost closed the discussion down completely: surely the cultural value of Shakespeare was merely axiomatic in twenty-first-century England? Unless, that is, one alters the meaning of 'culture' and 'value'. Each of the terms limits the instability of both the others, and holds them in a dynamic connection so that together they can refer to a phenomenon that might be investigated.

The purpose of our work, however, had been to explore rather than to confirm the Cultural Value of Shakespeare. We had been puzzled by the way that 'Shakespeare' continues, in the new millennium, to represent a marker of high cultural value in spite of the powerful anti-bardolatrous thrust of academic literary criticism in the late twentieth century. That work had questioned the value assigned to Shakespeare, making clear the historical conditions that had occasioned it and the interests that it had served.[1]

However describing the changing historical circumstances in which Shakespeare had been sustained over four hundred years could equally be cited as evidence of transcendent value and in the public discourse of publishing and reviewing and education, the claims for Shakespeare's value persisted. The celebrated 'Shakespeare' no longer referred only to the collection of texts written by an early modern playwright: the Shakespeare of the hip-hop performer Akala was getting as much attention as a new scholarly biography and the Royal Shakespeare Company was making its theatre spaces available to performances in a huge variety of styles including the iconoclastic inventiveness of the Kneehigh company and the international production of *A Midsummer's Night's Dream* in multiple Indian languages. Academic analysis since the 1990s had addressed 'popular Shakespeare' or 'Shakespeare without his language' as critiques or challenges to the idea of uniquely valued 'Shakespeare': now all of those varied forms that constituted Shakespeare's value co-existed quite comfortably within mainstream cultural organisations.

'Culture', too, we found, had expanded and diversified. Academic analyses in cultural studies of the second half of the twentieth century had addressed the complex intellectual history of the term and had made a powerful case to extend the term 'culture' (with its implications of value attached) to the tastes, practices and creativity of groups marginalised by ethnicity and class.[2] Yet in public discourse, that attention to the relations between culture and social power had disappeared. It has been replaced by a 'both/and' synthesis that includes 'the arts' as a category of leisure activity, as well as describing the practices of groups from commercial companies to whole nations. Depending on the context, the terms could designate the valued cohesion of a social group or the exclusivity and arrogance of the bankers who had, it was alleged, been responsible for the financial meltdown of 2008.[3]

The connection between culture and value caused more anxious analysis among the civil servants and politicians whose role was to oversee and establish policy for funding the arts. Though their primary task was to distribute money, their discussions repeatedly distinguished the 'cultural value' that they supported from the economic value of the resources at their disposal. In their discussions, as we will show in Chapters 1 and 6, 'cultural value' had to make the link between the forms of art that the funding agencies supported, their accountability to tax-payers for government expenditure and the larger political question of the state's responsibility for the well-being of its large and diverse population. In public, politicians could make that link work through their enthusiastic advocacy on behalf of culture, but we found that, behind the scenes, civil servants and social scientists were undertaking analytical work that exposed the very significant gap between commonplace ideas about the value of culture and the views and behaviour of the people that it was expected to serve. In the public discourse of newspapers and websites (that we have used very widely as our evidence) there seemed to be a consensus about the importance of culture and the value of Shakespeare within it but the nature of that value, the nature of the culture to which it referred, not to mention the nature of the 'Shakespeare' involved presented rather more intransigent social and intellectual questions.

The resulting controversies and debates in both public advocacy and academic enquiry have provided us with a rich resource for understanding the implications of recurring tensions between definitions of value, the role of culture in social life, the politics of demonstrable social benefit and the operational requirements of value for money. We will be arguing that value and culture require an analysis in their own terms. We need to address the different implications of formulating culture as both 'a way of life' and a canon of valued objects and of the tensions created by locating value both as inherent in valued objects and in the process by which that value is recognised, conferred or endorsed. By focussing on Shakespeare, we have been able to analyse the relationship between a particular object with a claim to cultural value, the agents and social processes that create that value, and its relationship to the larger questions about culture and value. In order to do so, we have had to place Shakespeare alongside a number of other forms and objects that compete for value in the twenty-first century.

At an early stage of his own investigation into culture, Raymond Williams wryly observed that 'When a particular history is completed, we can all be clear and relaxed about it'.[4] Writing in 1964, he was alerting his readers to the danger of that relaxed clarity: the way that it ignored or obscured the controversies and struggles that had informed the then 'completed' version of history. Conversely, we have tried to resist the backward pull of history, partly because narratives of change have been fully rehearsed elsewhere,[5] but also because rehearsing the history of an idea implies causation as well as narrative. We would find ourselves asking 'how did Shakespeare become such a valued part of world culture?', when what we want to know is 'what lies behind the commonplace assertion that Shakespeare is a valued part of world culture, how are these concepts being used and is their application to Shakespeare different from their application to other items included in "culture"?' By paying specific attention to the opening decade of the twenty-first century we will reflect on the way that history had informed the starting points of much contemporary discussion of cultural value, but we will also address the ways in which those starting points have been affected by the momentum of economic, institutional and technological change.

Our investigation will centre on England. Our decision to limit the investigation in this way does not stem from any sense of English exceptionalism or any disregard for the global implications of our enquiry. The limits of our discussion, rather, allow us to focus on the particular agencies and institutions that make and manage culture in a nation that regards itself as having a particular investment (in every sense) in Shakespeare. Questions about cultural value in England take a particular form because of the role of publicly funded organisations such as Arts Council England (ACE), and the institutions that it supports, in making and managing both culture and value. Their role in funding involves the potentially contradictory tasks of supporting and sustaining the heritage culture provided by established organisations and some newer ones, developing innovative management practice in arts organisations, and distributing the profits from the Heritage Lottery fund both to purchase heritage objects 'for the nation' and to allow artists to produce new work.

In order to keep the connection between cultural value and Shakespeare in view, we have begun the book with an account of the contemporary public consensus about cultural value and Shakespeare and the way that it is sustained by the rhetorics of advocacy as well as being challenged by more systematic analysis. In Chapter 2, we explore the implications of the often invoked distinctions between intrinsic and contingent value and the ways that they are played out through the idea of value in markets. In spite of the reiterated distinction between an absolute idea of value and contingent value in the market, we have found the distinct forms of value created in markets, and the distinctions they allow between producers and consumers, supply side and demand side, useful as a way of mapping the process of creating value in the transformation from raw materials into the complex products and services that circulate in the contemporary world. We have suggested that the market model reveals that value does not exist only in the inherent value of the product, or in the value conferred on it by the producer, but is significantly dependent on the value added by the processes of distribution that change the meaning and significance of the object in ways that make it acceptable, and, in conditions of oversupply, necessary to its consumers.

Chapter 3 deals with the discussion of value in Shakespeare's plays. We show how advocacy for Shakespeare's universal and transcendent value deal with the multiple forms of 'Shakespeare' in the present and the past by deploying the rhetorical techniques of narratives and extrapolation to insist on the connection between the historical Shakespeare and the 'Shakespeare' who is valued as 'our contemporary'. We will also show how the same techniques of narrative and poetic commentary structure the representation of values in the plays' dramatic form and create the potential for their emotional as well as intellectual endorsement. Shakespeare's plays, we suggest, have the potential to provide a tangible proxy for value that may (however temporarily) stabilise the contingency and uncertainty that attends the discussion of both value and culture in the twenty-first century. We go on to suggest that the devices that provide a proxy for value in the plays constitute them as a kind of 'raw material' whose relationship to the 'Shakespeare' that exists in modern times depends upon a value-chain of additional work on the part of identifiable agents and institutions that constitutes them as a form of 'non-rival' value, available to be deployed for a variety of different uses.

We turn to 'culture' in Chapter 4 to reopen the now commonplace distinction between its so-called anthropological and artistic meanings. We show how the discussions of culture involve both narratives of cultural change and ways of managing the knowledge in order to arrive at definitions of culture as valuable. Using specific examples of cultural contest, we explore the connection between the small scale, face-to-face experience of culture as a set of relationships and the larger discursive syntheses that grapple with attempts to frame cultural contests over value in contemporary discourses of politics and development. We then address the way that 'culture' is represented by cultural objects and content whose management and distribution have become a matter for political and organisational contest in twenty-first-century England. We use the idea of a 'value-chain' that we introduced in relation to the reproduction of Shakespeare to explore the process of linking the producers and consumers of cultural content and show how the supply side and the demand side ideas of cultural value have been influenced by what Mike Featherstone has described as 'the current over-supply of symbolic goods'[6] in twenty-first-century England.

Shakespeare appears again in Chapter 5, where we explore the intellectual, artistic, organisational and financial work that is deployed in order to assimilate Shakespeare into contemporary culture. We suggest that the different kinds of work undertaken significantly influence the value of the 'Shakespeare' that is produced by them. Since all these opportunities for work that add value to Shakespeare co-exist at the present time, their relationship to the value of Shakespeare can be assessed without recourse to the pre-emptive judgements implied in the contrast between authentic participation in 'culture' and the consumption of commodity production. The different ways that theatre and culture are valued in Shakespeare's plays and in the contemporary cultural moment can, we suggest, be accounted for by seeing all of that work as part of a continuing process of reproduction that is neither linear not teleological.

In the final three chapters, led by Kate Rumbold, we return to the contradictions of the present moment. Chapter 6 examines the new languages of value proffered by the previous Labour government in the first decade of the twenty-first century, and reveals the implications of the relocation of value to the 'experience', and even the 'creativity', of audiences and visitors. We show how both the languages and the practice of contemporary cultural policy have been drastically affected by economic pressures and the political changes occasioned by the post-2008 fiscal crisis. Chapter 7 explores the ways that institutions that reproduce Shakespeare have significantly altered their practices to respond to these changes in the definitions of cultural value, the demands of their audiences and the opportunities provided by new media. Chapter 8 shows how, in spite of the resource that 'Shakespeare' provides for culture, neither the name nor the content can be simply equated with commercial 'brands', but have a more complex relationship to the commercial realm and to the affective demands made of culture today.

In the Afterword, we focus more directly on the immediate impact of the public funding cuts that have followed both the financial crisis and the change of UK government in 2010. We suggest that, in spite of the significant decline in public funding for the arts, the state is still considered to have some responsibility for providing its citizens with the social goods now included in the category known as 'culture'. Those aspects of culture, however, no longer focussed on the arts as a category of particular value. As we argue throughout the book, the value attached to particular content that was viewed as beyond the market had been replaced by a value assigned to participants' and the audience's engagement with culture. Responsibility for managing that engagement had been transferred to the organisations and institutions who had curated and conserved it and, in a context of constrained government expenditure, that task could be equally effectively resourced by other funders, including the commercial sector.

If the boundary that had divided high from low culture is no longer so vigorously defended, the force of the division between culture as a canon of special objects and culture as a way of life is also less clearly the place in which value could be articulated. A way of life that included amateur engagement with the arts or with sport might remain as residual government responsibilities but the case for their value might have to be made in terms of their relative ability to attract commercial or philanthropic support.

These changes highlighted the important relationship between heritage collections of valued cultural objects and the capacity to leverage new sources of funding with which to realise their value. The value of cultural content may be asserted in terms of its appeal to those who might engage with it, but, without the capacity for distribution and informing display, its value is harder to discern. Those who resisted the cuts in public funding continue to insist on the value of heritage content as 'an end in itself', but without an address to the costs and work of making that content into culture the arguments have little purchase on the current scale for value.

The cultural value of Shakespeare is, we suggest, less affected by the current shifts in state funding. His works' capacity to play a part in both the small-scale, face-to-face cultural spaces of amateur performance and the high-gloss, high-value-added conditions of contemporary theatre may provide the flexibility with which to survive economic change. In the new economic climate, the tension between the small-scale experience of culture and the added value of institutional advocacy and innovation may well become the space in which culture and its value continues to be negotiated in twenty-first-century England. Its particular history remains far from complete and it may be some time before we can become relaxed about it.

Notes

1 The breadth of this discussion is usefully summarised in Graham Holderness, *Cultural Shakespeare: Essays in the Shakespeare Myth* (Hatfield: University of Hertfordshire Press, 2001).
2 This intellectual movement is usefully synthesised by Perry Anderson, 'A Culture in Contraflow', Part 1, *New Left Review*, 180, 1990, 41–78; Part 2, *New Left Review*, 182, 1990, 85–157.
3 See for example, Kimiko de Freytas-Tamura, 'How banking culture transformed over the decades', *BBC News* 05.09.12, www.bbc.co.uk/news/business-19463343 (accessed 07.01.13).
4 Raymond Williams, *Keywords: A Vocabulary of Culture and Society* (London: Fontana, 1976), p.16.
5 Eleonora Belfiore and Oliver Bennett have provided a summary view of the history of aesthetics from Aristotle to the present in *The Social Impact of the Arts: An Intellectual History* (Basingstoke: Palgrave Macmillan, 2008).
6 Mike Featherstone, *Consumer Culture and Postmodernism* (London: Sage Publications, 1991), p.13.

1

Advocacy and analysis

On 26 October 2004 the Arts and Humanities Research Board, the agency then responsible for research and postgraduate funding in UK universities,[1] hosted a seminar at which Estelle Morris, the culture minister, Neil MacGregor, the director of the British Museum, and Joan Bakewell, a journalist and media personality, engaged in a debate on 'Government and the Value of Culture'. The discussion had been triggered by the publication, in May, of a personal statement on the topic, written by the then culture secretary, Tessa Jowell, and circulated for comment to the UK's cultural institutions. Tessa Jowell's paper signalled the importance of the issue it addressed by linking the question of culture to the founding principles of the post-war labour movement. She quoted the 1942 Beveridge report's commitment to 'slaying the five giants of poverty – want, disease, ignorance, squalor and idleness'. The implementation of the Beveridge report had had real and lasting effects, establishing national insurance for those in want, a national health service that would combat disease, an education policy to address ignorance, a housing programme for the devastated cities that would eliminate squalor and a public work programme that would drive out idleness. Fifty years on, Tessa Jowell proposed to slay a further giant: 'the poverty of aspiration'. Her weapon, she said, would be 'Culture'.[2]

The Secretary of State was aware that 'culture' was 'a slippery concept'. She nevertheless proposed a comprehensive definition that included 'the cultural life of the nation' but almost immediately modified it to cover 'the intellectual and emotional engagement of the people with all forms of art, from the simplest to the most abstruse'. In shifting from 'the cultural life of the nation' to 'all forms of art' she deftly elided the more general and more limited uses of the term 'culture': 'the engagement of the people' was not to be separated from the material with which they would engage even though it became clear that her concern with the 'poverty of aspiration' was precisely with the difficulty of ensuring a connection between the 'cultural life of the nation' and the particular forms of cultural production that her department was tasked with supporting. Her definition thus shifted the application of 'culture' as an inclusive and unifying concept to a more specific and limited concern with the material with which they would engage. She referred to that material as 'the complex arts' and, as the paper developed, it came to include the canon of western music, fine art and theatre as well as more recent work that, she claimed, 'makes demands not only on the makers or performers but on those to whom the work of art is directed'.[3]

Jowell's statement signalled an important shift away from the reflexive populism of the previous minister's arts policy, and opened up the space for a renewed discussion of the role and value of culture. As the statement of a government minister, it raised concerns about the implications for government policy on funding, not only for producers of the arts but also for institutions responsible for their dissemination and reception. And yet, by invoking value as well as culture, it seemed to insist upon wider principles that were thought to be common to the whole population and to apply beyond the considerations of particular government policy.

Jowell's suggestion, that the value of culture lay in the desired connection between the work of art and those who engaged with it, was shared by the other speakers at the seminar, and by the audience. Estelle Morris agreed that value was to be found in the effects of the arts in the private world of personal taste and life-enhancing individual experience. Neil MacGregor extended this idea of value to the international arena in his characteristically passionate account of the British Museum's policy of national and international display of the objects in its care. It clearly mattered to him that the Museum's recently acquired Abyssinian tablet had been displayed across the nation in order to present a reminder of the rich and ancient culture of Mesopotamia that had been looted and destroyed during the recent war in Iraq. He celebrated the fact that the British Museum was able to lend an ancient Ottoman tunic to an exhibition in Kuala Lumpur in order to celebrate an international Muslim tradition that was not confined to the Arab world. Values associated with international education and global sharing of cultures were, he suggested, the foundations of the British Museum's curatorial care of the treasures in their collection. Those values, he asserted, could only be realised in an active programme of circulation and display, and he took evident pleasure in young people queuing up to learn how to write 'fuck off' in cuneiform at a schools workshop in Newcastle. Other participants in the seminar agreed that the arts demonstrated their value through the spontaneous engagement of children, and they offered moving accounts of disadvantaged youngsters whose creativity had been awakened by access to musical instruments or the chance to work in ceramics.

The discussion rehearsed familiar starting points for the discussion of cultural value. Cultural value was assumed to be located in the personal or collective experience of those who engaged with it: it could be a product of creative work (with music or ceramics, especially in the hands of children) but cultural experiences also included engagement with particular exemplars of culture (an Ottoman tunic or an Abyssinian tablet) that were already acknowledged as culturally valuable because of their ancient, unique or religious significance.

The participants did not suggest any hierarchy among those experiences. They did not value the experience of children entranced by music less or more than the value of children extending the range of their graffiti languages, and no one addressed the controversial topic of the historical provenance of the precious items from overseas that now constitute the global collections in British museums. Among the arts researchers, curators and educators in that gathering, controversies about high and low culture, pushpin or poetry, the ancients and the moderns, were forgotten or unmentionable in the demonstration of an open-minded celebration of cultural engagement wherever it was to be found.

The seminar participants' responses demonstrated an important distinction between advocacy and analysis. Their advocacy for the value of culture offered a *post hoc* justification for their existing enthusiasm rather than an *a priori* analysis of culture that called into question its definitions or addressed the process of assigning value in particular social and economic conditions. Consequently, their enthusiastic consensus about the role of the arts in creating cultural value by-passed the principal aim of Tessa Jowell's paper. By giving it the title 'Government and the Value of Culture', Jowell opened up the uncomfortable question of how the value of culture could be given priority in government policy and funding. Estelle Morris had reminded the audience of the fiscal constraints faced by ministers making a bid for the arts' share of 'the taxation pot', for which all of the arts organisations and practitioners in England competed in the zero-sum game of public funding. In spite of the year-on-year increases that had been allocated to the Department for Culture, Media and Sport since Labour took office in 1997, the re-allocations of those funds to arts organisations seldom satisfied the winners, always outraged the losers and could never completely rely on a supportive consensus in either Parliament or the general public. It was easy for a gathering of arts academics and cultural brokers to agree that a thousand cultural flowers should bloom; it was much more difficult for policy makers and civil servants to decide which of them should receive the sustaining subsidy that would allow them to flourish.

When Jowell's paper turned to the questions of subsidy and selection, the rhetorical alignment between 'the life of the nation' and 'the intellectual and emotional engagement of the people' was complicated by the contest for subsidy between particular works or forms of art.

> Why is it right for the Royal Opera House, to receive huge public subsidies? Why do we subsidise symphony orchestras but not pub bands or pianists? Why do we subsidise performances of Shakespeare and Mahler but not Coldplay or Madonna? Why do we spend millions on a square foot or so of a Raphael? Why is the *Madonna of the Pinks* more important than *The Singing Butler*?[4]

Her list of questions conflated cultural organisations (The Royal Opera House and some symphony orchestras), the performance of works from the classic repertory of western art (Shakespeare and Mahler) and an individual artefact (*The Madonna of the Pinks*) all of which had been priorities for previous public funding. They were contrasted with a commercially successful singer (Madonna), an 'indie' band (Coldplay) and a visual artist (Jack Vettriano). The principles of selection, however, were less to do with the artistic forms or their effects on audiences and more to do with the economics and politics of state support for the arts.

The Secretary of State's questions could have been answered in obvious, pragmatic terms: subsidy (whether provided by the state, philanthropic trusts or investing 'angels') is a means to meet the costs of acquiring, sustaining and conserving artistic products that may not be able to be met by ticket sales or other forms of return on investment. The Royal Opera House receives huge public subsidy because without it the range and quality of its productions, its ability to attract international performers for relatively short runs and its huge, enabling infrastructure of a city centre building, a chorus and orchestra, stage technicians and organisational overheads would be unsustainable. Symphony orchestras similarly need subsidy because the number of performers in an orchestra makes their performances more expensive than pub bands or pianists. Performances of Shakespeare and Mahler too, require larger numbers of more extensively trained performers than Coldplay or Madonna and have less capacity to balance the costs of live production with mass-market sales of recordings.

The *Madonna of the Pinks* involves a more direct form of expenditure. It includes the costs of acquisition as well as the subsequent costs of conservation, insurance and secure and controlled conditions of display.[5] There is no scope for a return on investment in an art market where accumulated value can only be realised, if at all, on re-sale. By contrast, *The Singing Butler* has achieved its fame through mass-produced prints that return annual royalties of £500,000 while also raising the re-sale value of the original painting.[6] In other words, Jowell's opposition between cultural forms that attracted state support and those that did not was less a matter of the particular characteristics of the art works and productions themselves than the costs of the infrastructure required to sustain them, the extent to which they could be disseminated by new technologies and the complex market relations that exist between the objects and their role in 'the cultural life of the nation'.

By posing the question of value in terms of an opposition between expensive, heritage forms of art and technologically distributed contemporary forms, Jowell was reiterating the early twentieth-century responses to mass production, when people were, by turns, fascinated and appalled by the capacity of mass production to meet the demand for cultural as well as material goods.[7] She acknowledged that debate by asking 'Why is mass public demand not the only criterion of perceived cultural "value"?'[8], but in the rest of her paper she clearly distinguished the demands of 'the mass' from 'the life of the nation' (p.3). The mass was assumed to be the generalised quantum of consumers who, as Featherstone puts it, are assumed to 'participate in an *ersatz* mass-produced commodity culture'[9] while 'the life of the nation' represented an aspirational idea of culture that existed in an ideal locus of value, located in individual life experiences: 'the *internal* world we all inhabit – the world of individual birth, life and death, of love or pain, joy or misery, fear and relief, success and disappointment'[10]. Unlike mass-produced artwork, the 'complex arts' apparently had the capacity to enhance these fundamental human life processes, and failure to engage with them was a regrettable result of a 'poverty of aspiration'.

Tessa Jowell's advocacy for a culture valued by 'the whole nation' was an attempt to argue that 'culture' that could be best ensured by the state's financial support for the complex arts. However, by the later years of the twentieth century, the political critique of the state's role in supporting failing industries had been extended to the state's support for culture, and, as cultural critics had observed, 'the status and the canonical force of "official culture", and the agenda set by the defenders of cultural orthodoxy'[11] had also been challenged by theorists and cultural activists making a case both for new commercial cultural products and the cultures of marginalised social groups. The calculation of resources or the potential conflicts between the tastes and experience of different groups of people existed in an entirely different frame of value that did not enter the discussion. In order to avoid any suggestion of bias in favour of any exclusive taste community, the advocates of 'culture' invoked a universal human experience that kept at bay questions about differences of taste and education, regions and location, language and ethnicity as well as the sheer scale of the task of offering a unifying experience of 'culture' to a diverse population of 60 million people.

Advocacy for a culture that would enhance the life of the nation or address 'the internal life we all inhabit' could not address the conflicts of interest that existed between audiences' sense of the value accorded to their tastes, artists' need for financial investment and the complex legal, administrative and financial procedures that governed the actions of the state and its agencies. The claim for the universally powerful effects of the arts could be asserted and might be agreed but it could not provide an analytical account of culture that would satisfactorily resolve the question of the role of government support in sustaining its value.

Making the case for culture

This special sphere for culture invoked by its advocates could appear universal and transcendent because it never engaged directly with the contingencies of economic and political change. Speaking at a conference on 'The State of the Arts' in 2012, following the economic crisis of 2008, and the change of government in 2010, the director of ACE, Liz Forgan, made the distinction clear:

> The instrumental value of the arts to wealth, to mental and physical health, to education, to social coherence, is real and enormously important. But today is about something else: today is about the extraordinary and essential role artists play in our society, their genius, their needs, their contribution to what matters in all our lives.[12]

She made a similar distinction between the admired characteristics of works of art and the economic conditions that supported them:

> Great art isn't about economics. It's about the ambiguity and restraint of Gerhard Richter's *September*; the lyrical insight of James McCarthy's *17 Days*, the breath-stopping horror of Jacobi's Lear, the exploration of personal landscapes of Akram Khan's Desh, the restless looking of David Hockney, or Lucien Freud. These works, these artists, some exalted, others setting out to develop their voices, tell us something about ourselves, about how we live and about what it is to be alive at this time.

By relegating more systematic analysis of the value of the arts to a generalised realm of 'economics', Liz Forgan's rhetorical advocacy for culture effectively marginalised political conflict over public funding priorities and aligned 'culture' with examples of works that had, in a variety of ways, already been valued by Arts Council funding, by press acclaim and by presentation in the prestigious venues of the National Theatre, the Tate Modern gallery and the Royal Academy.

The rhetorical exclusions involved in defining the sphere of cultural value were less to do with making a case for culture than for securing assent to the effects of Arts Council policy. As a funding agency, however, the Arts Council was informed in its work by a considerable body of knowledge, created by professional cultural analysts, and often commissioned by arts organisations themselves. This research addressed the effects and impacts of particular funding policies by analysing the actual cultural practices and behaviours of those who engaged with the arts, and had identified some the key problems with the generalised advocacy for culture.

The leading cultural statistician Sara Selwood had noted that 'Despite authoritative research reports by DCMS's and ACE's own researchers, the shortcomings of data on the cultural sector, including quantitative data are generally acknowledged'.[13] John Holden, from the think tank Demos, also mocked government ministers' assumption of authority in defining the realm of culture – '*We* will decide what has intrinsic merit and *you* will take two teaspoons a day'.[14] Most tellingly, the sociologists Miles and Sullivan had critiqued the 'deficit model' of culture that assumed a 'poverty of aspiration' on the part of those who did not engage with publicly funded 'complex arts'. They observed:

> Interviews with those who rarely or never interact with traditional or mainstream culture show that most are, nevertheless, positively engaged in informal social and cultural arrangements of their own. Largely focused on friends, relationships and ostensibly 'mundane' day-to-day activities, these can in fact be quite rich and involved.'[15]

None of these analysts dissented from the fundamental principle of state funding for the arts. However, they did separate the realm of advocacy with its aspirations for a universal cultural experience from the fiscal and organisation process that made cultural engagement possible. As John Holden explained:

> responses to culture are personal and individual; some people are radically transformed by a particular cultural experience while others are left unmoved ... it is the job of a gallery to put a painting on a wall, but it is not their job to determine what happens next. They cannot, and should not, require that 40% of viewers will have a spiritual experience in front of it.[16]

In his systematic analysis of the problems of 'capturing cultural value', Holden proposed a complex system of distinct forms of value that might be applied to culture. They would, he argued 'extend the range of factors that can be taken into account' (p. 56) in arriving at a robust definition of cultural value. This multi-faceted account of cultural value was designed to provide appropriate terms of engagement in the professional dialogue between government, funding agencies and the artists they supported and thus to ensure the authority and legitimacy of those who allocated public funds:

> The acknowledgement of Cultural Value addresses the issue of the legitimacy of institutions. The activities of funders cannot simply rest on devolved authority from Government. Legitimacy must be earned through practices and processes and a record of good decision making rather than being conferred from above. (p. 57)

The task of the cultural analysts was to facilitate what Stuart Cunningham, a sociologist of culture, has described as 'public processes involved in formulating, implementing and contesting governmental intervention in and support of cultural activity'.[17] They were concerned to suggest technical changes that would define cultural value in terms that might be acceptable to funders. In doing so they separated the effects of culture, and the organisations that created the conditions for those effects, into quite distinct analytical realms. The analysts dealt (in so far as the data allowed) with the facts of supply and demand, distribution and impact. The advocates, on the other hand, imagined a world of value in which giants were slain and artists, untrammelled by questions of economics, 'work to explore, to crash through our received ideas, to show us personal and unique perspectives, to express anger, love, fear and awe'.[18]

The analysts and advocates often worked in and for the same organisations and were equally aware of the others' claim for value. However, the different ways of expressing cultural value could not be reconciled. Governments and funding agencies demanded a 'return on investment' in the 'creative economy', while the champions of a universal culture insisted that culture 'is about something else'.

The case of Shakespeare

The 'something else' that both defined and inhabited the space of cultural value in public advocacy consisted partly of a list of psychological and emotional attributes that connected works of art to their audiences and partly of a list of individual works or artists that were thought to effect that connection. Shakespeare appeared in both. Tessa Jowell's list, in 2004, identified 'performances of Shakespeare and Mahler' as exemplars of activity that would attract public funding because they represented the antithesis of the commercially successful cultural forms and, by 2012, Liz Forgan simply celebrated 'the breath-stopping horror of Jacobi's Lear' that was, she asserted, 'not about economics'.[19] In both lists, 'Shakespeare' appeared as a standard reference point for cultural advocacy, secure within its defined rhetorical space as a default signifier of cultural value. The connection between advocacy and analysis that placed Shakespeare in those lists, however, still requires some analysis since it illustrates with particular clarity the need to refresh as well as assert the values that constitute a common-sense idea of culture.

The base-line for generally positive views about Shakespeare that extended beyond those of professional cultural advocates was readily identified in a vox-pop survey conducted in Stratford-upon-Avon on Shakespeare's birthday in 2007.[20] Asked 'how do you feel about Shakespeare?' people responded with recourse to familiar, collective valuations of his work: 'he's the greatest dramatist of all time', 'he's a national treasure' and, summing it up: 'he's a genius; that's all I know'. Many respondents nevertheless indicated that they had not read his plays since their school days and did not attend the Stratford-upon-Avon theatres, though they were able to quote some of the most familiar lines from the plays. They may have had more nuanced views about Shakespeare but there was no need to discuss them on that April afternoon.

A rather different kind of commitment to the case for Shakespeare was made by the participants at the 2007 meeting of the British Shakespeare Association (BSA). The teachers, practitioners and enthusiasts who attended the meeting had already identified themselves as advocates for Shakespeare's cultural value, and the discussion focused on reiterating and refining that advocacy through a dialogue with experts and with one another. The discussion on that occasion took the form of a response to a panel of three speakers who – in response to the question, 'is Shakespeare good for you?' – had offered analytical accounts of Shakespeare's value based on the use of Shakespeare in prisons' educational practice, an analysis of the audience for building-based theatre in the UK, and a critical investigation of the connection between the ethical and political ideas expressed in Shakespeare's plays and those of key twentieth century-thinkers.[21]

The different approaches of the papers indicated the extent to which any agreement about the value of Shakespeare was inflected by the knowledge on which it was based and the form in which the knowledge was communicated. The analysis of the audience for building-based theatre, for example, used data that was being gathered and was eventually published in ACE's *Theatre Assessment*

2003–2008. It indicated that a budget increase of 72%, awarding £25m of additional funding for theatre in each of the project's five years, had limited impact on attendances and audience profiles. Most mainstream work continued to attract largely white audiences, there was little engagement with diverse audiences, with the exception of some key venues, and programmers tended to target culturally specific audiences for culturally specific shows.[22]

This careful and systematic analysis of the relationship between public funding and the art form most closely connected to Shakespeare could not be endorsed by this audience's experience of Shakespeare in performance. Consequently, the data that informed its 'cultural value calculations' offered no intuitive connection to their continued advocacy for Shakespeare's value. Similarly, the account of twentieth-century philosophers' engagement with Shakespeare could not be corroborated by this audience's essentially personal engagement with Shakespeare's ideas even though it was well informed by knowledge of the plays and their contemporary performance. The participants in the seminar countered Arts Council England's expert evidence of a lack of engagement with theatre by explanations based on speculation about the respondents' limited opportunity to encounter Shakespeare's work, or taste deformed by mass culture or incompetent school teaching that prevented an appreciation of Shakespeare's genius.

The most engaged response to any of the papers was given to Bruce Wall, the prisons educator, who delivered an eloquent and moving account of the life-changing effect of Shakespeare performance workshops on prisoners.[23] He quoted at length from the prisoners' own accounts of the way that performing Shakespeare with the London Shakespeare Workout (LSW) had helped them to break established patterns of violence and recidivism, and included a number of stories of successful rehabilitation. The narrative form of both Wall's and the prisoners' own accounts made a direct connection between the experience of working with Shakespeare and the effect of spontaneous ethical and psychic transformation. His account was warmly endorsed by the audience who responded with narratives of their own experience of Shakespeare's transforming effect on children and other potentially recalcitrant groups of people.

The difference between engaged advocacy and social analysis is evident in the contrast between these affecting prison narratives of personal growth and the social research by two sociologists from the University of Manchester Centre for Socio-Economic Change.[24] Their work had been jointly commissioned by Arts Council England, the Department for Culture, Media and Sport, and the Offenders' Learning and Skills Unit at the Department for Education and Skills. As the report explained, it

> took place against the backdrop of the drive towards 'evidence based' policy and practice in the criminal justice arena and the recent Home Office review of the evidence base for the 'what works' agenda. (p. 8)

One of their conclusions was that the Home Office requirements for robust research quality on which to base funding decisions 'has resulted in the assertion of a set of standards for research quality which the arts in the criminal justice sector, as currently configured, has great difficulty in meeting' (p. 8).

The report's findings highlighted the gap between the demands of 'evidence-based policy' and the narratives provided by the engaged commitment of creative practitioners. Miles and Clarke were in some cases unable to gather enough data because of the logistics of working in a prison setting whose changing population made any consistent returns difficult to achieve. Their qualitative analysis, however, did allow them to record that

> Testimony taken from interviews and diaries across the study suggests that in the projects that were followed it was the culture of an arts intervention and its physical context as much as the specific content of the art form that made it effective. Participants felt that they were able to engage with the projects, develop self belief and build relationships because they were treated with respect and encouraged to make their own choices in a relaxed, non-judgemental space. (p. 12)

For the two sociologists, that evidence was not enough to establish the relevant level of knowledge required to make a definitive statement about the significance of cultural activity, not least because their role had been to test rather than to endorse the consensus among arts practitioners about the value of their work. The connection between their findings and the account of his work presented by Bruce Wall, however, did indicate that if the arts were to be presented as changing the lives of prisoners, a great deal of thoughtful work had to intervene between the activities that took place in prisons and the social outcomes that might be claimed in their name.

The nature of evidence for social research requires a sufficiently large base of data to make the findings robust and there is often a marked distinction, as in Miles and Clarke's study discussed above, between the scrupulous attention to the rigorous methodologies of the quantitative data and the imaginative potential of the qualitative evidence that is quoted. For people whose primary intellectual engagement is with narratives and other imaginative representations of human predicaments, it proved easier to weave a story about the prisoners who 'were able to engage with the projects, develop self belief and build relationships because they were treated with respect'. Engagement with that kind of detail is built into the syntax of causation and it offers the possibility of a narrative involving small numbers of individuals whose interactions would have identifiable outcomes. For an agency tasked with allocating significant public funds, on the other hand, the same small number of individuals would not constitute an adequate sample to provide the evidence necessary to support new prison management strategies, however emotionally persuasive the individual narratives of transformation might appear.

Value and knowledge

The responses of the BSA participants to the papers presented suggest some of the complexity involved in identifying the value of Shakespeare. The consistency of the audience response clearly endorsed the consensus that 'Shakespeare' was in some generalised way 'valued'. There was no dissent from the general consensus that his work could offer both spontaneous pleasure and personal transformation. The seminar participants acknowledged the importance of the work of effective educators and theatre practitioners in enhancing and ensuring those pleasures but this work was not felt to mitigate Shakespeare's claim to value and no reservations were offered about the relative value of this or that play or production.

The consensus within the group clearly benefitted from a high level of shared commitment to Shakespeare. Attendance at the conference indicated a level of professional and personal engagement and the responses also made clear a high level of regular and continued experience of reading and, in some cases, teaching Shakespeare. Moreover, engagement in the discussion itself reinforced the co-ordination of the group. Though the participants included some friends and acquaintances from earlier meetings of the BSA, they did not all work together and the group's (temporary) cohesion came from its reiteration of the idea of Shakespeare's value and its responses to different forms of knowledge about Shakespeare's value. The group was most sceptical of statistical and philosophical analysis and most responsive to narratives, including both Bruce Wall's account of the prisoners' transformation and their own narratives of children's and young people's engagement with Shakespeare.

In her contribution to an account of the 'cultural turn' in social analysis, Margaret Somers has suggested that

> Narratives ... not only convey information but serve epistemological purposes. They do so by establishing veracity through the integrity of their storied form ... in the first instance the success or failure of truth claims embedded in narratives depends less on empirical verification and more on the logic and rhetorical persuasiveness of the narrative.[25]

The narratives of Shakespeare's value that were accepted by the BSA audience added the corroborative authority of the speaker's experience to their own. When contradictory evidence – for example that theatre audiences were in decline – was presented, a different narrative (of inadequate teaching) or their own experience to extend and reinforce experience with cognate examples was deployed so that it could challenge the unfamiliar methodologies and be sceptical about data that seemed counter-intuitive.

Perhaps as a consequence, the respondents made no large-scale claims about 'economics' or 'mass demand' and they did not refer to the surveys of more than eleven thousand individuals which declared Shakespeare to be The Man of the Millennium[26] or the '37,000 people' who 'enjoyed a Shakespeare production for the first time' during the Royal Shakespeare Company's Complete Works Festival in 2006/7.[27] The consensus over value shared by the group did not depend on a mere aggregation of opinion. It is rather a shared frame of reference that defines both the group's agreement and the 'Shakespeare' that is its subject.

This shared frame of reference was both the strength and the weakness of the consensus established by the BSA group. It allowed a cohesive sharing of narratives that reinforced the group's commitment to the value of Shakespeare and their shared belief in the role of the arts as a source of psychic transformation. Those narratives however could not provide a sustained analysis of questions of social policy or the appropriateness of the balance of philanthropic and state funding that sustained the London Shakespeare Workout project. Similarly, the question of the economic base of theatre attendance in Arts Council England funding did not influence a fundamental agreement about the value of Shakespeare because it was difficult to create a narrative that linked the data being used with the personal experience of the Shakespeare enthusiasts in the group. The group's consensus about the value of Shakespeare did not depend on being endorsed by other people and did not, in that discussion, address any consideration of the enabling conditions that allowed it to thrive. The group was not provided with the information about the methodologies and scale of the research that might have allowed them to engage with data, and so drew their analysis from their extensive and well-informed life experience.

The distinction between narratives and the methodologies of social research has proved critical in public assessments of cultural value. John Holden has noted that the language used to identify the policy needs of the arts also inflects its relative authority:

> The vocabulary of culture reinforces the notion that money given to the arts, museums, libraries and heritage is a hand-out. The National Theatre and the army are paid for by tax, but only the arts are described as a subsidised sector. Theatres submit grant applications (every word needs weighing), whereas farmers receive top-up payments. Business schools use case studies, but culture puts together anecdotal evidence.[28]

In other words, Somers's assessment of the significance of narrative, the extent to which it 'takes on the mantle of epistemology and endows the information it conveys with the stature of knowledge, fact and truth' depends on the context in which the narratives are told and the other factors that support their consensual endorsement.

Narratives and the language of relationships imply the face-to face and local dimension of experience. They are granted only an illustrative, qualitative role in the reports that inform large-scale policy decisions even thought they are extensively used in the wider arena of culture. In the public forum of advocacy the case for the arts is made through a narrative that could be encapsulated in single images: 'going into the National Gallery or their local art gallery and discovering things they never saw before',[29] 'the breath-stopping horror of Jacobi's Lear'. Like the bright, clear images of advertising, these images depend upon recognition rather than analysis for their assent and endorsement. If that recognition is forthcoming, it fosters a consensus about value that is unaffected by the data on engagement with the arts.

This relationship between narrative and analysis is significant for accounts of the value of Shakespeare, whether the value of Shakespeare is being endorsed or critiqued. The consensual narrative of Shakespeare as an inspirational place of personal experience is held in place by a counter-narrative of the failure of that experience or by dissent from the version of 'Shakespeare' being proposed as valuable. Following the 'Man of the Millennium' contest, there was a flurry of journalistic commentary variously approving and deploring the choice of Shakespeare as winner. The approval reiterated the familiar consensus but even the disapproval secured the position of 'Shakespeare'. Some disapproval came, predictably, from advocates of competitor candidates, regretting that a figure from the arts won over figures from politics or science. Others disapproved because they wished to insist on the integrity of 'Shakespeare' as opposed to the re-working of the plays in the theatre. As one summary protest quoted in the *British Theatre Guide* put it:

> My Shakespeare is not Peter Brook's circus version of *A Midsummer Night's Dream*.
>
> My Shakespeare is not Ian McKellan's *Richard III*, set in 1930s England.
>
> My Shakespeare is not Adrian Hall's *Tempest*, with performers on stilts.
>
> My Shakespeare is not John Tillinger's *As You Like It*, with actors on rollerskates.
>
> My Shakespeare is not Peter Sellars' *Merchant of Venice*, with actors rapping while walking the boardwalk at Venice Beach.
>
> My Shakespeare is not Lee Breuer's *Lear*, whose mad King is an alcoholic Southern belle.[30]

The list demonstrated the diversity of forms in which 'Shakespeare' has been reproduced in recent years, but it insisted, too, on the significance of personal experience that had assessed a variety of contemporary productions and found them wanting.

The consensus about Shakespeare's value can co-exist with a diversity of views about what is being valued; it can circumscribe that value by excluding certain forms of knowledge from it or is can insist upon a purely personal informed view that is all the more emphatic because it is positioned either with or against an alternative version of a consensus. As Terry Eagleton put it, Shakespeare is 'at once ever new and consolingly recognisable, always different and eternally the same, a magnificent feat of self-identity persisting through the most bizarre diversions and variations'.[31] That diverse 'Shakespeare' itself creates the conditions for a consensus. It generated the localised debate that gave a dynamic quality to the necessary boundary setting and reinforced the enduring value of Shakespeare while at the same time requiring a combination of taste, knowledge and discernment for its justification.

Narratives of personal experience both limit the scope for systematic analysis of Shakespeare's value and ensure the continuity of the discussion that holds it in place. When the Royal Shakespeare Company, in 2006, launched a new initiative to develop Shakespeare teaching in schools, the programme was reported in a national newspaper with the rhetorical question: 'How is it that Shakespeare has become a byword for boredom among school children?' Again, it was not 'Shakespeare' that was to blame but 'a curriculum that, in many cases, allows pupils simply to learn, by rote, a few isolated scenes without appreciating context, the play as a whole or the dramatic power of the Bard's work'.[32] The fact that the National Curriculum documents explicitly include Shakespeare in the recommendations for drama education as 'one of the key ways in which children gain an understanding of themselves and of others'[33] and that 'rote learning' has virtually disappeared from pedagogy, was not acknowledged in the story. Similarly, historical information about the pioneering initiatives of earlier educators throughout the twentieth century[34] who had established Shakespeare as central to progressive child-centred education was not allowed to spoil the excitement that Shakespeare's value was at last being revived in schools.

Analysis of the enabling conditions of cultural engagement both undermines the personal agency of the central characters on which the narrative depends and limits its connection to the personal experience that is the foundation of the current model for consensus about Shakespeare and the arts. Individuals might dissent from particular judgements about the value of this or that work of art: they might prefer Madonna to Mahler or regard Shakespeare as dull. However, the central narratives of personal experience sustained both the idea that the arts are valuable and the idea that the value to be gained from them was fundamentally different from considerations of economic value or historical, sociological and aesthetic analysis that informed and sometimes determined the conditions of their existence.

The consensus that we have been proposing in this chapter highlights the difficulty of arriving at a way of talking about culture and value in the twenty-first century. When social scientists speak of a consensus, they do so with an acute sense of the difficulty of arriving at any account that is methodologically robust in both qualitative and quantitative terms and is framed sufficiently narrowly to eliminate ambiguity and error. The role of social analysis is usually to arrive at conclusions about human and social behaviour in specific domains that can provide empirically sound bases for comparisons and the mapping of change. By addressing questions of Shakespeare's value, by contrast, we have not been able to establish what two sociologists have defined as 'a single homogeneous domain' or 'a set of norms that pertain to a single area of behaviour'.[35] Both culture and value, as this chapter has suggested, are terms that are expressions as much of aspiration and self-reinforcement as they are of settled belief. Moreover, as we will show, culture includes value, value informs culture, and both of them have a complex relationship to the social practice that animates the dynamic relations between value, culture and Shakespeare.

Notes

1 The body became the Arts and Humanities Research Council in 2007.
2 Tessa Jowell, *Government and the Value of Culture* (London: Department of Culture, Media and Sport, 2004), p. 3.
3 Jowell, *Government and the Value of Culture*, p. 4.
4 A painting by the Scottish artist John Vettriano that is widely available in cheap prints. See Anthony Quinn, *Jack Vettriano* (London: Pavilion Books, 2005).
5 We discuss the case of the *Madonna of the Pinks* in chapter 4, pp. 97–100.
6 On 21 April 2004, *The Singing Butler* sold at auction for £744,500.
7 See John Carey, *The Intellectuals and the Masses: Pride and Prejudice*

among the Literary Intelligentsia 1880–1939 (London: Faber and Faber, 1992).
8 Jowell, *Government and the Value of Culture*, p. 4.
9 Featherstone, *Consumer Culture and Postmodernism*, p. 14.
10 Jowell, *Government and the Value of Culture*, p. 5.
11 John Frow, *Cultural Studies and Cultural Value* (Oxford: Clarendon Press, 1995), pp. 23–24.
12 Quoted in Mark Brown, Culture Cuts blog, *The Guardian* 14.02.2012, www.guard ian.co.uk/global/culture-cuts-blog/2012/feb/14/arts-funding (accessed 21.06.13).
13 Sara Selwood, 'The Politics of Data Collection', *Cultural Trends* 12(47) (2002): 13–24 (4).
14 John Holden, *Capturing Cultural Value: How Culture Has Become a Tool of Government Policy* (London: Demos Publications, 2004), p. 24.
15 Andrew Miles and Alice Sullivan, *Understanding the Relationship between Taste and Value in Culture and Sport* (London: Department for Culture, Media and Sport, 2006), p. 22.
16 Holden, *Capturing Cultural Value*, pp. 18, 22.
17 Stuart Cunningham, 'Cultural Studies from the Viewpoint of Cultural Policy', in Justin Lewis and Toby Miller, eds, *Critical Cultural Policy Studies: A Reader* (Oxford: Blackwell Publishing, 2003), pp. 13–22 (14).
18 Brown, Culture Cuts blog.
19 The sense in which *King Lear* precisely *is* 'about economics' is discussed in Chapter 3.
20 The survey was conducted by researchers involved with the AHRC-funded project 'Interrogating Cultural Value in 21st-Century England: The Case of Shakespeare'.
21 They were given by Bruce Wall from The London Shakespeare Workout (www.londonshakespeare.org.uk); Catherine Bunting, Arts Council England (for a full discussion of this work, see Chapter 6); and Paul Yachin, director of the Canadian SSHRC-funded 'Making Publics' project (www.makingpublics.org).
22 *Theatre Assessment 2009* (London: Arts Council England, 2009), www.artscouncil.org.uk/media/uploads/publications/theatreassessment.pdf (accessed 04.06.13).
23 The numbers of prisoners who have been recipients of this work now extends to 9,000 offenders and ex-offenders: www.lswproductions.co.uk (accessed 09.03.12).
24 Andrew Miles and Rebecca Clarke, *The Arts in Criminal Justice: A Study of Research Feasibility*, Centre for Research on Socio-Cultural Change, University of Manchester, www.cresc.ac.uk/sites/default/files/The%20Arts%20in%20Criminal%20Justice.pdf (accessed 21.06.13).

25 Margaret R. Somers, 'The Privatisation of Citizenship: How to Unthink a Knowledge Culture', in Victoria E. Bonnell and Lynn Hunt, eds, *Beyond the Cultural Turn* (Berkeley: University of California Press, 1999), pp. 126, 129.
26 'UK Bard is Millennium Man', http://news.bbc.co.uk/1/hi/uk/245752.stm (accessed 14.03.12).
27 Royal Shakespeare Company, *Annual Report and Accounts*, 2006–2007 (Stratford-upon-Avon: Royal Shakespeare Company, 2007), p. 9.
28 Holden, *Capturing Cultural Value*, p. 26.
29 One image in a list of desired outcomes of arts policy given by Tessa Jowell in an interview: Raymond Snoddy, 'The Interview: Tessa Jowell MP', *The Independent*, 18.10.04.
30 'Shakespeare: Man of the Millenium', www.britishtheatreguide.info/articles/100199.htm (accessed 14.03.12).
31 Terry Eagleton, 'Afterword', in Graham Holderness, ed., *The Shakespeare Myth* (Manchester: Manchester University Press, 1988), pp. 202–208.
32 Tim Walker, 'RSC/Warwick Diploma in Teaching: Shakespeare without Tears', *The Independent*, 12.10.06, www.independent.co.uk/student/postgraduate/rscwarwick-diploma-in-teaching-shakespeare-without-tears-419600.html (accessed 21.06.13).
33 Jonothan Neelands, *Learning through Imagined Experience: The Role of Drama in the National Curriculum* (London: Hodder and Stoughton, 1992), p. 6.
34 Discussed in Chapter 5, pp. 122–123.
35 Peter H. Rossi and Richard A. Berk, 'Varieties of Normative Consensus', *American Sociological Review*, 50(3) (1985): 333–347, p. 335.

2

The value of value

The account of cultural value provided by ministerial statements and groups of arts enthusiasts gives some indication of the difficulties involved in arriving at a stable definition of cultural value in twenty-first-century England. The value of selected examples of culture can be asserted, but the processes of evaluation in each case depends either on a consensus about the value assigned to their audiences and participants (children, reformed prisoners) or to the creative power of those who made the works (Shakespeare, Akram Kahn, David Hockney) or to those who made and produced them (a genius) or unexamined connection to 'the people', the nation' or 'the internal life we all inhabit'. The case that was made for cultural value took the form of corroborative narratives: the child or prisoner transformed by an encounter with Shakespeare; the connection between the work of art and the experience of 'anger, love, fear and awe'.

The narrative structure of these common-sense accounts of cultural value does not depend on evidence that is epistemologically distinct from them. Questions about whether taxation can legitimately be deployed in support of culture, questions of the relative benefit of Shakespeare workshops as opposed to other forms of prison recreation; questions about the most effective ways of overcoming the 'poverty of aspiration' cannot be independently addressed because, when they enter the narrative, they spoil the story and break the spell. Discussion of the enabling conditions of cultural engagement undermines the agency of the central characters on which the narrative depends; questions about the relative value of their activities are similarly fatal to the narrative's expression of value.

When the discussion took place in a small scale, face-to-face context, such as the BSA conference or AHRC seminar, individuals' accounts of these narratives of value coalesced into consensual agreement. When the assumed consensus was expressed at larger-scale events by authoritative public figures, the rhetoric they used established an explicit contrast between the direct experience of value and alternative, more abstract ways of defining it such as 'mass demand' or the pre-established criteria of public policy. These exclusions from the domain of value suggest that, in spite of its inclusive connection to 'the internal world we all inhabit', value is under threat. Invoking that threat gives greater rhetorical power to the case for value. It represents those who do not share this view of culture as people who, with the right opportunities or appropriate education, could overcome their 'poverty of aspiration', and thus reinforces the significance of the values that the consensus endorses.

However eloquently expressed or widely endorsed, a consensus offers neither a definitive nor a comprehensive account of value. By its nature, a consensus about value tends to identify and reiterate the shared assumptions of a group. It reinforces existing evaluations rather than systematically testing its own assumptions in the light of new knowledge. When those assumptions are tested by external analysts there is an inevitable gap between the group's advocacy for value and research that is framed by 'agreed indicators that substantiate value claims'[1] or, as we show in Chapter 6, the need to sustain the legitimacy of funding bodies' and arts organisations' practice.

This difference between the knowledge communicated through narratives and the knowledge that is the outcome of quantitative analysis is more than a matter of methodology. The first requires assent that arises from shared experience; the second depends on transcending individual or experience in order to arrive at conclusions that will meet the conditions of 'generalizability, explanations of causal change and contextual complexity'.[2] Each of these forms of knowledge may be used to make statements about the social impact of the arts in terms of their effects on people who engage with them, but each involves a different model of sociability. Narratives reinforce sociability through imaginative engagement and a desire for consensus; technical analysis attempts to account for the diversity and potential conflict of interest indicated by the behaviour as well as the interests of the different social groups that constitute the whole population.

The tension between ideas of value arrived at through consensus and those arrived at by systematic analysis was seldom a question of explicit disagreement about the value of this or that object. It was, we suggest, inherent in the idea of value itself. Using the term 'value' in a sentence such as 'I/we value X' implies more than 'I like X' or 'I enjoy X'. It suggests a higher level of commitment to the valued object than a reflexive and involuntary expression of taste or pleasure. However, the simple statement of value can give no indication that the value has any force or application beyond the statement itself. If the act of valuing is to be more than an idiosyncratic statement of preference, it must either be corroborated by others or it must exist in the object itself. If the value is located in the object itself, an assertion of its value might be presented as *recognising* that value. A shared consensus might be a matter of multiple, mutually confirming acts of recognitions but in the cases we looked at, it appears more often as a process of *conferring* value because the object of practice supports other social goods – such as the rehabilitation of prisoners, or a more open and internationalist perspective on world religions. So conferring value is often a matter of *endorsing* a value that has already been recognised or conferred by others.

All of those separate actions of recognising, conferring and endorsing are included in a kind of shorthand when assertions of value are applied to particular items such as Jack Vettriano's paintings or practices such as engagement with Shakespeare, but they do not in and of themselves provide a stable distinction between preference and value. A consensus among the valuers provides some measure of stability. It suggests that collective agreement about particular evaluations carries more weight because it is shared and endorsed by others. That sharing may occur on the small scale of a group of Shakespeare or arts enthusiasts, or on the more systematically identified scale of a social consensus that can be deemed representative enough to endorse or consent to public policy, undertaken on behalf of the whole population, including those who have not been directly engaged in the evaluative process. The sheer scale and diversity of the individual preferences of a whole population, however, cannot easily be assimilated into a unitary expression of value, so the stability and 'generalizability' of any collective agreement remains a critical question for any actions that take place in its name. If value is only an effect of evaluation, even of multiple evaluations over centuries, then it can be potentially overturned or at least modified by new evaluations and is therefore no longer an absolute value but is contingent on the relative strength of prior evaluations made by other people. It is precisely the instability implied by contingent (or relative) value that undermines its authority and makes the idea of intrinsic value at once so desirable and so vexing for analysis.

Steven Connor, for example, begins his analysis of *Theory and Cultural Value* by addressing head-on 'the conflict between absolute and relative value'. He observes that

> One of the features of this opposition between the absolute and the relative is that it provides no common frame within which to assess both claims, since each position derives its identity from its repudiative characterisation of the other. Any attempt to synthesize the rival claims of the absolutist and the relativist is always likely to be condemned by one side as itself tyrannically absolutist, or by the other as insufficiently armed against the corruptive force of relativism.

Connor is drawing attention to the fact that those who claim intrinsic value will not be convinced by arguments that assert that the value is not shared or perceived by others since intrinsic value inheres in the valued object and does not require endorsement by others. A claim for intrinsic value necessarily repudiates claims based on contingency and vice versa. He argues that any resolution of the debate between absolute and relative value is impossible since it constitutes 'a disagreement that cannot be brought to the bar of any higher argumentative authority'.[3] An appeal to a 'higher argumentative authority' is no more than a deferral of absolute value that leaves the impasse between the absolute and the relative positions securely in place.

Connor's view of this impasse makes clear that absolute value is identifiable only in theoretical terms. The endless deferral of authority that might endorse an absolute idea of value can only be halted if and when it arrives at authority that is similarly absolute. Such an absolute authority is only to be found in theology. As Terry Eagleton explains, societies that are, or were, organised on the hierarchical principles of Christian theology had recourse to a system of value that 'interweaves art, ritual, politics, ethics, mythology, metaphysics and everyday life, while lending this mighty edifice the sanction of supreme authority'. Eagleton then, characteristically, undermines the stability of this position by adding that it 'seemed to many decent, rational people remarkably benighted and implausible'.[4]

The absolute value created by theology is perceived by its adherents by virtue of their faith in its absolute nature and, in past theocracies, was reinforced by social structures of endorsement, and in some cases enforcement. In those contexts, any debate or dissention can be dismissed as the merely contingent expressions of disbelief. In more egalitarian, secular societies, on the other hand, where this value of last resort is unavailable, arguments that attempt to endorse value with reference to other desired effects or agreed methodological analysis merely defer the question of value in a process of infinite regression. If, for example, Shakespeare education is valued because it reforms prisoners, the locus of value is deferred to the reformation of prisoners and the case for that value (as well as the role of Shakespeare within it) must be separately argued until some sense of the absolute value is reached. That value might reside in contemporary social norms or the consensus of a small group discussion, or agreed analytical methodologies. Those contingent agreements, however, are not, in philosophical terms, absolute, and need to be re-established in the light of changing conditions.

The language Connor uses to identify the opposition between absolute and relative value gives some sense of what is at stake: he describes the proponents of absolute value as '*tyrannically* absolutist' while those who propose the contingency of value risk, he claims, sliding into 'the *corruptive* force of relativism'. An idea of absolute value might be rejected because it seems to speak of ancient structures of authority and belief and their disregard for informed consent, but relative value is always in danger of splintering into the individual ascriptions that comprise it, leaving the valued object terrifyingly exposed as valueless. Connor's invocation of political power-structures is not making the banal point that value is a product of particular forms of social power: that would be to concede the contingent case without argument. Rather, he is drawing attention to the relationship between independent acts of evaluation (using 'value' as a verb) and the products of particular but possibly multiple outcomes of evaluation ('values' as a plural noun). The idea of value seems to require an authority that may not have the absolute finality required for philosophical ideas of incontestable truth, but might have more pressure and purchase behind it than mere preferences of taste or practice. It requires a sense that value transcends the sum of individual acts of evaluation and is capable of existing beyond them.

One possible solution to the impasse between absolute and contingent value is to concede that value is contingent but to emphasise the significance of the negotiations that ensure that value (in one form or another) remains central to all human interactions. As John Fekete explains,

> The history of cultures and social formations is unintelligible except in relation to a history of value orientations, value ideals, goods values, value responses and value judgements, and their objectifications, interplay and transformations.[5]

By referring to 'value orientations' or 'value judgements' Fekete lifts the discussion away from particular acts of evaluation and particular objects that are valued to suggest the possibility of a kind of transcendent value that is evident in all social formations even if it produces very different outcomes in different times and places. 'Transcendent value' seems to offer a middle way in which objects and practices can be deemed to be valuable without depending either on an endlessly deferred absolute authority or on a mere aggregation of arbitrary individual opinions. The valued object or practice may be regarded as having transcendent value, not because its value transcends the whole spectrum of relative value, but because the act of valuing transcends the immediate instrumental interests of the person(s) making the evaluation. It suggests that there might be a kind of value that is collectively attributed over space and time, and therefore might begin to offer the possibility of a recurring consensus that will have a social as well as an individual application, a commitment to the common rather than the individual good.

The idea of transcendent value that is not absolute but nonetheless transcends immediate and instrumental utility is an attempt to hold stable an idea of value while acknowledging the contradiction between absolute and contingent value. An absolute value negates discussion; a completely relative idea of value creates the impasse between competing assertions of value. But a concept of a value that transcends individual preference and facilitates collective endeavour has a dynamic potential for continual negotiation and adjustment to different historical circumstances. It can thus avoid the limitations of absolute value that negates the possibility of negotiation while also insisting that there is more to value than the sum of competing evaluations. It is this idea of value that Connor also invokes when he speaks of an 'imperative to value' that is, he claims, as 'necessary as breathing':

> Value, in this imperative sense, is the irreducible orientation towards the better, and revulsion from the worse ... the irreducible principle of generalized positivity, the inescapable pressure to identify with whatever is valuable rather than what is not valuable.[6]

Connor may seem to overstate the force of this imperative, and it is easy to offer counter-examples of powerful individuals or even whole social formations whose actions and behaviours do not exemplify an 'irreducible principle of generalized positivity'. Connor supports his position by enclosing the idea of 'generalized positivity' within value, suggesting that 'Neither the suicide who believes that individual annihilation is preferable to continued existence, nor the philosopher who argues that it would be better for the human race, even life itself never to have existed, can resist the imperative of value.'[7] This imperative to value is different from the commitment to particular propositions about value: it suggests, rather, that the act of valuing is itself a demonstration of the existence of a realm of value in which such choices can be made but says nothing of the particular enabling conditions that will allow those choices to be acted on.

Connor's highly abstract concept of the universal nature of the tendency to value does not itself offer an absolute value. Rather, it provides another example of the tendency to defer the question of absolute value by pushing it back into a more and more abstracted location. His reference to 'generalized positivity' is needed in order to assert that the human capacity to make value-distinctions transcends individual acts of evaluation and thereby to avoid making judgements that appear to denigrate the practice of others and thus to impose particular ideas of value on others in a tyrannical fashion.

That sense of a transcendent capacity to value is essential for the model of social value described by Richard Flacks. He insists on the existence of

> an ethic of collective responsibility, a set of principles and rules that are morally binding on members, and that are capable of becoming obligatory for ever widening circles of non-members as well.[8]

By invoking considerations that go beyond the immediate instrumental needs and desires of individuals, Flack identifies transcendent value as the foundations of social living and collective endeavours of all kinds: it provides a stable point of reference from which particular actions and judgements can be assessed.

The understanding that these values are transcendent rather than absolute, that they were arrived at through the human and historically contingent process of reiterated evaluation, rather than being handed down by an absolute authority, leaves a space around them for the discussion and negotiation. It allows different advocacy groups to function peacefully and for adjustments to be made at the margins of social practice, without calling into question the fundamental principles within which the society functions. It is possible, for example, to hold that universal education or freedom of religious expression are transcendent values while holding divergent views on the value of particular educational or religious practices. This peaceful co-existence of a plurality of tastes and practices is both an expression of value and a value in itself. It is fundamental to the idea of value in liberal societies where values do not emanate from absolute authority but have been arrived at by historical struggles between groups who claimed value for their actions and the outcomes they desired and arrived at a negotiated agreement.

This dynamic quality of an idea of transcendent value creates both its strengths and weaknesses as a principle for judgement and action. It strengths are that it provides the possibility for a set of shared principles that facilitate social action: its weakness is that those principles cannot determine the conditions in which they take their social form. Invoking transcendent value offers a judgement of last resort, a place from which conflict might be resolved. It also expresses the utopian aspiration that the values of arbitrary and absolute authority might be replaced by a consensus formed of multiple individual acts of evaluation. It allows the everyday social practice of making choices and asserting preferences to continue untrammelled by cumbersome and inconvenient insistence on their historical and philosophical bases. However, the facilitating force of transcendent value, though it may provide the first step to establishing the consensus required for action, or act as the occasion for public debate, has no authority to enforce specific social behaviour.

This instability in the idea of transcendent value arises because the process of evaluation that produces transcendent value does not stop. The concept of value is always capable of further discursive splitting as different social practices and new objects of evaluation come within its scope. This unstable consensus over value, moreover, exists primarily in the ideal realm of discourse. The narratives, debates and rhetorical splitting that surround the idea of value take place exclusively in the realm of abstraction, where the human propensity for making value judgements can have free rein. As soon as the discussion moves to the conditions in which transcendent values might be actualised in effective social practice, the contingencies of particular social and historical conditions mitigate the claims to universality or transcendence of the value in question. In order to be transcendent, values must be free from the instrumental considerations of practice: the questions of implementation through adequate investment, or institutional capacity.

The dialectical gap between value that can be recognised as a philosophical concept and value that can be realised in particular social circumstances has profound implications for the location and operation of value. The assertion of transcendent value may act as a utopian imperative to improvement (Connor's 'irreducible orientation towards the better') but the gap between value and action equally offers examples of the worthlessness of values that cannot be realised in particular circumstances. The discursive effect of this separation of value from action or application is to place social, cultural and aesthetic values on one side of an intellectual and analytical divide and their effective realisation in social policy or cultural practice on the other.

The practice of value: water and diamonds

The gap between principles and practice is as fundamental to the nature of value as the gap between the absolute and the contingent: indeed, it may be the most profound version of it. Values that are claimed as absolute or even transcendent lose their authority and their capacity for consensus if the gap between them and contingent social practice becomes too great. The location of value in a separate realm from the contingencies of social practice is nevertheless a recurring feature of its expression since its status as a value would be compromised by the contingency of its effects.

As we saw in Chapter 1, the distinction between the realm of transcendent values and the social world of their implementation is reiterated in the almost axiomatic division between economic value and all other kinds of value. The values of the market are routinely characterised as the antithesis of intrinsic value since they depend on the completely contingent sum at which particular goods may be valued in a particular place and time. Terry Eagleton, for example, makes this division explicit when he contrasts 'the timeless values cultivated in the ethical, juridical, domestic and cultural domains' and 'the protean, diffuse, provisional forms of life bred by the marketplace'.[9]

However, the model of value created in markets cannot be so easily dismissed. It not only provides a symbolic opposition to absolute value, it also stabilises the contingency of competing valuations by providing a highly developed model for the consensual resolution of conflict over relative value. Moreover, since values in markets developed in the same social and ethical world as values in 'the ethical, juridical, domestic and cultural domains', their articulation and operations are diffused with the same dialectical and ethical complexity.

The most important of these dialectics is articulated in Adam Smith's famous distinction between use-value and exchange-value:

> The word value, it is to be observed, has two different meanings, and sometimes expresses the utility of some particular object, and sometimes the power of purchasing other goods which the possession of that object conveys. The one may be called 'value in use'; the other, 'value in exchange.' The things which have the greatest value in use have frequently little or no value in exchange; and on the contrary, those which have the greatest value in exchange have frequently little or no value in use. Nothing is more useful than water: but it will purchase scarce any thing; scarce any thing can be had in exchange for it. A diamond, on the contrary, has scarce any value in use; but a very great quantity of other goods may frequently be had in exchange for it.[10]

In this eloquently simple statement, Smith takes the long-standing classical distinction between use-value and exchange-value but rather than placing them in a single hierarchy where their relative value is a matter for debate or conflict, he proposes a relationship between them. By insisting on the un-exchangeable use-value of objects such as water he sustains the ethical evaluation of human needs as superior to the economic value released in exchange, but he suggests that exchange value can also meet human needs ('other goods may frequently be had in exchange for it'). By allowing that goods without immediate use-value can be transformed into exchange-value, he extends the value from the objects themselves (their intrinsic value) and suggests that value might be the product of negotiated social practice. Value-in-exchange has the capacity to increase the opportunities for acquiring further goods that might have value-in-use and, as a corollary, surplus quantities of goods with value-in-use can be offered for value in exchange, to create the multiple connections between use and exchange that constitute a market.

Value in Smith's model thus depends upon a set of *transactions* among those who hold exchangeable sources of value. By identifying transaction and exchange as a source of value, Smith's model challenges both the absolute idea of value as an intrinsic attribute and the complete contingency of value that is merely attributable to individual or multiple acts of evaluation. Smith's idea of exchange-value thus identifies a way of resolving the contest between value as an attribute and value as an effect. By using the vivid contrast between the value of diamonds and water, he breaks across traditional value-hierarchies that assign superior value either to rare and precious objects or to objects that meet fundamental human needs, and opens the possibility that value could be arrived at by negotiation among the values of different objects.

Conflicts of interest or disagreements about value can be resolved by negotiation and constant adjustment rather than rather than depending on a fragile consensus arrived at by argumentation and debate in the discursive realm or the deferral of value to a separate realm enforced by the authority of a higher power. Those negotiated adjustments, he suggests, are arrived at

> not by any accurate measure, but by the higgling and bargaining of the market, according to that sort of rough equality which, though not exact, is sufficient for carrying on the business of common life.[11]

Smith's pragmatic account of a rough and ready equivalence, 'sufficient for carrying on the business of common life' moves the question of value from the primary act of evaluation (with its attendant problems of principle and consensus) to the social practice that can negotiate the relationship between different orders of value. It offers a recognisable scenario of face-to-face social interaction that will provide the basis for amicable agreement about the relative value of equally recognisable familiar objects.

By identifying transaction and exchange as a source of value as well as use, and by describing them in recognisable social terms, Smith's model moves the question of value from the primary act of evaluation to the social practice that establishes the relationship between different orders of value. It can thus allay the anxieties about the equivalence of different evaluations or the difficulties of arriving at a consensus about them and provides a compelling instance of the operations of an 'ethic of collective responsibility'. His image of 'higgling and bargaining' indicates the importance of establishing acceptable and calculable equivalences between values attached to different objects, and depends on the assumption that the relationship between use and exchange value remains stable. For his model to be effective, the demand for goods with use-value needs to be balanced both by their supply and by 'rough equality' between those who hold goods for use and those who possess exchange-value goods with which to acquire them.

As Smith indicates in the larger argument of *The Wealth of Nations*, those ideal conditions seldom apply outside the bartering of simple economies. In complex markets there is seldom an exact or even a negotiable equivalence between different goods: how much water can be exchanged for a diamond? The relations between the value of different kinds of goods are also inflected by questions of supply and demand and the relative urgency of the need for use-value goods: How far might the exchange-value of a diamond be affected if those who hold diamonds were excluded from access to water?

An important mediating instrument managing the *in*equivalence between use-value goods and exchange-value goods is provided by money. Money separates the supply from the demand of goods, acting as a holding proxy for value, allowing both use-value goods and exchange-value goods to be exchanged in different places and at different times, and smoothing out the inequivalences in supply and demand by distribution in time and space. Using money as a proxy provides a calculable equivalence for value and allows multiple relations between sellers and buyers of different goods.

Money, however, could play no role in the management of conflicting interests and differential power that distort the process of negotiated exchange. That role was taken by market regulation. Prohibitions on hoarding foodstuffs in times of dearth, regulating access to water in an inland market and the regulation of usury are among the many early efforts to sustain the balance between value in use and value in exchange.[12] They represented efforts to manage the potential inequivalence of use- and exchange-value by excluding contingent imbalances of power between sellers and buyers of goods. In conditions where demand exceeded supply, they could give priority to the need for use-value among groups by establishing the idea of a 'just price' for basic use-value goods and in conditions of surplus supply, they could ensure the systems of distribution that would extend the range of the market to areas where there was further demand. These regulatory frameworks themselves were often articulated in terms of principles that identified the qualities of those who were allowed to enter the market: values such as honesty, trust, kinships networks, nationality or race. The effect was to assert a fundamental distinction between economic value – a matter of managed use and exchange, defined in terms of proxy values – and ethical or social value, whose frame of reference was focussed on the social, face-to-face relations between individual agents and the principles required to manage and control their behaviour in the market.

In the twenty-first century, it is not surprising that the division between the economic and the ethical domains of value should be most vehemently insisted upon. The global market in both mass-produced and primary goods has further expanded the market in both time and place on a scale that moves supply and demand into quite separate market arenas. Only a vanishingly small proportion of the multiple commodities available in modern markets can be categorically assigned to value-in-use. And even primary goods such as food and water seldom constitute use-value alone but require multiple interventions between suppliers and users in order to ensure safe and effective distribution to the whole population. The value that is experienced by consumers at the point of sale is entirely mediated by money and there is no direct relationship between its use-value and the multiple exchanges that have constituted its exchange-value. The price of goods also embodies the costs of distribution as well as other production costs such as interest on borrowing or return to shareholders so that the gap between use-value and exchange-value is no longer immediately visible. Consequently, concepts such as 'value for money' lose any real connection to the relative value of use and exchange. The value involved is conferred entirely by the user and is based either on the connection between the consumers' available store of money or on his or her (often limited) knowledge of existing markets for similar goods. The consumer's scope for 'higgling and bargaining' is limited to buying or doing without in an apparently intransigent market process.

The management and regulation of commodity pricing that holds the system in place are also largely invisible. They depend on systems of currency exchange and increasingly complex financial strategies of futures trading and debt management that are only called into question in times of systemic crisis or by activist groups who expose the most ethically reprehensible of market activities. Face-to-face market relations are replaced by economic systems that involve the activity of small and specialised groups of professionals who operate complex financial systems that are outside the control or comprehension of most producers and consumers. As John Lanchester explains in his account of the origins of the financial crisis of 2008,

> There is a much bigger gap between the world of finance and that of the general public ... Many bright literate people have no idea about all sorts of economics basics, of a type that insiders take as elementary facts about how the world works.[13]

This complete separation between use-value and exchange-value in the economic domain allows a similar rupture between the meaning of value as a product of economic transaction and its meaning in the domain of social relations. Value in the economic domain can be and is calculated in terms of the added-value of industrial and commercial processes and the relations of distribution and marketing world wide that will manage the relations between supply and demand. Value in the social domain nonetheless addresses human agency in which the relation to the market is still experienced as an aspect of social relations, personal choices and taste, and not merely as an aspect of managed supply and demand. The phenomenon of low demand for state-sponsored arts events, for example, could be managed by making supply-side interventions such as withholding goods until the market improves or reducing cost and price. These might be accompanied by demand-side interventions such as improving distribution, and increasing market share. As we will describe in Chapters 6, 7 and 8, many of these interventions did take place but they were accompanied by a residual rhetoric and narrative that spoke of personal and face-to-face social relations in which characteristics and attitudes of individuals could be held responsible for actions in the market, and economic concepts such as poverty, capital and value have only a metaphorical application.

Acknowledging both the connection and the disconnection between market relations and social relations without placing them into a value hierarchy is critical for understanding the location and operation of value. The two domains of value operate on different scales of time, space and volume, and the cross-over of language and metaphor between them confuses the existence of value in each. To use Smith's example, diamonds are able to command high prices in exchange because of the long value chain of skilled work and multiple traders that increases their value as they move from the mine to the market. Moreover, their value chain does not end with sale in the market. After they have been purchased, diamonds enter the social arena as proxies for wealth and social standing: the purchaser recognises the value of the diamond (or may be informed by expert authority) but may also confer further value on it by the symbolic uses to which it is put, and it may then be rendered literally 'priceless' by being removed from the market altogether and valued as an heirloom. Its value is constituted by market, social and symbolic relations at different stages of its existence and it may also be inflected by its intrinsic qualities that depend on the quality of the stone and the skill with which it has been cut.

This market model also allows us to pay attention to the structures of authority that attempt to manage and control the terms in which value is assigned to different objects in complex markets. The simple logic of production and consumption, where value is varied by supply and demand, has in modern times and in developed societies been replaced by massive overproduction of both commodities and symbolic goods. Managing that oversupply requires the intervention of 'cultural intermediaries', whom Featherstone describes as 'those in media, fashion, advertising and "para" intellectual information occupations, whose jobs entail performing services and the production, marketing and dissemination of symbolic (as well as material) goods'.[14] As we will discuss in Chapters 6 and 7, those cultural intermediaries include the policy-makers and government spokespeople whose statements on culture can thus be seen as a way to restrict, control and channel the exchange of goods in ways that change the value of cultural goods in contemporary markets.

This complex market, then, is less a single institution that exercises power than a chain of knowledge, work and interest that is constantly negotiating the relationship between producers and consumers. It provides the locus and conditions in which value is created and in which ethical and social values equally have a dynamic rather than an oppositional role. The resulting instability of unitary ideas of value indicates, once again, the extent to which value cannot be confirmed as absolute in secular societies, yet it is constantly subject to rhetorical, social and institutional attempts to secure its stability. These attempts may take the form of rhetorical distinctions (for example between 'the nation' and 'mass demand' or between ethical and economic value) that secure the stability of one form of value over another; they might involve establishing institutions that provide the authority from which conflict over value can be managed; or they might attempt to establish working equivalences between the relative value of one set of (material or conceptual) goods in relation to others. These recurring attempts to stablise value suggest, as Connor proposes, that value is an inherent social tendency that constitutes an 'irreducible orientation towards the better', a necessary concept for social existence that offers the possibility (however elusive) of a collective consensus that will provide the basis for ordering social life and for making judgements that transcend the mere wishes and desires of individuals.

The case of 'Friendship'

This rather abstract account of the ways that value is realised in markets can be illustrated with an example from the 2009 Reith lectures given by the Harvard philosopher Michael Sandel and broadcast on BBC Radio 4 in the UK. The title of the book in which was published an extended version of these lectures, *What Money Can't Buy*,[15] boldly announced the existence of social goods that had no place in the market and deplored the intrusion of the market into that realm, using examples drawn from social practices such as payment for surrogate mothers or for the right to violate international regulations on hunting endangered species or emissions of CO_2.

Sandel conceded that markets were effective 'for organising production and distribution' and generating 'affluence and prosperity', (p.5) but again and again he proposed that markets should not enter (though they have entered) the domain of personal and social relations that contribute to a more equitable and co-operative social existence.

Sandel's book cites numerous examples of revulsion against the commutation of social obligations to money payments as well as examples of the ineffectiveness of such payments in securing desired social results. These narrative examples provided support for his suggestion that objections to the market were both fiscal and ethical:

> From an economic point of view, social norms such as civic virtue and public spiritedness are great bargains. They motivate socially useful behaviour that would otherwise cost a lot to buy ... But to view moral and civic norms simply as cost effective ways of motivating people ignores the intrinsic value of the norms ... Relying solely on cash payments to induce [citizens to accept social responsibilities] is not only expensive; it is also corrupting. It bypasses persuasion and the kind of consent that arises from deliberating about risks ... and need. (pp.119–120)

The examples that Sandel chose focussed on particular shifts in the development of modern markets where the maximisation of opportunities to create financial products and the collusion of regulatory authorities in permitting those developments have produced perverse incentives, bogus forms of insurance and the replacement of fees to allow anti-social behaviour rather than fines to prevent it. These mechanisms are sometimes the result of simple corruption but they are also used to control a market that is too large and involves too many players to be managed by face-to-face social agreements.

Sandel's lectures made a passionate case for the intrinsic value of social norms that would in and of themselves ensure a productive and harmonious society without the incentives developed through the calculations of technocratic public management. His central case was that the 'intrinsic value' of social norms are recognised and endorsed, and can be relied upon to result in appropriate behaviour. Using the example of 'Friendship', he argued that friendship could not be contaminated by market considerations or it would cease to be friendship. He provided, in other words, an *a priori* definition of friendship as a social relationship that did not exist in the market and the argument merely confirmed that distinction. He was thus able to marginalise consideration of the enabling social conditions that will allow friendship to exist.

Once the discussion moved beyond the idealised domain of intrinsic value, the contradictions of Sandel's argument become apparent. Friendship may be the desired basis of personal relations but its existence cannot assure the material conditions that will allow it to transcend competition over access to social goods or assure their distribution beyond the immediate friendship group. Historians of friendship have described the complex relationship in earlier societies between friendship and gift exchange and their role in structuring the exchange regulation in markets and economies through friendship and kin.[16] Like 'trust' or 'honesty', friendship is a value that can offer a way of regulating the connection between use and exchange value, but in the social world 'friendship', particularly when it is institutionalised, is as likely to distort the market with cronyism and exclusion as it is to work on behalf of the 'common good' of all participants. Rather than establishing the priority of 'Friendship' as a value that transcends markets, Sandel's lectures demonstrate the way that the boundaries between the ethical and the economic, and their effects on one another, require constant surveillance and regulation in order to ensure that they do not produce unintended and deleterious social consequences.

Sandel's examples, like those of the advocates for cultural value discussed in Chapter 1, show how claims for a transcendent value always depend upon limiting the rhetorical range within which value can function, and defining value by what it is not. He asserts the transcendence of 'friendship' only in respect of an economic realm that has been established *a priori* as its opposite. Ethical and cultural values are separated out from the calculations of the exchange economy and asserted to be beyond measure, beyond the market, beyond the contingencies even of time and place. The distinction between the exchange-value of the market and the use-value of social interactions seems axiomatic. It is supported by a social consensus, reinforced by emotional commitment, and deviance from it is met with an apparently involuntary repugnance.[17]

By locating those values deemed to be beyond exchange in the private sphere of personal relations, Sandel limits their scope for application to the social world of conflicting interests where value is a matter of negotiation and transaction. In a further example he refers to a system of ensuring conformity to the regulations regarding 'late pick-up' at a children's nursery. He deplores the practice of fining parents who infringed the 'late pick-up' rules, arguing that the system of fines commodifed child-care and substituted a cash relationship for the collective responsibility of parents for the welfare of children and the working conditions of care-workers. The example is telling because it illustrates the problem of the social location of value. A small-scale, face-to-face social world managed by personal relations such as friendship may be able to establish (or coerce) commitment to shared value that would be reflected in social behaviour. If the value of children's welfare and care-workers' convenience can be recognised and endorsed without coercion, the system he proposes might be effective, though it would still involve an exchange: the exchange of one form of labour for another. If, on the other hand, the parents do not have any relationship other than as users of a nursery, they might in certain instances value their time more highly than the cost of additional hours of child-care. The organisation can then exchange the additional cost of care for a higher payment that might allow them to hire more care-workers, resulting in a more efficient system that meets the needs of the parents, the workers and the providing organisation. The market in child-care can grow. The higher market value of the organisation can then extend the provision and increase opportunities for women to enter the labour market, exchanging the pleasures (or tedium) of unpaid child-care for higher family income and enhanced social and economic status. In those circumstances, it is less easy to establish a clear difference between the value of friendly co-operation, which takes no account of differential interests or the need to provide market proxies for time, and the value of an effective exchange system in meeting the need for social goods.

In his antithesis between the ethical value of the common good and value in the market, Sandel fails to acknowledge that the system of child-care that he describes has already created an exchange-value for the care of children. His concern about commodification only applies to the regulation that will reduce anxiety about the potential inequivalence of the exchange between the users and the employees of the organisation. How many hours as a worker can be exchanged for hours as a carer? Sandel tilts the argument in favour of friendly co-operation and away from the efficiency of exchange, but the impulse to do so reveals the desire to locate value in intuitively perceived equitable relations located in the world of small-scale, face-to-face interactions rather than in already existing negotiations between the value of different kinds of work. His example, however, reveals unease at the flexibility of a market that can manage the relationship between the use and exchange value of social relations, as easily as it can those of diamonds and water. Discussion of value stands in for a discussion of the more complex questions of managing a market in which the differential power of producers and consumers and the role of the mediating organisation is at stake.

Sandel's lectures provided a challenging reiteration of the continuing problem of value. Though his arguments were informed by philosophy, his examples of friendship and child-care were deployed in a similar way to the government ministers' advocacy of the arts or theatre enthusiasts' commitment to Shakespeare discussed in Chapter 1. They identified consensual values that seem intuitively endorsed and are felt to be at odds with the values of the market that identifies only the contingent values that result from particular negotiations. The desire for human-scale, face-to-face expressions of value and the creation of consensus that appears to arise from it, can then be set against the alienating calculations of efficiency and effectiveness that drives organisations and institutions that operate in the market. That face-to-face version of value, however, tends to obscure precisely the protean capacity of markets that allows them to be changed so as to devise new ways of managing the relationship between use- and exchange-value, and the distribution of social goods. The capacity of markets and their intermediaries to manage that change in the interests of what Sandel calls 'the common-good' needs constant surveillance and discussion (for example of the differential social as well as market power of care-users over care-workers) but the axiomatic separation between market value and an idealised abstracted value cannot effectively replace that surveillance of value in practice.

The instability of all ideas of value, their dependence on consensus and transaction and their dynamic relationship to historical evaluations may simply have to be accepted as part of the condition in which value can function in society. The potential for conflict of interest between use- and exchange-values and the anxiety of equivalence that it generates can recur as even the most consensual values are challenged by new social circumstances and by the scale and complexity of contemporary social existence. Whether those challenges to the stability of value are regarded as part of the dynamic balancing of inequivalent values essential to a changing society or as signs of serious social crisis, will depend on the extent to which they can be resolved by argument and debate rather than by coercion and the unmediated exercise of power.

The exercise and expression of value in a secular society are not undermined by disagreement and debate. On the contrary, the instability that allows the debate is a mark of the dynamic social capacity that repeatedly negotiates a collective consensus to provide the basis for ordering social life and for making judgements that transcend the mere wishes and desires of individuals. As we have seen, simple oppositions between different valued objects, between past and present value judgements or between the interests of privileged and less-privileged groups contain the discussion of value in manageable terms. However, alongside this discursive circulation of value judgements, there exists the more fundamental dialectic between institutions that embody and reproduce value and markets that create value out of the transactions between use and exchange. By keeping both markets and institutions in the frame of our discussion of value, claims to value can be tested not only by setting valued objects one against another but by examining the transactions and locations in which their value is realised and expressed.

Notes

1 C. Scott, 'Exploring the Evidence Base for Museum Value', *Museum Management and Curatorship* 24(3) (2009): 195–212, p.198.
2 S. Galloway, 'Theory-Based Evaluation and the Social Impact of the Arts', *Cultural Trends* 18(2) (2009): 125–148, p.129.
3 Steven Connor, *Theory and Cultural Value* (Oxford: Blackwell, 1992), p.1.
4 Terry Eagleton, *After Theory* (London: Penguin Books, 2004), p.99.
5 John Fekete, 'Introductory Notes for a Postmodern Value Agenda', in John Fekete, ed., *Life after Postmodernism: Essays in Value and Culture* (London: Macmillan, 1988), pp.1–23(1) (in Connor, *Theory and Cultural Value*, p.8).
6 Connor, *Theory and Cultural Value*, p.2.
7 Connor, *Theory and Cultural Value*, p.2.
8 Richard Flacks, *Making History: The American Left and the American Mind* (New York: Columbia University Press, 1988), p.168. Quoted in Michael Denning, *Culture in the Age of Three Worlds* (London: Verso, 2004), p.128.
9 Terry Eagleton 'Capitalism and Form', *New Left Review* 14 (2002): 123–136, p.127.

10 Adam Smith, *An Enquiry into the Nature and Causes of The Wealth of Nations*, ed. R. H. Campbell and A. S. Skinner (Cambridge: Cambridge University Press, 1978), p. 47.
11 Smith, *The Wealth of Nations*, p. 49. Discussed in Nicholas Phillipson, *Adam Smith: An Enlightened Life* (London: Allen Lane, 1978), p. 219.
12 See Joyce Appleby, *Economic Thought and Ideology in Seventeenth Century England* (Princeton, NJ: Princeton University Press, 1978).
13 John Lanchester, *Whoops: Why Everyone Owes Everyone and No-One Can Pay* (London: Penguin Books, 2010), p. xv.
14 Featherstone, *Consumer Culture and Postmodernism*, p. 17.
15 Michael Sandel, *What Money Can't Buy* (London: Allen Lane, 2012).
16 See Alan Bray, *The Friend* (London: University of Chicago Press, 2003) and Daniel T. Lochman, Maritere López and Lorna Hutson, eds, *Discourses and Representations of Friendship in Early Modern Europe, 1500–1700* (Farnham: Ashgate, 2011).
17 Ways of managing these exchanges through non-financial market mechanisms are discussed by Alvin Roth, 'Repugnance as a Constraint on Markets', *Journal of Economic Perspectives* 21(3) (Summer 2007): 37–58.

3

Value and Shakespeare

'Shakespeare' presents a particularly intractable example of the problem of value. As we saw in Chapter 1, 'Shakespeare'[1] appears to be an incontestable location for value: even people who have little direct engagement with his plays in the theatre and have not read his plays since their school days are willing to agree that he is 'a genius', while those who are more enthusiastically committed are keen to rehearse and corroborate the narratives of transformation that reinforce and reiterate the value of Shakespeare in intuitive and consensual terms. The cycle of recognition, conferral and endorsement of value has been reiterated over centuries until the unstable connection between the valuers and valued seems to disappear. Yet, as we suggested in Chapter 2, though the reiteration of value may add weight to the authority required for claims to absolute value, a sum of evaluations, however large, cannot add up to an account of absolute value: it always depends upon the contingency of continuing evaluation that remains open to disagreement and dissent.

When disagreement and dissent occur, advocates for Shakespeare's value, as we have seen, shift the terms of evaluation from 'Shakespeare' to the particular experiences and education that reduce the authority of the dissenters and allow their evaluations to be discounted. Commenting on Wayne Booth's assertion that the value of Shakespeare is something 'that every person who undergoes a proper apprenticeship and comes to understand enough about Shakespeare's culture can discern', Connor observes the 'immaculately self-confirming' tautology that defends intrinsic value from the 'yawning abyss' of relativism.[2] If Shakespeare's value depends upon 'a proper apprenticeship' and an understanding of Shakespeare's culture, then its intrinsic character must be called into question.

The philosophical neatness of denying the absolute, intrinsic value of Shakespeare has had interesting intellectual consequences. It has opened up a new field of enquiry in which scholars have investigated the continuity of Shakespeare's reproduction in the eighteenth-century 'making of the national poet', and the nineteenth-century development of 'big-time Shakespeare' in the publishing and entertainment industries.[3] This work has shifted the focus of attention from the plays that constitute 'Shakespeare' to the social and economic processes and the negotiations of authority and expertise that assign value to Shakespeare, showing how these forms of reproduction have developed the tastes and capacity of those who value 'Shakespeare' and providing an audience for the developments of cheap print and other technologies of distribution that extended the scale of market for Shakespeare.[4]

In spite of this emphasis on the contingent circumstances that generate the effect of value, the special character of Shakespeare's value continues to be insisted upon. Even when that value is described in the language of markets, the commodity identified as 'Shakespeare' seems to have a value that transcends particular market transactions. As Terry Eagleton describes it,

> Shakespeare is the quintessential commodity, at once ever new and consolingly recognisable, always different and eternally the same, a magnificent feat of self-identity persisting through the most bizarre diversions and variations.[5]

By describing Shakespeare as a *quintessential* commodity, Eagleton articulates the sense that, behind every particular manifestation, there nevertheless exists an essential Shakespeare that transcends each one. The object of value appears as a portmanteau term that includes all the individual productions and versions of the plays whose value might be called into question, but none of them could deny the value that transcends time and place and can be claimed to be 'universal' because it is always greater than the sum of its particular instances. As Graham Holderness describes, 'Shakespeare' acts as 'a sign post pointing towards something greater and more complete than itself'.[6]

This elusive, ideal, quintessential Shakespeare seems almost like value itself. It can be identified only by its effects; its material manifestations are always the result of contingent historical circumstances and its existence becomes a matter of belief. The value is

Value and Shakespeare 53

thus unavailable for analysis, a value of last resort that authorises and sustains all of the actions undertaken in his name.

In the latter part of this book, we will pay close attention to some of the manifestations of this essential Shakespeare in cultural reproduction, to show how they are effects of particular institutional and material processes. At this point, too, it is important to arrest the drift towards abstraction and idealism by paying attention to the discursive as well as the material work that sustains the connection between Shakespeare the universal signifier and the material existence of Shakespeare in his published poems and plays.

Negotiating Shakespeare's value

As we found at the BSA meeting described in Chapter 1, expert accounts of Shakespeare and social analysis of his theatrical reproduction, however intellectually authoritative, no longer have a direct impact on the advocacy of value. Rather, it is the form of the knowledge applied that allows it to connect with and reinforce the value of the elusive essential Shakespeare. Narratives of conversion seem to have a significant corroborative effect but so too do accounts that present a persuasive analogy between the historical existence of Shakespeare and his role as 'our contemporary'. Stephen Greenblatt, for example, in a collection appropriately entitled *Shakespearean Negotiations*, distinguished Shakespeare's work from other 'collective expressions' that, he finds, 'when moved from their original settings to a new place or time are dead on arrival'.[7]

In order to do so, he developed an analytical method that linked unfamiliar early modern printed texts with the themes of Shakespeare's plays. For Greenblatt, the unexplored repository of early modern texts was not the source of information about Shakespeare's theatre and his theatrical contemporaries: that resource had been fully explored earlier in the century; even less was it the source of quantitative data about early modern social relations whose findings on the whole demonstrated the difference between Shakespeare's fictional narratives and the lived experience of early modern people. Rather, the non-Shakespearean texts that Greenblatt connected to Shakespeare's plays provided a store of narratives, such as the strange tales of egregious popish impostures, or, in his biography of Shakespeare, the dangerous link between Jesuit missionaries and a Lancashire family who left a legacy to one Shakes-shaft, that gave a fresh new meaning to the familiar play texts. His work highlighted the verbal and ideological connection between these narratives, their real-life preoccupations with religious and social change, and the themes and preoccupations of Shakespeare's plays. By a process of analogy and extrapolation, he made a compelling and eloquent case that the identified connections constituted a shared 'social energy' that had both produced the plays of Shakespeare and made them into exemplary paradigms of early modern social existence that continued to speak to contemporary audiences.

In his acclaimed literary biography of Shakespeare, moreover, he established similar connections between the known events of Shakespeare's life and the narrative of the plays. The deaths of Shakespeare's father and son and the death of Hamlet's father, for example, are connected by an alliterative phrase that points away from the detail of Shakespeare's biography or the events of the play towards an experience that appears universal because of the abstractions in which it is expressed:

> the death of his son and the impending death of his father – a crisis of mourning and memory – constitute a psychic disturbance that helps to explain the explosive power and inwardness of *Hamlet*.[8]

The 'Shakespeare' re-animated by Greenblatt's account exists less in the historical seventeenth century than in a neutral space of recognition in which the commentator can identify not only with the play's narratives but with values developed out of nineteenth-century liberal social thought. In Greenblatt's biography of Shakespeare, modern preoccupations with the co-existence of different races in developed societies are echoed in his account of Shakespeare's eloquent empathy with 'the wretched strangers' imagined in Sir Thomas More's appeal on behalf of immigrants (p. 263) or his capacity to call 'laughter into question, to make the amusement excruciatingly uncomfortable' (p. 278) when dealing with the story of Shylock. Those liberal humanist values, their concern for individual rights and freedoms that underpin the idealised, if not always realised, value system of twenty-first-century democracies, can be extrapolated from individual speeches in the Shakespeare text. In turn, they allow directors and critics to align the plays with events in the modern world that neither Shakespeare nor his characters could possibly have envisaged or understood.

In spite of the learning that informed Greenblatt's work, his tone was less authoritative scholar and more persuasive storyteller. The work of academic experts, who might have cavilled about the provenance and transmission of his sources, was gently dismissed as the 'dogged archival labour' of 'eager scholars' (p.212). Greenblatt's method instead offered a form of expert authority that did not depend upon assertions of fact or robust analysis of effect, but shaped the contours of a possible shared relationship with a Shakespeare who was both 'our contemporary' and a spokesman for the past. His Shakespearean negotiations are both between Shakespeare and his present and between Shakespeare and our present. They are led but not imposed by the informed and eloquent critic and they create a new form of knowledge that can stand in for the (often puzzling) process of reading and responding to the plays.

This eloquent critical work of contemporary literary analysis is not explicitly acknowledged in the consensual account of 'Shakespeare's' 'explosive power' or its connection to 'the inner life we all inhabit'. However, the connections it makes between historical texts and their metaphorical 'social energy' provide the intellectual underpinnings for the value of 'Shakespeare' in the present.

This persuasive deployment of new knowledge to reconstitute the value of Shakespeare was different from the extrapolation of singular truths from Shakespeare's plays in the form of collections of quotations. It required eloquent argumentation that enacted rather than simply advocating the value of Shakespeare. It depended on the particular discursive techniques that turned the plays' narratives into allegories of the present as well as paradigms of a recognisable past. In 2011, the leading Shakespeare scholar, Jonathan Bate, for example, was commissioned by the AHRC to promote and celebrate the value of the research that they fund. In the course of that defence, Bate invoked Shakespeare not only as valuable object for research but as spokesman for the fundamental priority of intrinsic over relative value. He quoted from the discussion of value from Act 2 of *Troilus and Cressida*, concluding that for 'Shakespeare'

> The relativism of Troilus (things only have value in so far as they are valued by particular people who prize them) is replaced by the proposition that there can be essential values, that a thing might be intrinsically valuable ('precious of itself').[9]

Bate's expert knowledge of the histories of publishing and theatrical transmission was not invoked in this allocation of cultural authority to Shakespeare.[10] For the purposes of this polemic, 'Shakespeare' was presented as a defining voice whose statement about value could resolve division and silence intellectual dissent. No case needed to be made for the specific value of Shakespeare: rather Shakespearean eloquence was deployed as a way of substituting rhetoric for analysis, substituting a statement about value made in the course of a Shakespeare play, for a systematic analysis of the relations between cost and value in the case of academic research. The quotation from Shakespeare was offered as a rhetorical supplement to a familiar position in the value debate, giving weight to the idea of an immeasurable and intrinsic value and the suggestion of a truth that had stood the test of time.

Identifying that intrinsic value, however, cannot be solely a matter of endorsing critical opinion, however authoritative. In Greenblatt's case the intrinsic value of Shakespeare is re-negotiated as the 'social energy' with which the plays engage subsequent readers; in Bate's case it is identified by selective quotation, glossed and explicated for particular rhetorical purposes. Both critics sustain the value of Shakespeare by adding the value of their knowledge and argument to make a case for the continuing relationship between Shakespeare's own time and ours. Their negotiations with Shakespeare, however, could not take place if Shakespeare was an empty signifier: their discussion depends upon the choice of example from the range and variety of Shakespeare's plays and their particular expression of the ideas that can be selected to make the connection to the present time. The cases that they make depend not only on their own skills and knowledge but also on the plays' formal characteristics of speech, narrative and dramatic action that constitute the printed texts.

Value in Shakespeare

For all their alleged difficulty, which we will discuss in Chapter 5, the texts of Shakespeare's plays offer an extraordinary, but not unique,[11] asset from which value can be created. Unlike other valued historical remains, their dramatic form allows them, as Bate's example shows, to present characters who speak of value (as well as other social ideas) as well as being objects on which value can be conferred, negotiated and exchanged. The play texts themselves present only set of speeches preceded by their speakers' names. Together those speeches communicate an action, evoke the past that might explain it and describe the emotion that connects speaker to narrative. Since their literary and narrative effects depend upon conflict, the speeches often put into question the most settled of social values, including the divine rights of kings, the power of witches and the allegiance that women owe to men. Their speakers who enact, dramatise and comment on this conflict are manifestly not our contemporaries, and in many cases were not Shakespeare's. When those characters speak of value they never speak with the voice of Shakespeare and nor can the sum of their statements add up to a unitary statement about the value of Shakespeare in spite of the hermeneutic and creative ingenuity that has been applied to that end over the centuries.

Nevertheless by resisting the tendency to interpret the plays' meanings and paying attention instead to their formal particularity, it is possible to identify the specific ways in which their speeches and narratives are organised to dramatise conflict within the question of value. Those conflicts present the question of value in ways that are different from and offer a challenge to the discussion of value at the present time, but it is possible also to discern the points of connection that make the contemporary discussion possible.

In *Troilus and Cressida*, for example, the Act 2 debate over the value of Helen of Troy canvasses a wide range of assertions about value. It is possible, as Bate's analysis suggests, to extrapolate individual arguments that eloquently support contemporary ideas of value. However, the scene as a whole offers a much more confused and confusing image both of possible arguments for value and the connection between those arguments and the case in point: whether to return Helen to the Trojan camp. The Trojan king, Priam, indicates that the Greek general, Nestor, has proposed terms for the return of Helen:

> Deliver Helen, and all damage else
> As honour, loss of time, travail, expense,
> Wounds, friends, and what else dear that is consumed
> In hot digestion of this cormorant war
> Shall be struck off.
>
> (2.2.3–7)

The list of items that might be set against the value of Helen includes a variety of proxies for value, which are more (loss to time, travail, expense) and less ('honour', 'wounds' and the lives of friends) easy to quantify. The list concludes with the term from simple accounting 'struck off', as if Nestor hopes that the war can be ended by a simple transaction.

Hector's response makes clear that the Trojans must 'Let Helen go' (2.2.16). In his speech to justify the decision, the language of accounting becomes completely confused:

> Since the first sword was drawn about this question,
> Every tithe-soul, 'mongst many thousand dismes,[12]
> Hath been as dear as Helen – I mean, of ours.
> If we have lost so many tenths of ours,
> To guard a thing not ours – nor worth to us,
> Had it our name, the value of one ten –
> What merit's in that reason which denies
> The yielding of her up?
>
> (2.2.17–24).

His language confuses a quantity of value (a tithe or a dime) established by long-standing social practice, with the legal question of ownership that conveys value to the owner. A tithe was an exact proportion of variable values for land that was owed to the church or other landowner so its value was proportionate rather than the same sum in every case. It offered no exact sum that could be used for a simple, arithmetical calculation of value. Hector's confusion arises from a lack of understanding of the symbolic nature of mathematical calculation. In his speech 'a tithe soul' represents a person, so in the rest of the speech when he speaks of 'one ten' he is referring to each individual ('every soul 'mongst many thousand') Trojan who is 'as dear as Helen' (2.2.19) but is also trying to convey that the number of Trojans makes them even more dear. The maths merely provides him with generalised hyperbole that cannot provide a persuasive analogy with the fundamental question that ends the speech: 'What merit's in that reason which denies/The yielding of her up?' (2.2.23–24).

Troilus, on the other hand, is on less intellectually treacherous ground when he simply denies that any system of measurement could provide a proxy for the 'worth and honour of a king':

> Weigh you the worth and honour of a king
> So great as our dread father in a scale
> Of common ounces? Will you with counters sum

The past-proportion of his infinite?
And buckle in a waist most fathomless
With spans and inches so diminutive
As fears and reasons?

(2.2.25–31)

The shifting metaphors, however, give an almost comic sense of the impossibility of stable measurement: he suggests that even the scales for measuring weights and lengths cannot act as proxies for value, but his metaphorical connection between 'fears and reasons' (2.2.31) and 'spans and inches' (2.2.30) leads him to suggest that King Priam's 'waist' is fathomless.

What is dramatised in these exchanges is the complexity, if not the impossibility, of arriving at an effective metaphorical proxy for value, or even an agreed scale with which to measure equivalence. Priam's account of the offer to return Helen presents an extended articulation of the modern metaphor of 'cutting one's losses' but that concept, so commonplace after 300 years of professional accounting practice, makes no sense to Shakespeare's Trojan warriors, whose language is permeated with metaphors for the connection between goods and value. Priam's speech includes the image of 'this cormorant war': this is not a war in which expenses can be rationally exchanged but resembles a paradigm for voracious greed.

In the absence of stable proxies for value, the debate veers off into personal insults about the connection between reason and sheer cowardice, along with unstable analogies between the case in point and the behaviour of merchants or lovers. Helen's value is described both an equivalent for 'an old aunt whom the Greeks held captive' (2.2.76) and, in an image that echoes Dr Faustus's breathless eulogy of his vision of Helen of Troy, as 'a pearl,/Whose price hath launch'd above a thousand ships,/And turn'd crown'd kings to merchants' (2.2.80–82). The value-calculations that the warriors present are no more precise than analogies that equate Helen's value either with already highly valued objects (the 'pearl/Whose price hath launch'd above a thousand ships') or objects that are obviously denigrated ('an old aunt whom the Greeks held captive').

The warriors' debate reveals the fundamental instability of proxies for value rather than a preference for absolute over contingent value. In the imagined world of *Troilus and Cressida*, value is fought out in physical action that is only tenuously contained by rules of war that allow a system of negotiated equivalence to manage the exchange of prisoners. That world includes the contracts among buyers and sellers that prevent the return of 'silks upon the merchant,/When we have soil'd them' (2.2.68–69) and a system of 'law in each well-order'd nation' that is designed to resolve conflicts among 'those raging appetites that are/ Most disobedient and refractory' 2.2.179–181). Nevertheless, by the end of the scene, none of those attempts to establish a firm and reliable set of agreed proxies for value, or systems of authority with which to manage it, can overcome the overriding claim of 'the joint and several dignities' (2.2.191–192) of a group of powerful and pugnacious warriors. In the world of the Trojan war, the question of value cannot be resolved by accounting measures that provide an agreed proxy for a variety of disparate elements, by negotiated compromise or by the structures of social consensus that allow ideas of value to function in modern societies.

The warriors' discussion is interrupted by the crazy wailing of Cassandra: 'Cry, Trojans, cry'. She makes no intellectual case for handing Helen back. Rather, her prophecies dramatise the ineluctable force of events that will make argument irrelevant in the face of an already determined future in which 'Troy must not be, nor goodly Ilion stand'. The disputatious contestants in the debate will face death and mutilation in the case of Hector and sexual humiliation in the case of Troilus. Their relative positions in the debate over value will have no bearing on either fate.

The dramatic events of this scene, in other words, offer no easily recognisable connection either to a bureaucratic requirement for public accountability, or to the modern challenge of explaining the relationship between free intellectual enquiry and the public resources that fund it. Rather, the world of Shakespeare's plays, where value is literally fought out as a matter of life and death, instead highlights the *difference* between modern social struggles over value and those dramatised in Shakespeare's plays. *Troilus and Cressida* dramatises the characters' failure to resolve the confusion caused by an offer of negotiation because the terms of value that are offered cannot easily connect with their warlike ways of dealing with conflict. The equivalences that the Greeks propose between Helen, whose abduction occasioned the conflict, on the one hand, and 'honour, loss of time, travail, expense,/Wounds, friends, and what else dear'(2.2.4–5) on the other, cannot be managed or even fully understood: the warriors attempt to assimilate them into the more familiar values of honour and reason or the protocols of prior possession, but their disputation offers no peaceful way of resolving the overriding realities of brute power and the historical circumstances of the action in which they are embroiled.

Troilus and Cressida is not, of course, the last or only word on the question of value in Shakespeare. The warriors of the Trojan play have a particular difficulty with numbers and their attempts to make a case for value reach for analogies with the mix of trade and prisoner exchange that provide the most pressing contemporary circumstances in which a stable idea of value is at stake. In other plays the arithmetic of value is more clearly understood, but the proxies for value that it provides cannot resolve the connection between value and action in terms of the deferred value of social hierarchy.

In Q2 of *Hamlet*, as the play moves towards its conclusion, Hamlet, banished from Denmark, encounters a Captain, sent by Fortinbras to seek a safe passage over the kingdom of Denmark as he marches on Poland. The captain explains that the land that Fortinbras is out to conquer is

> A little patch of ground
> That hath in it no profit but the name.
> To pay five ducats, five, I would not farm it;
> Nor will it yield to Norway or the Pole
> A ranker rate should it be sold in fee.
>
> (Q2 4.4.11–15)[13]

For the Captain, acquiring land through conquest should return some 'profit' beyond its name: the profit created by the use-value of agriculture or the exchange-value of sale 'in fee'. The Captain's numerical calculation of the value of the disputed land is taken up by Hamlet, but his enumeration brings him to the opposite conclusion. For Hamlet, the 'Two thousand souls, and twenty thousand ducats' that would be spent defending the land is a tribute to the value of human aspiration and active resolve:

> Rightly to be great
> Is not to stir without great argument,
> But greatly to find quarrel in a straw
> When honour's at the stake.
>
> (4.4.44–47)

It is precisely the *in*equivalence between Fortinbras's military action and the worthless plot of land that strikes Hamlet as heroic.

Fortinbras's honour however, is not a vaguely transcendent value: it can, in the circumstances, be precisely measured against

> The imminent death of twenty thousand men
> That for a fantasy and trick of fame,
> Go to their graves like beds, flight for a plot
> Whereon the numbers cannot try the cause,
> Which is not tomb enough and continent
> To hide the slain.
>
> (4.4.51–56)

In the imagined world of Shakespeare's plays the characters present value as highly contingent on the status and interests of those making the evaluation. For Hamlet the death of common soldiers, referred to by numbers, is incommensurate with ideas of aristocratic honour; for the Captain, the effort of a war can be calculated against the profit or fee that the land will produce.

Market value: the prizer and the prized

The discussion of value in *Hamlet* and *Troilus and Cressida* reveals some of the complex entanglement of comparisons used in Shakespeare's characters' speeches in order to present an idea of value stable enough to support action. Their accounts demonstrate that fixed numerical scales cannot fully establish value in ways that will be accepted by everyone involved and the ultimate authority for value depends upon the standing of those who assert it: the 'joint and several dignities' of the Trojan warriors or the 'divine ambition' of Fortinbras that cares nothing for the 'imminent death of twenty thousand men'. Hector makes a case for a distinction between the intrinsic value of an object 'wherein 'tis precious of itself' and the 'particular will' of what he calls 'the prizer', but he finds no stable proxy for that distinction that will allow his distinction to resolve the action. The language and actions through which the characters negotiate those disagreements offer vivid images of the connection between those who confer value and the unstable measures of the proxies that hold their idea of value in place.

In the opening scene of *Antony and Cleopatra*, for example, the Egyptian Queen demands 'If it be love indeed, tell me how much?' (1.1.14) Antony's riposte, 'There's beggary in love that can be reckoned' (1.1.15), echoes Troilus's insistence that the 'worth and honour of a king/So great as our dread father' cannot be measured 'in a scale/Of common ounces' (2.2.25, 27). Antony's use of the term 'beggary', however, also suggests a patrician association between 'reckoning' and the action of beggars: adding up sums of value is not the behaviour of lovers who rule the known world and could 'find out new heaven, new earth' (1.1.17) before a limit or 'bourn' (1.1.16) on their love could be set. Antony and Cleopatra did not need to reckon their love or any of the other necessaries of their lives that came from the surpluses provided by conquered land or the spoils of war.

The security of Antony's confident distinction between himself and a beggar has, of course, been destabilised from the beginning of the play's action. Philo's opening lines have established a completely different scale of value in the contrast between the 'triple pillar of the world' and 'a strumpet's fool' (1.1.12–13): the value of a conquering soldier is for Philo axiomatically higher than that of a lover and the judgements that he makes themselves affect his status. The prizer is not so easily distinguished from the prize.

As we suggested in Chapter 2, the connection between value and valuer is critical not only for establishing a stable concept of value but for managing early markets. When Othello, for example, castigates himself for the death of Desdemona, the language he uses to articulate his loss presents his mistaken evaluation of his wife as a miscalculation in a market:

Had she been true,
If heaven would make me such another world
Of one entire and perfect chrysolite,
I'd not have sold her for it.

(5.2.150–153)

He has not, of course, *sold* Desdemona: he has murdered her. This connection to a market, however, is elaborated by his language and its unsuccessful attempt to distinguish between buying and selling and the value of the objects of exchange. He elaborates the analogy – I would not have sold her for the world – with the image of 'one entire and perfect chrysolite',[14] an unimaginable valued object, worth more than all the world. The use of an analogy as a mark of value, however, though it might express the speaker's eloquence does not actually stabilise value: analogies can go both ways as Emilia's witty play on the same image demonstrates when she and Desdemona discuss the value of marital fidelity. Desdemona asks 'Would'st thou do such a deed for all the world' (4.3.62), and Emilia's response presents a set piece that reverses commonplace ideas of value:

> The world's a huge thing: it is a great price.
> For a small vice...
> By my troth, I think I should, and undo't when I had
> done. Marry, I would not do such a thing for a
> joint-ring, nor for measures of lawn, nor for
> gowns, petticoats, nor caps, nor any petty
> exhibition; but for the whole world, – ud's pity, who would
> not make her husband a cuckold to make him a
> monarch? I should venture purgatory for't...
> Why the wrong is but a wrong i' the world: and
> having the world for your labour, tis a wrong in your
> own world, and you might quickly make it right.
>
> (4.3.67–81)

Emilia's spirited mockery of the transcendent value of chastity is a familiar trope for a witty servant or a clever child: the structural position of Emilia in the narrative of the play. It situates value in what Claudius calls 'the corrupted currents of this world' (*Hamlet*, 4.2.164) in the prayer scene of *Hamlet*. Recognising the contingency of the world 'as it is' is necessary to hold in place the divine absolutes that assure a value of last resort. Emilia boldly claims that she would not only exchange her chastity for the world but would 'venture' or risk 'purgatory for't': but she does not blaspheme against the possibility of salvation and her place in heaven.

Again and again the metaphors of value indicate analogies with the market that negotiate the connection between absolute and contingent value as a set of unstable rhetorical comparisons but also determine the fitness of individuals to take part in market exchange. Once Othello is finally convinced of Desdemona's virtue, the metaphors he uses to express her value shift from 'the world', represented by a perfect chrysolite, to an implied comparison between himself and others whose understanding of value seems to him less secure. He asks to be remembered as 'one whose hand,/ Like the base Indian, threw a pearl away/Richer than all his tribe' (5.2.345–347). The 'base Indian' is part of the nexus of value: misrecognition of value, as much as attempts to calculate it, is enough to indicate baseness that is further endorsed by racial difference. In the First Folio printings of the text, the word 'Indian', found in the Quarto and Second Folio printings, is printed as 'Iudean'. Turned letters (n for u) were a common printing variation but 'Indian' and 'Judean' equally designate marginalised groups, whose recognition of value might be presented as unreliable. Othello's speech indicates a shift in the stability of value from appropriate analogue to the authority as a prizer. In Othello's case that authority does not come from aristocratic status: it is established only by his difference from the base Indian/Judean. He, unlike the base Indian, can see the value of the world as 'one perfect chrysolite' and he, along with Troilus and Faustus, recognises the 'priceless' value of the pearl, a value that was further endorsed by the parable narratives of the Christian gospels.[15]

The metaphors used both by Othello and by the writers of the gospel give both a vivid and a confused sense of value: they are vivid because of the precision of the objects being invoked but they are obscure because a metaphorical connection does not depend upon a clear correspondence between tenor and vehicle. Like value itself, the effectiveness of metaphors depends on accepting the suggested relationships between rubies and wisdom or between pearls and the kingdom of heaven, or, for that matter, between Shakespeare and transcendent value. As we suggested in Chapter 2, it is impossible to identify value that is completely transcendent without either an accepted consensus or a defining authority. If that correspondence is denied (pearls are nothing like the kingdom of heaven; the worth of a dread king cannot be measured 'in a scale/Of common ounces') the basis for assigning value is destabilised. It is the authority of holy writ or historic texts that sustains the necessary stability of those connections, while their frequent reiteration renders them proverbial long after the material conditions and the value systems within which they were articulated cease to exist.

Within the plays' action, these values remain conditional. One some occasions the security of the metaphors that hold them in place is explicitly called into question by presenting, as Emilia does, possible alternatives to the familiar connections that have brought them into being. At others, the plays' narratives and the situation of the characters within them demonstrate the gap between the metaphors used to establish value and the situation in which the characters have to act on their values. The Trojan warriors' invocation of honour as the authorising value is set against the inevitability of their defeat; Hamlet compares Fortinbras's secure sense of honour with his own failure to endorse that value with action; and both Antony and Othello endorse their own sense of value by contrast with the beggar, Indian or Iudean whose misjudgements of value shore up the comparative authority of the misguided evaluations they make. The prizers' authority may be endorsed by high-sounding comparisons within established hierarchies of value, but it cannot ensure that values that they so eloquently claim will be endorsed either by other characters in the plays or by subsequent readers.

Narratives of value

The connection between value and action is further tested by the narratives in which these statements about value are made. As we suggested in Chapter 2, assertions about value, however eloquent or authoritative, can always be countered and denied by counter-assertions or, more powerfully, by analysis that reveals the gap between those values and the facts of social existence. The social power of values depends upon securing a consensus that requires a tolerance for contingency and a willingness to accept (however temporarily) a scale of equivalence that can provide an accepted proxy for value and thus reduce the potential for continual social conflict. Shakespeare's plays, on the other hand, address the question of value from the other end. Their structure depends on conflict for the narrative drive that would be pre-empted by premature consensus or compromise. The passion with which their protagonists refuse to accept the contingency of the values that inform their behaviour gives the narratives their particular urgency, and the failure of proxies to provide resolution is central to their dramatic effect. In the closed world of Shakespeare's dramatic narratives, value can, for the duration of the story, seem completely transcendent, and is the occasion for struggle, fighting and death. Whether death or compromise is the outcome is determined by the genre, the way the story goes, the division of emotional attention between one character and another.

The dramatisation of value is clearest in two plays whose conflict depends upon the tension between value and terms in which it is established in the contracts that control its social operations over time. Both the love test in *King Lear* and Shylock's bond in *The Merchant of Venice* enact the operations of contracts intended to provide clear, shared and binding agreements that will be stable enough to resolve the balance between value and time. Lear announces that he will 'publish/Our daughters several dowries,/ that future strife may be prevented now'(1.1.43–45),[16] and Antonio's bond with Shylock is also a standard instrument for solving cash-flow problems:

> a month before
> This bond expires, I do expect return
> Of thrice three times the value of this bond.
>
> (1.3.156–158).

The agreements themselves are commonplace ways of managing the social effects of debt and inheritance by adding the dimension of time to the exchange value of commodities. In a fictional narrative, of course, the uncertainty of time, which contracts are designed to overcome, can be managed for emotional effect, and their limitation to the objects for exchange can equally be compromised for the sake of surprise and suspense. It is Lear's rage at the failure of his proposed bond and Shylock's attempt to use his bond to resolve an 'ancient grudge' that vitiates the bonds' roles as proxies for value, but that same emotional dimension gives the narratives the emotional dimension.

Proxies such as bonds, contracts and money itself also function as symbolic equivalents of social relations that allow them to be managed effectively. In both *King Lear* and *The Merchant of Venice*, the turns of the plays' events work to expose the gap between these symbolic values and their all too material outcome. The ensuing conflict produces, in the case of Lear, the complete collapse of social relations into violence and death and, in the case of Shylock, the return to value imposed by the authority of Venetian law. The failure of literal calculation in these plays' narratives, however, is less an indication of an absolute ethical divide between social relations and the calculation of value and more a dramatic account of the emotional and affective significance of that failure.

The distinction between calculation and social relations that has become axiomatic in contemporary discussions of value is much less evident in Shakespeare's plays as both their language and their narratives elide and interchange them. In *King Lear*, the opening conversation between Kent and Gloucester elides 'affect' and 'value' in a casual fashion, substituting the one for the other without comment:

> **KENT** I thought the King had more *affected* the Duke of Albany than Cornwall.
> **GLOUCESTER** It did always seem so to us: but now, in the division of the kingdom, it appears not which of the dukes he *values* most; for qualities[17] are so weighed that curiosity in neither can make choice of either's moiety.
>
> (1.1.1–6).

In *The Merchant of Venice*, too, Bassanio opens the play with a similar elision of the values of love and the credit relations that they support:

> To you, Antonio,
> I owe the most, in money and in love,
> And from your love I have a warranty
> To unburden all my plots and purposes
> How to get clear of all the debts I owe.
>
> (1.1.130–134)

Antonio's love provides Bassanio with a 'warranty' that is both a social permission to speak of his debts and a 'guarantee' of his financial support.

These double entendres that play between the affective and financial meanings of bond, warranty and debt set the terms for the dramatic transactions of inheritance and credit that have both material and affective consequences. The dramatic crises occur when the metaphorical connections are put to the test: Cordelia abruptly refuses to articulate the connection between love and inheritance, and the enmity between Antonio and Shylock exposes the instability of the equitable relations essential for the effective operations of contracts.

Antonio is initially clear that the distinction between friends and enemies need not impede the exchange of money. He tells Shylock:

> If thou wilt lend this money, lend it not
> As to thy friends; for when did friendship take
> A breed for barren metal of his friend?
> But lend it rather to thine enemy,
> Who, if he break, thou mayst with better face
> Exact the penalty.
>
> (1.3.130–135)

Money can provide a stable proxy for value only if it is clearly distinct from the social relations among friends.

In *King Lear* family relations are placed outside the realm of calculation with rather more complex effects. Goneril expresses her love for her father by removing any consideration of the social and economic relations that might give it substance. Her speech deploys rhetorical hyperbole whose comparisons set love higher than things whose value, like Othello's priceless pearl, is claimed to be axiomatic but can only be expressed in comparisons with other items of value

> Sir, I love you more than words can wield the matter;
> Dearer than eyesight, space, and liberty;
> Beyond what can be valued, rich or rare,
> No less than life; with grace, health, beauty, honour;
> As much as child e'er loved, or father found;
> A love that makes breath poor and speech unable.
>
> (1.1.55–60)

As Peter Brook has pointed out, it is impossible, in theatrical practice, to connect Goneril's rhetoric with an innately evil character. At the opening of the play, her speech alone cannot indicate her future behaviour and presents only the high-flown language of 'a lady of style and breeding, accustomed to expressing herself in public'.[18] Her speech offers a metaphorically eloquent account of 'inexpressible value' that presents a rhetorical contrast to Cordelia's abrupt offer of 'Nothing' (1.1.89). Cordelia stages a more literal dramatisation of a love that 'makes breath poor and speech unable' but one that consequently disobeys Lear's command to speak.

The theatrical structure of the scenes where value is discussed, range from the casual and rhetorically smooth use of the metaphors seen in the examples discussed above to episodes that overdetermine the significance of the value transactions. When Bassanio first approaches Shylock for his loan, Shylock's repetitive, slow motion responses both effect narrative suspense (will Bassanio get the money he needs for the play to continue?) and provide the starting pace for the scene:

> **SHYLOCK** Three thousand ducats. Well.
> **BASSANIO** Ay, sir, for three months.
> **SHYLOCK** For three months. Well.
> **BASSANIO** For the which, as I told you, Antonio shall be bound.

SHYLOCK Antonio shall become bound. Well.
BASSANIO May you stead me? will you pleasure me? shall I
know your answer?

(1.3.1–8)

The pace picks up as Shylock shifts the conversation to the metaphorical meaning of 'good' as a marker of credit value, and Bassanio confuses the distinction by insisting on the social rather than the technical economic meaning of 'assure':

SHYLOCK Three thousand ducats for three months and Antonio
bound.
BASSANIO Your answer to that.
SHYLOCK Antonio is a good man.
BASSANIO Have you heard any imputation to the contrary?
SHYLOCK Oh, no, no, no, no: my meaning in saying he is a
good man is to have you understand me that he is
sufficient. Yet his means are in supposition. He
hath an argosy bound to Tripolis, another to the
Indies. I understand moreover, upon the Rialto, he
hath a third at Mexico, a fourth for England, and
other ventures he hath, squandered abroad. But ships
are but boards, sailors but men. There be land-rats
and water-rats, water-thieves and land-thieves – I
mean pirates – and then there is the peril of waters,
winds and rocks. The man is, notwithstanding,
sufficient. Three thousand ducats; I think I may
take his bond.
BASSANIO Be assured you may.
SHYLOCK I will be assured I may; and, that I may be assured,
I will bethink me. May I speak with Antonio?

(1.3.9–29)

The economic significance of assurance, in this case, cannot be fixed through a proxy: Shylock needs assurance of face-to-face connection with Antonio. Bassanio, however, misreads the terms of that face-to-face relationship and suggests a more intimate social connection than Shylock can consent to:

BASSANIO If it please you to dine with us.
SHYLOCK Yes, to smell pork; to eat of the habitation which
your prophet the Nazarite conjured the devil into! I
will buy with you, sell with you, talk with you,
walk with you, and so following, but I will not eat

with you, drink with you, nor pray with you. What
news on the Rialto? Who is he comes here?

(1.3.30–37)

Shylock separates completely the world of business transactions, and the social world of sharing food and prayer. The calculations of credit exchange require the assurance of a face-to-face confirmation among the parties to the bond but this transactional relationship is distinguished from the affective world of social interaction that might include enmity as well as friendship, each of which confuses the clarity necessary for the equity that is essential for smooth business transactions. The hatred between him and Antonio, so vividly expressed in their first encounter, mixes religious prejudice and competitive business relations. The possibility of negotiating an agreed equivalence of value, which connects the sum lent to the time when it is not available for the lender's use (three thousand ducats, for three months), is displaced by the angry accounts of past confrontations and their theological dispute over the meaning of the biblical analogy with Laban's sheep.

The ridiculous inequivalence of the ensuing contract dramatises the complete breakdown of market relations. As Shylock makes clear (1.3.162–168), Antonio's flesh has no value in the market: the 'merry bond' Shylock proposes instead, offers only a ghastly travesty of the idea of credit relations based on human worth. Antonio's value as a good, sufficient man cannot be assured by a proxy note of credit; it must be literally based on his flesh. The social relations of friendship and shared religion can provide a stable basis for credit relations only among peers: those, like Antony's beggar or Othello's base In(u)dian, who are not part of the legitimate circle of social relations are excluded except in cases where value can be agreed on through neutral proxies, unencumbered by the emotional considerations of either friendship or enmity.

In the drama, of course, the emotional dynamic of the scene and its position in the narrative are much more significant than any implications that the discussion might have for the abstract analysis of value. The rhythm of the scene – its carefully paced build-up to the crescendo of Shylock's passionate recall of past humiliations and its second movement into the calculations of the bond – addresses the fate of the characters as the story of fulfilling the bond unfolds. The effect of testing conflicting values and their proxies in a dramatic narrative is to assign emotional authority to characters according to their affective role in the play rather than on the intellectual coherence of their value analysis. Antonio's and Shylock's different accounts of the nature of value are structured by their roles as hero and villain of the story. The story of the bond acts as a frame for the play's other actions where the familiar narratives of triumphant love, though the language and the terms of that triumph are complex and contradictory,[19] once again reinforce the claims of affect over those of analysis. The effect is to marginalise the figures that have no place in the final resolution: Morocco, Aragon, Tubal and Shylock himself, none of whom participate in the play's joyful final scenes.

The framework of affect and its reinforcement through the plays' action is equally powerfully realised in the dramatic structures of *King Lear*. There, too, the play's management of the theatrical point of view and structures of sympathy assert the priority of affective bonds over the question of their relative value or the material conditions on which they depend. The connection between affective bonds and bonds of credit is hinted at by Cordelia's statement that she loves 'your majesty/According to my bond, no more no less' and her formal use of Lear's title signals the social relations of fealty within which her love exists as much as in family relations. Nevertheless, the dramatic and narrative force of her uncompromising position is managed by the connection created by her asides and the mounting suspense of her commentary on her sisters' performances.

When Lear himself is confronted by the non-negotiable reality of dependence on his daughters, a similar crescendo of enumeration marks its emotional impact. His cry 'O reason not the need' is the culmination of a conflict that has escalated in inverse proportion to the number of Lear's knights. Regan has approved her sister's reduction of his knights from 100 to 50, and further diminished them to 'five and twenty'. When Goneril exposes the false analogy between service and numbers of knights ('What need you five and twenty, ten, or five,/To follow in a house where twice so many/Have a command to tend you?') Regan takes the argument to its numerical conclusion: 'What need one?' (2.2.435–438).

She denies the incalculable nature of service based on traditional fealty that is quite different from the sufficiency provided 'in a house where twice so many/Have a command to tend you'. For Regan and Goneril their 'half of the kingdom' is an asset that can be transferred, leaving no residual claim on 'The offices of nature, bond of childhood/Effects of courtesy, dues of gratitude' (2.2.351–352). However, at this point in the action, questions of analytical claims to consistency are swamped by the emotion of Lear's response: Regan's and Goneril's cold response to his distress make any endorsement of their analysis impossible. The social world of affective relations is clearly distinguished from the arena where market relations provide both a proxy for value and a way of ensuring that the material conditions of the social world can be sustained.

The beggar and the king

Lear's emotional rejection of the connection between 'need' and 'reason' marks a critical point in the play. Stripped of the symbols of his social status and authority, he insists that a reasoned calculus of need does not apply even to those at the farthest end of the social scale from himself:

> The basest beggars are in the poorest things superfluous
> Allow not nature more than nature needs,
> Man's life is cheap as beast's.
>
> (2.2.438–441)

The hierarchical distinction between men and beasts remains in place, assured both materially and symbolically by a superfluity albeit of 'the poorest things'. Even on the heath, where Lear has most in common with the basest beggars, he continues to insist on the importance of material surplus as the basis for effective social relations. Considering the 'poor naked wretches … That bide the pelting of this piteous storm' (3.3.28–29) he imagines them as objects for his 'care', and calls on a personified 'pomp' to 'shake the superflux to them/And show the heavens more just' (3.4.35–36). The fundamental scale of value is social hierarchy, whose material differences both symbolise and sustain the social relations that are destroyed by a calculus of need. Without that material resource, the bonds of loyalty and love can provide the emotional support that Kent and Cordelia give him, but they cannot protect him from madness and death. The distinction between social bonds and the economic bonds that both symbolise and secure them is taken to its terrible logical conclusion.

Lear's 'basest beggar' is different from Antony's beggar, who is imagined as 'reckoning' love, or Othello's 'base In(u)dean', who misrecognises the value of the pearl richer than half his tribe. He is, rather, a figure whose capacity to be human depends on the superfluity of uncalculated philanthropy. There is nothing egalitarian about Lear's connection between himself and the beggar. His speech comes at the most moving moments in the play's narratives, when the loss of his authority makes the connection to the beggar most poignant. However, the terms of that association also indicate that the fellow-feeling that authorises the sympathy he invokes depends on the kingly wealth that will allow him to act. The scale of social value that creates the relation between king and beggar holds in place the hierarchies of wealth and power, and the authority to speak persuasively of value is endorsed dramatically and rhetorically by a contrast between Shakespeare's 'prizers', and their social inferiors: Hamlet's Captain, Othello's base In(u)dian, Shylock, or Lear's and Antony's beggars.

More recent historical shifts in the authority of royal and racial social power have left the hierarchies that inform value in Shakespeare's plays feeling more problematic. The rhetorical and dramatic force of Shylock's claims for human and cultural integrity has had a particular resonance in more egalitarian societies, and, from the late twentieth century, the impact of the women's movement has called into question Lear's right to the unquestioning fealty of his daughters. However the plays' narrative structures, their dramatic and emotional endorsement of the prizers' authority, complicate attempts to align the plays' emotional dynamics and their accounts of value.

The hierarchies of value implied in the antithesis between the king and beggar, between value that is endorsed by recognisable social hierarchies and value that must be explicitly calculated, provide a structure for the narratives and imagery of Shakespeare's plays. Value may be recognised in a familiar rhetorical comparison ('more than words', 'all the world', 'richer than all his tribe'), challenged in alternative comparisons (a 'joint-ring', a pound of flesh) and the connection between value and social action tested in narratives that align ideas of value with emotional engagement. The passion that the characters bring to the discussion, the significant actions of life and death, and the feelings of relief or disappointment that the narrative structures around the events, bring a sense of dramatic urgency to the questions of value that is absent from more measured philosophical or economic analysis. The effect of the emotional and narrative role played by discussions of value in Shakespeare's plays is to emphasise that value cannot be defined in the abstract but operates within particular social relations where it has a symbolic function that endorses the emotional effects of the play's action.

In presenting the contradictions of value in these emotionally loaded ways, Shakespeare's plays offer a representation of value that, like other proxies, temporarily stabilises the inequivalences that are, as we suggested in Chapter 2, built into an idea of value. The plays dramatise the emotional struggle involved in giving priority to social needs and personal relationship over the rational calculations associated with markets and exchange. Individual dialogues articulate fully the recurring competition between value as an attribute (where in a thing is precious in itself), value as an effect of valuation ('attributive/To what itself affects') or value as the ratio of price to cost ('worth what she doth cost', 'the holding'). The plays' comic or tragic conclusions, however, resolve the inherent inequivalence of different ideas of value in favour of those who assert the significance of socially authorised value, as against those who challenge that authority by asserting the possibility of a value that can be calculated and reckoned. The language of value slides between its social and its enumerative meanings, and the authority to make value judgements is sustained more by the status (both social and dramatic) of those who make them than by the coherence or consistency of their ideas of value. Above all, judgements about value are part of the negotiations with which the characters establish their authority, and make their claims for the sympathy not only from other characters but from the plays' audience.

Models of value

The structuring of emotional effect in Shakespeare's dramatised narratives has played an important part in sustaining the authority of Shakespeare's account of value. As we described in Chapter 1, narratives offer a more intuitive, understandable account of value. They present a version of value that can relate to the day-to-day, face-to-face, experience of social existence that does not need to take account of the unimaginable scale encompassed by contemporary forms of social knowledge. The plays' presentation of the conflict between emotional commitments and value calculations is always resolved in favour of the emotional, and the balance of sympathy built into their comic and tragic conclusions appears to endorse and affirm the now axiomatic separation between value in social situations and values agreed through systematic calculation in social analysis and markets.

A similar negotiation between narratives and calculation seems necessary in order to create a model that will explain the value of Shakespeare in the twenty-first century. As we described at the beginning of this chapter, that explanation can be offered as a narrative, in which an object of enduring value is transported into the present and arrives, miraculously, alive with its value intact. That narrative, because of its imaginative power, does not need to deal with the historical processes that have made possible the transmission of 'Shakespeare' to the present day. It can be used to assert the continuity between the Shakespeare of the past and the Shakespeare who is 'our contemporary', and to close the gap that exists between particular products and the elusive, timeless 'Shakespeare' that authorises them.

This double existence of 'Shakespeare' makes the value attached to it different from other cultural objects such as paintings or sculptures that have a direct material existence in time and place and, as we describe in Chapter 4, can find their value altered as they are moved in and out of the markets which exist in different places and times. 'Shakespeare' exists as multiple copies of early texts in European and North American libraries that provide free access to them, on the free space of the world wide web, and in educational settings where they are 'free' at the point of use, because the underlying costs or provision are supported by the market or mediated by the state. At the same time, as W. B. Worthen has pointed out, 'Shakespeare' also appears 'as a mass market product in an economy dependent on the diversification and multiplication of target audiences'.[20] The connection between the 'free' Shakespeare and the 'market' Shakespeare needs to be mapped in order to understand the economic as well as the social processes that create its value in the twenty-first century.

One way of explaining this process is to invoke the economic concept of the 'non-rival' good.[21] A non-rival good is an identifiable asset whose relation to the market depends on the fact that its consumption by one person, unlike the consumption of commodities, does not diminish the quantum available for others. Where most commodities exist in a market in which they are consumed and replaced by other commodities, the value of non-rival goods can be identified in terms of the numbers of its consumers whose engagement does not diminish the supply. Indeed additional consumers of a non-rival-value good increase rather than diminish its value, and additional investment in the good increases both its asset value and its use-potential.

The concept of a non-rival good is especially useful for a discussion of the value of 'Shakespeare' in that it clarifies the distinction among the diverse connections between 'Shakespeare' and the market. The non-rival nature of the value of 'Shakespeare' is critical in that it need bear no relation to the original costs of production and need not be located in particular editions or texts. Instead it forms the basis of the value chain in which its position is closer to that of a natural resource that requires additional, quantifiable, work to be transformed into a useable commodity.

A comparison might be made with the marketisation of a raw material such as oil whose function in the market place depends upon complex market relations of extraction and processing to create products from petroleum to plastics. That comparison is, of course, seriously limited by the fact that the markets in oil and its products are entirely controlled by large-scale capital investment with serious geo-political implications. Shakespeare may be a highly visible element in the cultural markets of developed societies but it has neither the economic nor the material scale of key commodities. Nevertheless, the idea of a value chain can account for the relationship between non-rival Shakespeare and the plethora of competing new forms whose value-added in production and distribution costs can be clearly identified even when they are not directly returned in consumer purchase.

As we will discuss in Chapter 5, the connection between non-rival Shakespeare and the finished products created through the value-chain changes over time and depends on the dynamic relationship between different and competing kinds of added-value provided by new knowledge and new forms of production. Inserting the idea of the value-chain between the 'free' out-of-copyright texts and the particular products of the twenty-first-century market goes some way to clarifying the terms of the recurring contest over Shakespeare. The new products add value to non-rival Shakespeare by working to identify useable elements that will suit the predilections of their contemporary consumers: textual difficulties are smoothed out by modern editions, the hints of racism or misogyny can be dealt with through ingenious adaptation and production, contradictions in narrative or ethical consistency can be addressed by annotation and various forms of critical special pleading.

From time to time, creative practitioners will reach beyond non-rival Shakespeare to introduce elements from non-Shakesperean traditions of performance or analysis that extend the range of non-rival Shakespeare and give it scope for further innovation. This resource can then be used not only for follow-on products in the market but also for the generalised sense of a Shakespeare that is accessible, of our time, contemporary and therefore available for extended, if not completely limitless, reproduction, in varied adapted forms that increase the value of non-rival Shakespeare the more often it is invoked.

Engagement with Shakespeare by a wide range of people actually increases his value as a non-rival good but this same non-rival value depends upon an access that appears to be free, not only of monetary exchange but of intervening information that will draw attention to the intellectual and historical processes that have made the free access both possible and pleasurable. In the case of other consumer products the free moment of pleasurable consumption made possible by developed markets depends upon consumers ignoring, wilfully or otherwise, the more or less exploitative relations of production and environmental damage that accompanies it. The pleasurable 'engagement' with 'Shakespeare' similarly depends upon its consumers' ignorance of the complex procedures of textual analysis, literary abstraction and expensive and sometimes undervalued artistic experimentation that have made their engagement possible.

The long value-chain that lies between non-rival Shakespeare and the free out-of-copyright Shakespeare is as invisible to the experience of new Shakespeare forms as the questions of the social processes and physical work that creates a public park out of a wilderness or a palliative drug out of a publically funded university laboratory. Making the value-chain invisible closes the gap between the historic Shakespeare and Shakespeare our contemporary, but it also closes the gap between producer and consumer, locating Shakespeare's value in the consumer's pleasurable experience.

In the cultural market of the twenty-first century, adding to the sum of value attributed to Shakespeare as a non-rival good is only part of the aim of investment. Competitors in the cultural market build on the non-rival value of Shakespeare and compete to manage access to it by adapting it to different forms, creating claims for new and added value that exist in the this or that edition, theatre production or museum display. The market relation to those new Shakespeare goods is determined by their distribution, together with the additional value that can be added and charged for by creating a value-chain of additional services from the non-rival good to the ultimate consumer.[22]

This account of the relationship between free 'out of copyright' Shakespeare, 'non-rival' Shakespeare and the Shakespeare of particular instances in the contemporary market illustrates some of the difficulties inherent in establishing Shakespeare's value. All the transactions that make each kind of Shakespeare take place in markets; all involve costs and investment (including costs paid for by public subsidy and philanthropic sponsorship); together they create a sense of a social good that appears to be 'outside the market' both because it can be located in a cultural frame of reference that is greater than the sum of particular instances and because, at the moment of satisfied consumption, the illusion is created of a direct emotional engagement with ideas of values that transcend the market and speak beyond it to the world of honour, need, love and death.

The capacity for the emotional engagement that will release the non-rival value of Shakespeare, of course, depends on more than the capacity to pay for a ticket to a show or buy a book. The non-rival value that is the foundation of the value of 'Shakespeare' depends on the active engagement of all the people involved in the social and market transactions that constitute its value. This process takes place in time but its effect is not to waft Shakespeare's value intact from one historical moment to another. It is a process that creates and transforms that value and makes it useable as well as exchangeable in the present. It assures not only the reproduction of value but the creative link between the valued object and the new valuers that endorses non-rival value with emotional satisfaction.

The capacity of Shakespeare's plays to present affecting narratives of the comic and tragic consequences of the instability of value and the capacity of readers and audiences, informed by the work of educators and theatre companies, to undergo the 'proper apprenticeship' that will ensure their engagement, together create a mutually confirming endorsement of the priority of emotional over analytical knowledge and personal over market relations. Once that process is complete, 'Shakespeare' can be used, as we have seen, as the authority for a contemporary commitment to non-market values. Shakespeare's account of the instability of value increases its authority as an account of value that is outside of time, open to interpretation and therefore continually refreshed, while the eloquence with which it is expressed gives it the pithy, repeatable characteristic of indisputable truths.

In Chapter 5 we will explore in more detail the connections between Shakespeare's writing and the different kinds of work required to sustain its position an active part of contemporary culture. Before that, in Chapter 4, we will explore the complexity involved in dealing with the affective and market dimensions of culture that help to structure the space that 'Shakespeare' occupies within it.

Notes

1. The scare quotes around 'Shakespeare' distinguish the contemporary object of value from the early modern playwright.
2. Connor, *Theory and Cultural Value*, p. 18.
3. See Michael Dobson, *The Making of the National Poet: Shakespeare, Adaptation, and Authorship, 1660–1769* (Oxford: Clarendon Press, 1992); Michael Bristol, *Big-Time Shakespeare* (London: Routledge, 1996).
4. Andrew Murphy, *Shakespeare for the People: Working-Class Readers, 1800–1900* (Cambridge and New York: Cambridge University Press, 2008); William St Clair, *The Reading Nation in the Romantic Period* (Cambridge: Cambridge University Press, 2004).
5. Eagleton, 'Afterword', p. 184.
6. Holderness, *Cultural Shakespeare*, p. 107.
7. Stephen Greenblatt, *Shakespearean Negotiations* (Oxford: Clarendon Press, 1988), p. 1.
8. Stephen Greenblatt, *Will in the World* (London: Jonathan Cape, 2004), p. 318.
9. Jonathan Bate, *Public Value in the Humanities* (London: Bloomsbury Academic, 2011), p. 5.
10. Jonathan Bate, *Shakespearean Constitutions: Politics, Theatre,*

Criticism 1730–1830 (Oxford: Clarendon Press, 1989) examines the role of key eighteenth-century institutions in securing the supremacy of Shakespeare in literary and theatrical culture, while *The Genius of Shakespeare* (London: Picador, 1997) shows how key nineteenth-century critics endorsed and managed Shakespeare's critical standing.

11 The plays of many of his contemporaries, including Ben Jonson and John Webster, share many of the same characteristics. Jane Austen and Dickens are also being used in similar ways, though, as prose, the structures of their texts present different opportunities for negotiation.

12 The OED cites this word under 'dime', noting this spelling as obsolete. Early uses of the word are cited with reference to 'tithes', the tenth of income granted as a tax to church or landlord. OED further cites this phrase as figurative, meaning 'a tithe of war; a tenth man sacrificed' www.oed.com/view/Entry/54766 (accessed 05.11.13). Even with this gloss, Hector's exact calculation remains far from clear.

13 This passage is printed only in Q2. Wells and Taylor include it in 'Additional Passages': see Stanley Wells and Gary Taylor, eds, *William Shakespeare: The Complete Works* (Oxford: Clarendon Press, 1988), p. 689.

14 The sense of instability is further reinforced by the fact that chrysolite is not the name of a particular single stone but 'a name (before 1790) given to several different gems of a green colour' OED, qv chrysolite, www.oed.com/view/Entry/32640 (accessed 05.11.13).

15 See Matthew, 13, 47–8 KJV and the long note on the Indian/Judean crux in *Othello*, ed. E. A. J. Honigmann, The Arden Shakespeare (Walton-on-Thames: Thomas Nelson and Sons, 1997), pp. 341–342.

16 These lines are from the Folio text, *The Tragedy of King Lear* in Wells and Taylor, *Complete Works*, pp. 945–974.

17 The Q text reads 'equalities', suggesting an equivalence between the dukes that refers to their share of the kingdom rather than personal qualities. Compare *King Lear*, ed. R. A. Foakes, The Arden Shakespeare (Walton-on-Thames: Thomas Nelson and Sons, 1997), 1.1.5 textual note and collation.

18 Peter Brook, *The Empty Space* (London: McKibbon and Kee, 1968), pp. 13–14.

19 Critical accounts of the play have explored these contradictions fully: see especially Richard Halpern, 'The Jewish Question: Shakespeare and Anti-Semitism' in *Shakespeare Among the Moderns* (Ithaca, NY: Cornell University Press, 1997), pp. 159–126.

20 W. B. Worthen, 'Hyper-Shakespeare', *Performance Research* 7(1) (2002): 7–21, p. 15.

21 For a useful summary discussion of 'non-rival' goods see, http://en.wikipedia.org/wiki/Rivalry_(economics) (accessed 07.06.13).
22 For a full discussion of the Shakespeare value chain, see Emily Linnemann, 'Culture and Carparks' in *The Value of Shakespeare in Twenty-First-Century Publicly-Funded Theatre in England*, PhD thesis, University of Birmingham, 2011.

4

Value and culture

Narratives

In Chapter 3, we suggested that the eloquent account of value in Shakespeare's plays can be redeployed in the twenty-first century, because the metaphors and analogies that the characters use bring together poetic images that represent enduring value – the pearl without price, the honour that will 'greatly find quarrel in a straw', the incalculable worth of a great king – with the pressing material and psychic demands of their particular circumstances. Though the authority of these accounts of value has been endorsed by centuries of repetition and reproduction in the market for cultural goods, their capacity to replay the contradictions that are inherent in the idea of value – between the valuer and the valued, between the absolute and the contingent – also depends on the narratives and metaphors that create the conditions for the perception of an emotional and intuitive validity in the terms in which value is expressed.

In this chapter, we will explore the extent to which the narratives and the uses of metaphor that structure the terms of the value equation in 'Shakespeare' are also relevant to an account of the value of culture. In Chapter 1 we found culture, like Shakespeare, being referred to as 'something else' (possibly with both its literal and slang meaning) and in Chapter 3 we addressed the way that Shakespeare often acts as 'a sign post pointing towards something greater and more complete than itself'. For culture, the elusive object of cultural value is even more comprehensive. It was described in the twentieth century, in T. S. Eliot's influential formulation, as 'the way of life of a particular people living together in one place', 'the assemblage of its arts, customs, religious beliefs'. Moreover, according to Eliot, 'these things all act upon each other and to fully understand one you have to understand all'.[1] Eliot's formulation posits a symbiotic relationship between a 'way of life' and the 'arts, customs, religious beliefs' that allow it to be perceived. As with Shakespeare, the individual instances of culture in practice and artefacts all but disappear behind the elusive signifier that gives them all authority.

As in the case of Shakespeare, too, the contemporary artefacts that indicate the presence of culture are only part of the signifier's frame of reference. 'Culture' also includes representative objects from past cultures and from geographically distant places that signal their 'way of life' and have been included in the 'way of life' of the present by processes of veneration, conservation and evaluation. 'Culture' as a result includes some consideration of the continuities of the 'arts customs and beliefs' across time and space to assess their relationship to the present.

Dealing with this vast array of possible objects, which are both discrete and interconnected, presents analytical problems that exceed the possibility of quantitative methods: of evaluating the precise relations between production and consumption or between the value of individual objects and the value-added required to sustain its value in the present. The solution, as we have found in relation to other forms of evaluation, is to resort to narrative and metaphor. We have already discussed Greenblatt's story of how 'the social energy encoded in certain works of art continues to generate the illusion of life for centuries'. In making that statement, he was drawing on narratives of transmission that had been used to represent the continuities of culture from the past to the present and the changes that had occurred in modern times. In one of the foundational texts of modernism, Walter Benjamin had described how even the multiple versions of a work of art, diversified and distributed by mechanical reproduction, 'in permitting the reproduction to meet the beholder or listener in his own particular situation, *reactivates* the object *reproduced*'.[2] Some forty years later, Pierre Bourdieu echoed the story of a work of art staying alive across time by observing that

> the most audacious intellectual breaks of pure reading still help to *preserve the stock* of consecrated texts from becoming dead letters.[3]

The mixture of metaphors shows these writers struggling to find appropriate terms with which to describe the anomaly of the continuing status of older cultural material in contemporary culture and the ways in which its value had been affected by changes in the technologies of reproduction and in interpretative innovation. In their effort to link the old and the new, the metaphors encapsulated familiar stories: of bringing the dead to life, of analogies with selective breeding, a new message created from an old consecrated text, of galvanic reanimation or the story of Frankenstein, brought to life by a lightening bolt of electricity. The relations between these metaphors and sacred narratives of resurrection, commonplace agricultural practice, the revision of consecrated texts and anxious responses to new technology give some indication of what is at stake in coming to terms with an idea of culture.

The problem was addressed more explicitly by Raymond Williams in 1977 in the distinction that he drew between 'archaic' and 'residual' cultural forms:

> I would call 'archaic' that which is wholly recognised as an element of the past, to be observed, to be examined, or even on occasion to be consciously 'revived', in a deliberate, specialising way ... The 'residual' ... has been effectively formed in the past, but is still active in the cultural process, not only and often not at all as an element of the past, but as an effective element of the present.[4]

Williams makes a distinction between the 'archaic' elements – which are not really part of culture, except for specialists – and the 'residual' ones that are. However, in making that distinction, he indicates the difficulty and the importance of making a case for a synchronic symbiosis between 'culture' and its representative objects. For Williams, cultural objects that are merely 'revived, in a deliberate, specialising way' would not be 'still active in the cultural process ... as an effective element of the present' and therefore could not claim a place in culture. Culture had to be more than a mere agglomeration of cultural objects: the objects and practices in which it is expressed are not discrete objects that may or may not be valued by those people. In order to become culture, past objects must be transformed into 'an effective element of the present' in order to become part of a 'way of life'. Only then can cultural objects and ways of life, as Eliot puts it, 'all act upon each other' so that 'to fully understand one you have to understand all'.

The metaphors that are used to express this imagined and desired synergy of objects and 'way of life' suggest an important connection between the idea of culture and the idea of value. As we have been suggesting, a stable idea of value depends upon a constant, undisputed equation between the valuers and the valued. The idea of culture as a symbiosis between a way of life and its expression offers a powerful image of value in practice where the cultural objects are so integrated into the way of life that it is impossible to separate the two and no distinction is made between a canon of valued content and the activities of the groups who value them. The troublesome gap between the valuers and the valued that complicates the value equation thus disappears and a 'culture' can be imagined to embody a complete synergy between the two.

This imagined synergy between the members of a culture and its representative activities had also been articulated by the anthropological work that influenced T. S. Eliot's account and continues to provide a model for ideas of culture. Expounding the founding principles of the new discipline of anthropology in 1871, E. B. Tylor indicated that its scope would extend to

> that complex whole which includes knowledge, belief, art, morals, law, custom and any other capabilities and habits acquired by man [sic] as a member of society.[5]

Behind the particular beliefs and practices that Tylor identified in the 'Primitive Culture' he studied, he was looking for a more abstract idea of 'the capabilities and habits acquired by man as a member of society'. Critics of Tylor's work have claimed that he provided only an inventory of practices rather than a coherent theory of culture.[6] His work was limited by the sheer scale of the ethnographic research required to arrive at systematic conclusions about 'man as a member of society' from the accumulation of particular instances. However, by the mid-twentieth century, as Adam Kuper has described,[7] the accounts of different cultures from all over the world were brought together to establish the systemic character of social structures by extrapolating the elements that they had in common. The elements chosen tended to illustrate practices rather than objects but their extrapolated organising principle emphasised symbolic rather than instrumental significance.

Marshall Sahlins, following his teacher, Leslie White, explained the process of extrapolating principles from practice:

> Christian men take off their hats when entering a house of god and Muslims wash their feet. The difference in customs in incidental to

the expression of deference to the divine master of the house, which is their common raison d'etre. Indeed as customs, these acts are altogether distinct as well as historically contingent; whereas, the social relations they manifest are of a type and generalisable across societies.[8]

The structuralist methodology that systematised contingent customs into generalisable characteristics provided an important structure for the developing discipline of anthropology. The same process of abstraction from particular customs to essential human capability could be applied to other defining practices: kinship patterns, forms of religious observance, ways of selecting, preparing and serving food, the rituals associated with coming of age, birth and death, could similarly be generalised 'across societies' even when the forms of behaviour itself were very different.

These accounts of cultural practice produced a persuasive model of social relations in part because the knowledge that they provided was organised in ways that had identified activities that seemed to illustrate core human activity. The accounts scrupulously avoided judgement or evaluation that came from outside the cultures being described and they provided the evidence for the allegedly essential human 'faculty for symbolizing, generalising and imaginative substitution'.[9]

The process of abstraction in this structural definition of culture has important parallels with the abstraction of absolute value. Rather than defining culture as the *sum* of individual customs, structural anthropologists were able to use ethnographic research to identify social behaviours that appeared reflexive, ingrained, consensual and shared and therefore seemed to point to a satisfactory definition of the human.

This image of a mutually confirming, essentially human, form of existence is similar to the definition of transcendent value: its defining 'capacity for signification' has parallels with the essentially human 'imperative to value', and its basis in communal forms of life is similar to the distinctive character of value which is shared rather than individual. This abstracted view of culture can thus stand in for a statement of value: it reiterates the aspiration for the possibility of a consensual existence and marginalises the historical contingencies of struggle and change as well as the agents and institutions of power and authority that hold it in place.

The appeal of this abstracted model of culture and value was that it focussed on an idea of human existence that could be seen as distinct from both history and power. As Clifford Geertz put it,

> No matter how much one trains one's attention on the supposedly hard facts of social existence, who owns the means of production, who has the guns, the dossiers or the newspapers, the supposedly soft facts of that existence, what do people imagine human life to be all about, how do they think one ought to live, what grounds belief, legitimizes punishment, sustains hope, or accounts for loss, crowd in to disturb simple pictures of might, desire, calculation and interest.[10]

Geertz's work became hugely influential in the late twentieth century as a form of cultural analysis that provided a link between exemplars of human behaviour and representative practice from Bali to New York by turning each of them into a connecting abstraction of supposedly universal traits. The twentieth-century abstractions of anthropology could thus be used to create an inclusive field of culture that would avoid contentious hierarchies of value based on the specific historical characteristics of different cultural practices. All and any culture could thus be admired and valued as an exemplar both of culture as a signifying practice and culture as an example of human aspiration and endeavour.

Politics

The narratives, metaphors and abstractions that structured accounts of 'culture' in the twentieth century were the source of both its strength and its weaknesses. Its strength was that it created a utopian image of culture as a way of life in which the shared human experiences of 'belief, hope and loss' could be distinguished from the operations of 'might, desire, calculation and interest'. Its weakness was that these rhetorically separable characteristics of human societies co-existed in all actual cultures and the relations between them were the sources of frequent and sometimes deadly conflict. The capacity of any cultural group to continue with practices that embodied their own sense of 'belief, hope and loss' has, historically, been significantly constrained by the 'might, desire, calculation and interest' of those with whom it has interacted. Geertz had earlier acknowledged that in the late twentieth century

> The transformation ... of the people anthropologists mostly write about, from colonial subjects to sovereign citizens has ... altered

entirely the moral context in which the anthropological act takes place.

It was, therefore, inappropriate to discuss human cultures through the nineteenth-century paradigm of 'a sweeping, up-from the-ape, study of mankind sort of business'. He nevertheless aspired to use anthropology as the basis for

> the possibility of intelligible discourse between people quite different from one another in interest, outlook, wealth and power, and yet contained in a world where, tumbled together as they are into endless connection, it is increasingly difficult to get out of each other's way.[11]

Geertz's image of social interaction between different people as an amiable 'intelligible discourse' was presented in more tragic terms by other anthropologists. Marshall Sahlins, for example, late in his career, has re-defined the study of culture as the

> field on which indigenous peoples struggle to encompass what is happening to them in terms of their own world system ... not only apart from or before Western imperialism but even as they endure the world-capitalist juggernaut.[12]

Sahlins's image of a field of struggle reintroduces the idea of conflict within a vivid imagined narrative of vulnerable indigenous peoples in the path of a 'world-capitalist juggernaut', an image of global modernity as an unstoppable machine. The distinction between 'culture' as the human domain of 'belief, hope and loss' and political economy as the domain of the mechanistic non-human force of dominant global economic systems, is as intellectually and ethically distinct as the domains of value and commerce. The images used by Geertz and Sahlins vary between a possible conversation and a narrative of tragic defeat but the value opposition remains clear.

James Clifford, writing in 1988, made this sense of the ethical force of the idea of culture explicit:

> The reason that we still need the notion of culture is a moral one, or a political one. The concept of culture provides us with the only way we know to speak about the differences between the peoples of the world, differences that persist in defiance of the processes of homogenization. And cultural difference has a moral and political value, making a political commitment to the power of culture to

resist Westernization (or modernisation, or globalisation or, simply, misrepresentation).[13]

This sense of culture as a field of resistance was particularly significant in the late twentieth-century struggles for autonomy among marginalised groups, both in the post-colonial nations and in the multi-ethnic societies of the west. Since the justification for their oppression had often taken the form of denying the value of their cultures, the assertion of cultural value carried a powerful ethical force. It offers the possibility of a stable means of valuing multiple practices and behaviours and allowing their continued co-existence in contemporary society. It builds on the idea of culture's association with a generalised 'human' realm but also acknowledges the role of culture as a resource for political conflict. The idea of culture, however, provided a resource for both sides in the conflict.

As Adam Kuper has shown, the politics of a homogenised idea of culture that elided practices and objects with groups could as easily be used for oppressive as for egalitarian political purposes:

> In South Africa the language of cultural identity, the ideology of cultural destiny, supported a hideous tyranny. Immigrants to the West might also be troubled by the exhortation to cherish and build upon their differences, when they would, perhaps, enjoy the opportunity to become unhyphenated citizens.[14]

The mid-century turn to an eclectic definition of culture attributed value according to prior political imperatives. Kuper is suggesting that they did not always work to support the wider political and economic aspirations or needs of the groups whose culture was so valued. The attribution of value to culture, like any other attribution of value, is a recurring process of negotiation between historical agents and institutions, but the ethical and political trajectory of those negotiations cannot be assured any more than their value.

Culture, value and knowledge

The ethical claims of culture as a locus of value have, since the end of the twentieth century, derived a good deal of their authority and effect from international agencies that are tasked with managing conflict in the contemporary world. Their role is both to articulate an international consensus about the values that might ensure the stability of the global world order and to provide limited resources to support national governments in implementing them. The gap between these high-minded principles and the possibility of their implementation is, perhaps inevitably, very wide, and this applies as much to the domain of culture as it does to the arenas of politics and economics. The frequent critiques of the resolutions that articulate their aspirations indicate not only the instability of ideas of value but of the kinds of knowledge and understanding required to negotiate between authoritative general statements about cultural value and the practices of particular groups.

For example, a critique of a proposed United Nations (UN) declaration on 'traditional cultures' noted that

> Traditional cultural practices reflect values and beliefs held by members of a community for periods often spanning generations. Every social grouping in the world has specific traditional cultural practices and beliefs, some of which are beneficial to all members, while others are harmful to a specific group, such as women. Despite their harmful nature and their violation of international human rights laws, such practices persist because they are not questioned and take on an aura of morality in the eyes of those practising them.[15]

This critique of the ethically positive view of culture was co-ordinated by an association committed to women's rights. It sought to protect women from practices such as non-consensual marriage, honour-killings and female genital mutilation (FGM) while at the same time acknowledging the value of 'traditional cultural practices' that were, in good faith, being championed by the UN resolution. The arena of conflict had evidently moved from the field of 'indigenous groups' and the 'world-capitalist juggernaut' to the conflict within the groups themselves.

The critique from the women's rights organisation did not challenge the value of culture as a 'traditional practice ... spanning generations': instead, it made the challenge from the alternative, equally authoritative value-position of individual human rights supported by international law. The values of and rights to culture, endorsed by a UN declaration, were challenged by the values and rights of individual women over the integrity of their bodies and their choice in matters of sexual behaviour, endorsed by international law. Moreover, the women's rights organisation not only included representatives from cultures who used this practice, it deployed the ethical and social authority of the international women's movement to challenge the authority of the UN who, they claimed, were defending existing structures of authority within cultures whose practices 'harm' their participants. The conflict was no longer between the clearly defined and ethically differentiated 'west and the rest'. Like other disagreements about value, it involved an attempt to adjudicate between contingent values, by invoking what Connor calls a 'higher argumentative authority':[16] the case for traditional culture was endorsed by the 'higher argumentative authority' of the UN declaration, while the women's organisation invoked the 'higher argumentative authority' of international agreed human rights. The disagreement, moreover, called into question the ethical authority of a consensual value by indicating the possibility of conflict between that consensus and the aspirations and needs of a group within it.

This conflict could not be resolved by adjusting definitions of culture or placing different cultural practices in competing hierarchies of evaluation. As Henrietta Moore has shown, in her ethnographic analysis of the campaign against female circumcision in (the Kenyan district of) Marakwet, the contest over the cultural practice of FGM involved more than an external group imposing one evaluation of a traditional practice on another. The direct engagement in the Marakwet case, of the young women themselves and of other community leaders, involved a more fundamental realignment between custom and culture.

In her analysis, Moore addresses the question of the knowledge rather than the value that is involved in cultural practice. She contrasts the knowledge of culture that is 'a type of practical understanding' based on the repetitions of day-to-day practice, and knowledge 'imagined as an extant body of information that can be drawn on and elaborated on in the manner that text-based religions can be'. She argues, further, that culture, for its participants, involves

> forms of knowledge that are bound together not by rules or by systematic relations between the system's components but rather cohere ... through situated practice that is often discontinuous in space and time, and yet always potentially applicable.

This knowledge, she argues, is inseparable from the cultural traditions but, more than that, it depends for its success on a consensus, on the part of the practitioners, that was not explicitly articulated or evaluated, even though its application was constantly debated and not always put into practice. When those practices were evaluated by international agencies, she suggests, 'something had to happen which made these practices cultural objects around which contests of value could legitimately take place':

> These contests of value were not like the old ones concerned with the appropriateness or not of specific situated practices, but were rather about the nature of knowledge itself and its effectiveness in modern contexts.

Contests about value, she argues, created 'the idea of culture, as opposed to that of the lived world' as an object of knowledge, that 'in this form proved more amenable to change because it could be acted on in a new way'.[17] The international and government agencies who acted on the Marakwet community from the outside not only deployed the knowledge of 'culture' to negotiate changes in traditional practices, they engaged the participants in alternative forms of knowledge that substituted for traditional practices and offered instead the possibility of being seen 'as part of a larger world'.

The larger world in which the contest over cultural practice takes place is the world of globalised modernity in which 'culture' is built into a hierarchy of valued knowledge. The knowledge constituted by the definition of culture as lived practices had explicitly excluded the applications of scientific education and social management, that might have indicated 'the harmful effects of FGM, respect and discipline, the rights of the child, HIV/AIDS, personal hygiene and courtship'.[18] This excluded form of knowledge, as Moore explains, is outside the boundaries of 'culture' but it had nevertheless been made available to the people of Marakwet and become 'both continuous and discontinuous with traditional ideas of the community and its values'.[19]

This new knowledge is often championed by community leaders and, like traditional knowledge, it offers skills and satisfactions that can facilitate living 'as part of a larger world' which include, but are not restricted to, access to the financial resources provided by NGOs and their government and international sponsors. As such, it offers less scope for the tragic late twentieth-century narrative of the coercive power and authority of 'the west' imposed on 'the rest'. Instead, the version of cultural knowledge developed in the case of Marakwet people arrived at a compromise through a process of adaptation and negotiation rather than coercion or the direct imposition of power. This version of the process of cultural change makes identification of its agents easier and allows a more analytical understanding of the specific relationship between knowledge and power in particular historical circumstances.

Culture and culture

Henrietta Moore's discussion of the role of knowledge in the process of cultural change offers a useful analytical model with which to understand the conflict over cultural value as it occurs in twenty-first-century England. Her suggestion that 'something had to happen which made these practices cultural objects around which contests of value could legitimately take place' shifts attention from the static model of culture 'as a way of life', that can only change as a result of the more or less traumatic exercise of external power, in order to pay attention to the scope for negotiated transactions among different agents of change and the different forms of knowledge that they bring to bear on the idea of culture.

Though the transactions that Moore observes have more immediate material consequences for the lives of the people she studies, the connection between culture and knowledge that she describes provides a useful way of mapping the negotiation that takes place in attempts to establish a connection between 'culture' and the vast array of made-objects – books, paintings, sculptures, play scripts, songs – that have been accumulated throughout history and from across the world and are being added to at an ever greater speed by new forms of production. Categorising these objects – for example, by provenance, or age or maker or form – has, in the contexts of learned analysis, constituted a form of knowledge that could be disputed, corrected and confirmed. Identifying them specifically as *culture*, on the other hand, involves a form of knowledge that cannot easily be disputed by alternative information. Rather, it presents an important instance of a recurring negotiation between facts and values: the facts about the production and distribution of cultural objects and the values associated with an idea of culture as a way of life.

Objects such as Assyrian tablet or an Ottoman tunic, to return to our examples from Chapter 1, might be valued, in the name of a politics of cultural diversity, as exemplars of the universal human ability to communicate over space and time. The specific skills of their unknown makers or the wealth and power of those who employed them or the economic conditions that allowed such a high level of specialised work to exist would have been relevant knowledge about those objects and would certainly have been collected by their curators in the British Museum. However, when they were being presented as culture they became representative objects that were both substitutes for the knowledge of their originating cultures and symbolic representations of the essential human capacity to connect the present to the past and people of one nation to the world.

Walter Benjamin had described this process of changing the values and the knowledge associated with works of art as the shift from 'cult value to exhibition value': the process whereby, for example, the music for an eighteenth-century Catholic mass, preserved in the great collections of European museums, is changed by its performance in the concert hall from an act of worship to an arts event. A similar process occurs when a sacred relic is removed from its ritual function, often associated with celebrating particular saints' days, to an existence as an object in a cathedral treasury or a museum collection. Benjamin not only described that process: he celebrated its potential for change. It might, he proposed, 'emancipate the work of art from its parasitical dependence on ritual' and allow a new relationship between the arts, which were formerly the preserve of an elite or served the superstitious purposes of religion, and citizens who would, he claimed, make 'revolutionary demands in the politics of art'. The exciting, democratising possibilities of emerging technologies would, as we described earlier, like electricity, 'reactivate the object reproduced' and the process would 'lead to a tremendous shattering of tradition':

> Its social significance, particularly in its most positive form, is inconceivable without its destructive, cathartic aspect, that is, the liquidation of the traditional value of the cultural heritage.[20]

Benjamin's heroic vision of cultural and technological change that would change the connection between art and 'the masses' is informed by film's technical potential for mass distribution: his hopes for a consequent effect on culture, however, are a statement of value. A similar connection between value and distribution informed the British Library's extraordinarily successful 'Sacred' exhibition of 2008, which exhibited the sacred books of the four world religions. The objects displayed were rare and beautiful so were admired by those for whom they had no ritual association as well as providing an opportunity, in many cases for the first time, for people of all those faiths in multicultural London to see ancient versions of their sacred books. The cultural value of celebrating the faiths of many cultures, though, seemed to have been realised without the complete liquidation of tradition. It had been made possible by the long and complex history of the Library's acquisition of objects from all over the world, together with the institutional structures and funding provided by its relationship to the government funding bodies.

The items in the British Library's 'Sacred' exhibition were able to become part of twenty-first-century culture as a result of complex negotiations between knowledge and value. The process involved an interaction between the library curators' knowledge and the consensual values of multiculturalism that had informed their decision to select these items for exhibition from the Library's enormous collection. None of this negotiation was made explicit to the audience for the exhibition, many of whom may have felt that these ancient objects were indeed being 'reactivated in the moment of their reproduction' in order to become what Raymond Williams described as 'an effective element of the present'. The shift from 'cult value' to 'exhibition value' involved more than historical changes in technology. It involved more active management of objects from the past in order to make them into culture.

This active management of cultural objects complicates the late twentieth-century dystopian view that 'Aesthetic production today has become integrated into commodity production generally'.[21] As Mike Featherstone has described, the creation of value for works of art can be achieved by managing their relationship to the market not only in the work of curators but by the prior process he describes as 'decommodification':

> Art objects or objects produced for ritual, and hence given a particular symbolic charge, tend often to be the ones excluded from exchange, or not permitted to remain in the commodity status for long. At the same time, their professed sacred status and denial of the profane market may paradoxically raise their value. Their lack of availability and 'pricelessness' raises their price and desirability.[22]

As Featherstone makes clear, this 'pricelessness' is less to do with the particular qualities of the objects under discussion, or their symbiotic relations to the cultures in which they are valued, than with a relationship to the structures of contemporary markets. It can apply to the ritual object from the past, or the expensive items made in markets for printed books or foreign curiosities and exotica. Equally, it can apply to

> The way bike boys make sacred the original 78 records of Buddy Holly and Elvis Presley and refuse to use compilation albums which may have better reproduction.[23]

The unified model of 'commodity production' imagined in Jameson's statement has been replaced by a set of relations in time between producers, consumers and cultural intermediaries. As the cultural economists Jeffcutt and Pratt explain, contemporary arts markets

> span a diverse range of activities ... [that produce] a terrain with a very mixed economy of forms – from micro-businesses, through micro-enterprises to transnational organisations – encompassing the range from sole artists to global media corporations ... sustained in diverse communities of activity, from project based/hybrid/virtual organisations to cultural quarters and digital media hubs.[24]

The complex relationships between cultural objects and markets can be illustrated by the case of the purchase and display of the Raphael painting *The Madonna of the Pinks*, referred to in Tessa Jowell's list of valued art objects discussed in Chapter 1. The painting was acquired 'for the nation' at a cost of £38.44m in 2004. Of this, £11.5m was paid for by money from the Heritage Lottery fund, the bulk of whose tickets are bought by lower-income individuals betting on the possibility of winning the multi-million weekly prize.[25] £403.895 was provided by the Art Fund, a membership organisation whose members pay an relatively low annual subscription (£37.50 in 2011) and are entitled to free entry to some museums in the UK; the remainder of the cost was met by tax remission for the painting's owner.[26]

The painting was put on the market by the Duke of Northumberland, whose family had acquired it in 1854 when the fourth duke acquired the collection of the painter Vincenzo Camucinni. Its attribution to Raphael had been controversial throughout the twentieth century and the painting was valued at £6,000 in 1986. In 1992 the Raphael attribution was confirmed by the then curator of Renaissance art at the National Gallery though it continued to be contested even after the sale.[27] The change in market relations over a century was clear: removing an art object from the market in 1854 could be achieved by a single transaction from seller to buyer. By 2004, the process of placing it in a public collection where it could be identified as 'culture' required a complex negotiation between controversial curatorial finding, the Art Fund's small-scale sponsors, the larger-scale accumulation of finance by the National Lottery and the legal framework that permitted art objects to be taken into public ownership in lieu of tax.

These negotiated arrangements are structured and planned by the bureaucrats who manage the Art Fund, the Heritage Lottery Fund and the relevant civil service departments, and are analysed in the academic literature. However, they are too complex to have played a direct part in the discussions over value that took place in the discussions surrounding the painting's display. The National Gallery's public-facing website describes Raphael's achievement in this painting in the present tense and emphasises its immediate connection to the viewer's possible experience:

> Raphael transforms this familiar subject into something entirely new. The mother and son are no longer posed stiffly and formally as in paintings by earlier artists, but now display all the tender emotions one might expect between a young mother and her child.[28]

The knowledge relevant to its attribution was quite literally held in a separate domain located on the 'in depth' section of the site, which offered information about 'how to spot a Raphael'. What mattered more was the contrast between the 'stiff and formal' poses found in other paintings (dead on arrival, in Greenblatt's terms) and the immediately recognisable 'tender emotions between a young mother and her child' that signalled the painting's cultural value.

This relation between knowledge and value came together in an extensive *Evaluation of the Education and Community Strategy for the Madonna of the Pinks 2004–2007*, the research of which was designed to assess 'the short-term and long-term impact of engagement' with the painting. Confirming the value of the cultural object required not only the knowledge of curators and the structures of finance, it also involved knowledge of the 'impact' gathered by researchers. The painting was circulated on a tour of galleries outside London and was accompanied by a series of workshops involving school children, 'new audiences', unsupported mothers and young people in the care of local authorities. The evaluation's findings showed that the impact of the painting depended to a very large extent on the skill and experience of the workshop leaders, their commitment to the project and the amount of time spent both on studying the painting and on the related creative activity engaged in by participants. The significance of culture could no longer be left to assertions about a 'way of life' or the role of cultural objects 'in the present'. It required a managed process of accumulated and distributed knowledge.

As the evaluation's conclusions noted, respondents to the comments questionnaires used by the researchers

> commented frequently on the style and general impression of the painting (colour, light, size), more rarely describing what they could actually see, and frequently using the language of the National Gallery leaflet to express themselves.[29]

The circle between the ancient work of art and contemporary culture could be closed by linking forms of knowledge even if that link in practice could not clearly identify its connection to the 'way of life' of the majority of the people in twenty-first-century England.

The symbiotic relations between art objects and culture, imagined and hoped for in the aspirations of twentieth-century cultural analysts, had been managed by the knowledge-based interventions of twenty-first-century cultural managers working, in good faith, to sustain some coherence between the complex market for art objects from the past and the larger society. The terms of valuation for cultural objects among non-experts could be satisfactorily managed within the domain of public-sector engagement with the arts because the activity took place in a relatively limited domain, both in terms of the numbers involved and in terms of the relatively small sums of money involved as a proportion of national GDP or total government spending. The successful engagement of a relatively small number of school children and even smaller numbers from groups identified as disadvantaged had to stand in for the painting's role in the way of life of the larger nation. The carefully managed engagement provided a proxy for value that was entirely incommensurate with the costs and was thus able to reinforce the idea that culture and markets had no connection.

Much more pressing contests over value occurred in the wider markets for cultural content distributed by television. There, the contest moved from the 'priceless value' of individual items of content and was dominated by equally questionable ideas about a direct relationship between supply and demand. Delivering the keynote McTaggart lecture at the Edinburgh International Television Festival in 2009,[30] James Murdoch, heir to the Murdoch media empire, championed the principles and the business models of commercial media by placing its values firmly on the demand side: 'The right path', he said, 'is all about trusting and empowering consumers':[31]

> People who buy the newspapers, open the application, decide to take out the television subscription – people who deliberately and willingly choose a service which they value. (p. 19)

Murdoch's robust but reductive presentation of the simplest of market transactions was presented as the antithesis of the public sector's management of cultural value. He drew attention to the levels and extent of companies' accountability to regulatory agencies and the limits on competitive management posed by the requirement that produce a fixed number of programmes for identified groups such as children. His solution to creating a managed consensus over value was simply to allow an unconstrained relationship between TV companies and their customers.

Murdoch's critique of a regulated market, however, was disingenuous. He drew no attention to the differential power of companies and their customers: the companies' control of content and their capacity to manage its distribution by market mechanisms of bundling and exclusions in order to secure maximum profitability. His attack was primarily directed at the BBC. He claimed that the company's long-standing support from the licence fee amounted to unfair competition even with global media companies such as the Murdoch empire. His homely narrative of a direct relationship between suppliers and consumers negotiating in an open market obscured the complex value-chain that managed the connection between content and consumers: the issue was whether management was to be influenced by the state, regulating on behalf of consumers, or by companies working to secure the most advantageous conditions in which they could increase their share of a global market on a huge scale.

By focussing on programme content, the part of the TV business that was most visible to consumers, Murdoch was able to perpetuate the idea that culture could best be managed by acknowledging and catering for the whole range of tastes and judgements:

> As originally with news and sport, so now with the arts and drama. Sky now offers four dedicated arts channels. Original commissioning by channels that customers choose to pay for is expanding and will continue to do so, not just from Sky but from the likes of National Geographic, History, MTV and the Disney Channel, to name a few. Sky alone now invests over £1 billion a year in UK content. (p.11)

The focus of Murdoch's speech obscured the fact that the differences between the content of different channels, or between 'information', 'sport' and 'the arts' was insignificant in a market whose scale made the engagement with individual items (valued because they were ancient or sacred or new) or small, socially defined groups (encouraged to engage with a work of art because it would enhance their lives), both invisible and irrelevant. In this argument, the abstractions that had informed the attempts by anthropologists or cultural critics to define 'a whole way of life' or 'human capacity as a member of society' had been replaced by the abstractions of market categories, linked by the numbers (in billions) that represented financial investment.

Murdoch's description of the value of consumer choices provided a proxy for value in an argument that was making a case for eliminating what he saw as the anachronistic anomaly of the compulsory licence fee that provided the BBC with an annual income stream of £3 billion. This annual investment had allowed the BBC, acting as both a producer and distributor of TV content, to accumulate an extensive archive of intellectual property that gave them considerable competitive advantage in the new contest over content in the market. In Murdoch's view, the licence fee constituted an inappropriate subsidy that distorted the market for cultural production and constrained the competitive capacity of commercial organisations. He claimed that by paying for Sky TV packages, including packages labelled 'Culture', consumers were not merely purchasing a commodity, they were endorsing the value of 'investment, innovation and independence'. He implied that their engagement with television was part of a commitment to a modern opposition to 'creationism', his term for 'the belief in a managed process with an omniscient authority' (p.4). He was thus able to align the values of consumers against the forces of reactionary and unscientific views that stood in the way of innovation and the process of competitive natural selection that, in his view, characterised the unconstrained market.

Murdoch's account of the fundamental market contest that he thought should apply to culture as to any other sector revealed the way that a discussion of culture and the market involved a scale of investment and activity that could not easily be aligned to the experience of individual evaluation of cultural objects. Discussion of the value of 'culture' now involved a quite different negotiation between knowledge and values but the discussion confused the ethics of equal distribution of social goods, the aesthetics of the distinction between different forms of content and the political economy of their distribution by agents working on radically different scales.

This sense that the scale of cultural production had made old accounts of culture irrelevant was shared by the Oxford critic, John Carey in his 2005 polemic *What Good Are the Arts?*

> My answer to the question 'What is a work of art' is 'a work of art is anything that anyone has ever considered a work of art, though it may be a work of art only for that one person' ... It follows, of course, that the old use of 'work of art' as a term of commendation, implying membership of an exclusive category, becomes obsolete. The idea that by calling something a work of art you are bestowing on it some divine sanction is now as intellectually respectable as a belief in pixies.[32]

Carey offered a challenge to what he regarded as a moribund debate about the value of particular objects in the cultural domain. He suggests that because the tastes of the art establishment have been marginalised by the experience of larger numbers of people (which he calls 'the masses') who receive 'art on a scale and of a kind undreamed of by the official art world', the value of art can only ever be an expression of individual taste. In making that case, Carey echoed the dismay of modernist artists and cultural critics who felt that traditional cultural values could no longer be sustained in the face of a new market in culture created by technological change. Some residue of those feelings is echoed in Carey's own observation that 'Poetry readers and theatre goers are as rare as practitioners of origami compared with the global hordes who live their imaginative lives through TV soaps' (p.29).

In spite of his insistence that the hierarchies of value no longer carry any weight, his residual sense of modernist cultural crisis may be shared by those who continue to see the social world of the twenty-first century as one of conflict between small groups engaged in 'rare' activities and the 'global hordes' who have no taste for them. His analysis divided those who engaged with culture into broad-brush categories of taste and (since he was not engaged in systematic sociological analysis) did not consider that those who read poetry might also watch TV soaps or that TV soaps might provide as engaging imaginative representations of the contemporary social world as other forms of narrative drama. His alignments of culture with taste, and his segmentation of the market only in terms of content, obscured, once again, the important relations between cultural content and the institutions, technologies and markets that manage its value on a global scale.

Cultural relations

The management of cultural value by the state agencies, the market triumphalism of Murdoch's speech and John Carey's iconoclastic rejection of any collective agreement about the status of a work of art all reveal the difficulty of arriving at a coherent account of culture that can take account of the scale of cultural production and engagement in contemporary society. The contemporary mass-market in cultural goods operates on a global scale where production and consumption are not analogous in any way to the individuals engaged in what Adam Smith called 'higgling in the market' or the face-to-face discussions about the interpretation of a play or enjoyment of a visit to a gallery. These changes of scale make clear that a single stable and consensual ideal of culture that could gain universal assent is as impossible to achieve as a single consensual agreement about value. The diversity of cultural activities that take place in contemporary developed societies is on a scale that requires any analysis to take the form of proxies, whether those proxies are drawn from the mathematics of accounting, from the abstractions of anthropology or from the vivid imagery of metaphors that attempt to bring together experiences of individual experience and their larger significance. The resulting analytical oscillation between the individual experience, the requirements of a group and the whole 'way of life of a particular people living together in one place' indicates the constant adjustment of focus between the face-to-face scale of individual acts of consumption and the mass scale of production, distribution and regulation that is involved in different accounts of contemporary culture.

The contests that emerge periodically between those different accounts are less to do with the knowledge of culture than with the values involved in the supply-side management of cultural resources. In the case of the discursive conflict between Murdoch and the state-supported agencies that he regarded as competitors, the discussion of markets were a proxy for political values: they involved a contest between the state agencies' accountability to government and, through them, to the tax-paying public and the primary accountability of global companies to their shareholders and financial investors. In the case of the complex management of funding and evaluation required for the purchase and display of *The Madonna of the Pinks*, the whole extended exercise enacted an idea of the value of the arts for the nation but the discussion did not apply the same scales to the value achieved by removing the painting from the market, the aspirations of the outreach strategy or even the raw data of numbers of visits. Carey's argument imposed a single scale that measured value by numbers of people engaged but he offered no data with which to test the connection between numbers and taste, and reversed without questioning the traditional aesthetic hierarchies between poetry and TV soaps.

On the demand side, engagement with cultural activity is, for adults unconstrained by a school curriculum, a matter of open choice from within eclectically diverse cultural offering. As Bourdieu put it in 1993,

> One of the most significant properties of the field of cultural production, explaining its extreme dispersion and the conflicts between rival principles of legitimacy, is [that] ... the extreme diversity of the 'posts' it offers ... defies any unilateral hierarchisation.[33]

The absence of 'unilateral hierarchisation' certainly creates difficulties for accounts of culture that attempt to align cultural consumption with a unitary 'whole way of life', or 'man's capacities as a member of society', or supply-side efforts to manage its distribution.

Bourdieu himself had used a system of 'unilateral hierarchisation' in his early work to identify the alignment of taste for particular kinds cultural production with other forms of social hierarchy and to establish the distinction between those groups in terms of their access to what he called 'cultural capital'. For Bourdieu there was a direct analogy between 'cultural capital' and finance capital in terms of the way that each of them influences access to markets. However, his metaphorical use of the term 'capital' to refer to the combination of taste, education and wealth that tends to accompany the choice of particular cultural items suggests a prior evaluation of those items as more desirable. His concept of 'cultural capital' became very influential among cultural intermediaries who wished to increase the take-up of the limited cultural repertoire managed by state resources. The metaphorical use of the concept of capital not only reflects prior evaluation of the value of those resources: it also provides a useful rationale for governments who find the redistribution of cultural capital more acceptable than the redistribution of wealth.

Mike Featherstone's analysis confirms Bourdieu's earlier findings that consumers' choice in cultural goods is driven by the same calculus of money, time and social relations as the consumption of other social goods.[34] However, the range of goods available and the greater diversity of the supply undermine any simple 'deficit model' of culture that connects the choices of the less affluent with deprivation. As Featherstone and others have shown, the eclectic consumption of cultural goods, like other social practices, takes place in a variety of settings that both structure and are structured by social relations that extended beyond the simple connection between the individual and the object being consumed.

Cultural goods are consumed as part of a range of leisure activities that take place in and outside the market. Cultural consumption includes not only goods such as origami and TV soaps that are restricted in the social interaction they require, but may also involve more communal activity, such as music festivals, theme parks, amateur theatricals and sport, that can only with difficulty be abstracted into a representation of a unitary definition of culture. Attention to the consumption side of the market equation has produced a much more diverse idea of the social relations produced by culture than the model that opposes production-led content, to which consumers passively respond, against a unified culture in which the arts are a necessary and inseparable component.

The mix of market and non-market, individual and communal, heritage and contemporary forms that constitutes 'culture' in the twenty-first century does not fit easily into either the historical or the market analysis that was applied to it in the twentieth century. John Frow noted in 1995 that it was no longer possible

> to employ the traditional value-laden opposition between the disinterested, organic, original, self-governing work of art and the interested, mechanical formulaic and commercial mass cultural text.[35]

However, he framed his account of the new market-driven economy of culture in the context of a historical movement away from a more coherent culture in which 'high culture was unequivocally the culture of the ruling class'. Yet, as the case of *The Madonna of the Pinks* showed, objects from 'high culture' were a matter of markets in the past and remain so in the present. The 'ruling class' (itself a totalising concept) continue to be engaged in that market, though their role in it is now often mediated by the state. That highly specialised market for unique heritage objects is quite different from the forms of engagement in which most other people, not merely those who are socially disadvantaged, engage with culture. Their engagement with both heritage culture managed by the state and diverse cultural products managed by a variety of providers of different sizes and organisational models is more likely to be the result of a series of choices that are driven partly by income but also by time, taste and inclination.

The absence of a single scale or 'unilateral hierarchisation' for culture is partly to do with the diversity of supply but it may also have to do with a less authoritarian structure of values more generally. Featherstone for example, has noted this trend that, he finds, began in the counter-culture of the mid-twentieth century:

> The less strict canons of behaviour and relaxation of codes that accompanied the informalization process demanded that individuals show greater respect and consideration for each other as well as the ability to identify with and appreciate the other's point of view ... that would make them more open to emotional exploration, aesthetic experience, and the aestheticisation of life.[36]

His observation suggests that absence of 'unilateral hierarchisation' may be connected to the dispersal of what Connor called '*tyrannically* absolutist' values and their replacement by a structure that will only appear to represent '*corruptive* relativism' to tyrants.[37]

In using the term 'aestheticisation of life', Featherstone may have been referring to Benjamin's critique of the aesthetics of fascism that, he suggested, 'sees its salvation in giving these masses not their right, but instead a chance to express themselves'.[38] Writing in 1936, Benjamin was particularly concerned that the achievement of mass culture was highly dependent on the political conditions in which it might be realised: the model of a mass consensus was, for Benjamin and for the generation that succeeded him, fatally contaminated by images of the Nuremberg rallies. In the political context of the late twentieth and early twenty-first centuries, however, that anxiety may be less pressing, particularly when the eclecticism of contemporary culture can include forms of resistance to authoritarian politics such as political rallies or the festivals that coincided with meetings of the world leaders, as well as engagement with large-scale cultural markets.

The political terms in which this new cultural eclecticism is configured indicate the importance of understanding a diverse contemporary *economy* (rather than simply, a market) of culture. In her summary review of economic sociology, Nicole Woolsey Biggart suggested that

> The outstanding discovery of recent historical and anthropological research is that man's [sic] economy is submerged in his social relationships. He does not act to safeguard his individual interest in the possession of material goods; he acts so as to safeguard his social standing, his social claims, his social assets.[39]

The historical and ethnographic research on which these findings are based deal, for the most part, with the practices of face-to-face relations that characterise the day-to-day human experience of leisure. In those contexts, Biggart argues,

> the functions of an economic system proper are completely absorbed by the intensely vivid experiences ... which offer superabundant non-economic motivation for every act performed in the frame of the social system as a whole. (p. 42)

Her emphasis on the structural *conditions* that allow the symbiosis between economic and social existence is critical. In developed societies, the market of gain and profit creates the conditions for cultural exchange by reducing the costs of distribution and creating financial rewards for increased production. However, the market does not completely dominate the terms in which cultural interaction takes place. As Marshall Sahlins's analysis has shown, participation in the market, including in the mass markets of developed economies, are based on choices that can be described in cultural as well as market terms. He concludes the preface to the 2004 reissue of *Stone Age Economics* by noting that

> In The West as in The Rest, rationality (that determines choice) is the expression of the culture, of its meaningful system of utilities, not the antithesis.[40]

Sahlins's polemical case is supported by the examples he chooses: the purchase of food in supermarkets, which he describes as the 'code of motivated relationships between men and animals prevailing among the Western natives', and the choices of clothing 'that mark the social distinction between men and women, holidays and ordinary days, business men and policemen, work and leisure'. Sahlins acknowledges that those social and cultural choices are not entirely unconstrained and that the supply side of the market is constantly seeking to influence their choices: 'Granted that producers are always looking to invent new differentiations for their own profits.' However, he suggests that the means that markets deploy to engage their potential consumers reinforce his view that those choices are part of culture that is built into and inseparable from economic relations: 'all the more reason that they have to operate on the same cultural wavelength as consumers'.[41]

Sahlins's assimilation of cultural value into market-dominated cultural production appears to resolve the troublesome split between market value and cultural value by focussing on the use-value even of the objects of commercial and mass production. Thus, the value of objects in culture lies in the meanings that are made from them and the uses to which they will be put. This is distinct from the value that has been assigned to them by institutions of culture or the supply side of market relations and requires no dominating authority from either to endorse it. These analytical attempts to identify a stable location for cultural value on the demand side are equally open to questions of the scale of the analysis and the universal applicability of the proxy for value that it implies. They do, however, indicate a trend away from ideas of cultural value that can be located either in the formal characteristics of particular objects and events or in the authority of value assigned to them that derives from the status and intentions of its valuers.

These shifts in ideas of cultural value from an authoritative, if challenged, hierarchy of cultural goods to a more tolerant and eclectic recognition of the diversity of use, has been reflected both in media discussions of the question and in the new forms of engagement exercised by cultural institutions. In a 2007 BBC Radio 4 series called *National Treasures*, panellists were invited to allocate an imaginary £50,000 to capital projects in the cultural arena that involved either major purchases or infrastructure projects. None of the participants protested at the connection between value judgements and finance, since the programme format was familiar from television game shows including one called *Restoration* in which communities competed for funding to refurbish a local historic house or monument. In *National Treasures*, at least one project in each programme involved a community venture and these were set against an individual work of modern or heritage art or a public space for leisure activities of the kind made familiar by the changing role of the National Trust as it transferred resources from conserving historic great houses to conserving landscapes and city streets.[42]

The possibilities of a commitment to culture that did not merely polarise heritage art and mass production provided an opportunity to extend the debate beyond the high and low culture opposition. By the end of each programme, the panellists had to make a choice to allocate their funding to one object or another: the industrial museum *or* the old master painting, the restoration of Canterbury Cathedral *or* Damien Hirst's *Diamond Glitter Skull*.

The structure of the debate, the field that it defined, was more revealing than the final judgements made among competing objects. The field of culture was opened out so that it did not depend on category distinctions between the built environment, the cultivated landscape of rural England or the canon of made-objects structured by the contemporary art market. The success of the programmes depended on the participants' ability to place these different elements in a single hierarchy and to create controversy and debate through the eloquence and, occasionally, the vehemence with which their views were expressed. The format created a sense of a zero-sum game in which the hierarchy had to be absolute: it offered no possibility that the participants could agree to differ, that the competing objects could be judged to be so different that comparison was impossible, or that different ideas of value might be applied to each of them. Above all, there was no acknowledgement that the wealth historically accumulated through finance capital or industrial mass-production might provide more than enough resources to fund all of the projects being proposed. The programme had no scope to envisage a different material reality and it created a set of oppositions that could be rehearsed but not resolved.

The format both popularised and trivialised intellectual enquiry and the process of fiscal decision-making. Their form and structures, as much as their particular conclusions, revealed the extent to which commonplace ideas about cultural value swing between a sense that any authoritative and absolute value that could resolve competing claims is more or less arbitrary, and that competing claims must themselves make a case for a more authoritative idea of value in order to take part in the debate at all. None of the participants undertook a formal analysis of the characteristics of any of the objects discussed and no detailed cost-benefit assessment or investment-return analysis was offered.

Neither the format of the programme nor the tastes of the participants allow any consideration of the politics or economics that might inform particular funding decisions, nor of the formal differences among the items that might provide a robust basis for a meaningful comparison. Cultural value, it appeared, existed in a place that transcended (or at least avoided) systematic calculation or rational choice. There was no question of rejecting or preferring an object or a practice on a principled or informed commitment to one type of project or another, or on the basis of those who championed it. Each programme came to its own decision about the relative values of the objects in questions and it was impossible to discern any consistency or system in the application of value.

The presentation of cultural value in these radio debates neutralised the conflict over cultural value. Though the differences of opinion were clear, they were treated even-handedly and without invoking the absolutes of existing specialised authority. The programmes' final judgements always involved discreetly triumphant winners and disappointed losers who accepted the decisions good naturedly without any sense that the loss of funding might jeopardise people's livelihoods or the security of their way of life. The question of value was limited to the moment of the discussion, which could range over a random selection of objects taken from any or all definitions of culture. In that regard, the programmes were analogous to the opportunities for cultural consumption that co-exist in developed societies: individuals might enjoy a Bach concert on Monday, watch the Brit Awards for rock music on TV on Tuesday, go to Glastonbury in June and perhaps celebrate the summer solstice at Stonehenge on the way over. The precise culture value of these events cannot be defined by the demographic of the groups who attend them: they are too diverse to be placed in a single hierarchy of value and they are engaged in as a matter of free choice, neither enforced nor denigrated by any determining cultural authority.

The process of making culture a desired and important but ultimately optional choice was equally evident in Neil MacGregor's 2010 book and radio programmes, A *History of the World in 100 Objects*.[43] The book, and the radio programmes that both publicised it and shared its findings with the larger and more public media, juxtaposed unique items from the British Museum's collection with mass-produced commonplace objects. Each of the 100 objects discussed was given the same level of detailed expert attention, but imputations of authoritative selectivity were deflected by an invitation to members of the public to submit their own items along with a story that demonstrated their significance to the individual concerned.

The 100 objects of the title were limited only by the constraints of the programmes' time and the book's space: the question of value, conceived of as a hierarchy of relative judgements, was abandoned in favour of an eclectic consensus that value could be equally be assigned by the director of the British Museum and any individual whose story invited the listeners and the visitors to the programme's website to share in its claim to value. Many of the stories included moving accounts of the individuals' family past, usually when that past connected with similarly emotionally loaded experience such as war or migration. The value of the object discussed, though it was seldom asserted as such, consisted in the appeal that its significance might be recognised as it stood in for familiar images of the past.

The programme created an image of an immensely appealing world in which cultural objects could act as triggers for shared meaning that owed nothing to institutions, markets or the process of purchase, selection and conservation. These objects constituted completely stable instances of value in which the potential instability of consensus, the conflict of interest over established and changing values and the anxiety of equivalence that characterises markets were, albeit temporarily, absent. They suggested a utopian vision of a world that is profoundly attractive, partly because it provides an emotionally powerful antidote to the vision (or indeed the experience) of a social life that is riven by conflict and struggle. It offered the possibility that principled and consensual social action could align, on the one hand, the sum of individual evaluations and, on the other, the values enshrined in the tradition and authority of institutions, including, in this case, The British Museum and Radio 4. To raise the question of power or institutional or market authorisation would have been an impertinent intrusion on deeply held private evaluations that were generously being shared with the public at large.

A History of the World in 100 Objects thus provided some indication of what was at stake in the public articulation of cultural value in the twenty-first century. It brought together the major constituents of both culture and value: a commitment to shared practice that is more than a reflexive and involuntary expression of individual taste or pleasure and an assertion of the claim to value of particular activities and objects as narratives that transformed them into expressions of 'culture'. The British Museum project showed how the value of culture might be given transcendent, if not absolute, authority by virtue of its identification with the practices of particular people, whether those people were Assyrian kings or random individuals from the contemporary population. It suggests the ways that culture could be aligned with practices of both groups and individuals and depended less on the object or practice itself than on the shared respect and consideration that other groups might afford it. It offered an image of culture easily aligned with the dream of transcendent value: consensual, uncompetitive, outside the market and with no visible signs of coercion or the exclusive authoritarian exercise of power.

The defining characteristics of cultural value remain fluid, contested and open to constant negotiation. In the following chapters, we will explore the particular conditions in which those unstable relations between use and exchange value, intrinsic value and contingent value, cultural value and the value of particular cultural practices are being negotiated by the supply side of culture in twenty-first century England, as Shakespeare is assimilated into culture and twenty-first-century institutions, and markets and technologies are managed in ways that are inflected by government investment in culture. Government interventions cannot ultimately resolve the inherent instability of the idea of cultural value. However, their efforts to do so articulate and in some cases regulate the ways in which ideas of cultural value provide some response to political and economic change in the opening decades of the twenty-first century.

Notes

1 T. S. Eliot, *Notes Towards a Definition of Culture* (London: Faber and Faber, 1948), p.120.
2 Greenblatt, *Shakespearean Negotiations*, p.1; Walter Benjamin, *The Work of Art in the Age of Mechanical Reproduction*, trans. J. A. Underwood (London: Penguin, 2008), p.8.
3 Pierre Bourdieu, *Distinction: A Social Critique of the Judgement of Taste*, trans. Richard Nice (London: Routledge, 1979), p.496.
4 Raymond Williams, *Marxism and Literature* (Oxford: Oxford University Press, 1977), p.122.
5 E. B. Tylor, *Primitive Culture*, 2 vols (London: John Murray, 1871), vol. 1, p.1, quoted in Adam Kuper, *Culture: The Anthropologists' Account* (London: Harvard University Press, 1999), p.56.
6 See Kuper, *Culture*, p.57.
7 Kuper, *Culture*, pp.24–47.
8 Marshall Sahlins, *Culture in Practice* (New York: Zone Books, 2005), p.15. Compare the principle of 'generalizability' that informed social analysis of culture, discussed in Chapter 2, p.30.
9 A. L. Kroeber and Clyde Kluckhorn, *Culture: A Critical Review of Concepts and Definitions*, Papers of the Peabody Museum, vol. 47, no. 1 (Cambridge, MA: Harvard University, 1952), p.153, quoted in Kuper, *Culture*, p.57.
10 Clifford Geertz, *After the Fact* (Cambridge, MA: Harvard University Press, 1995), p.43.
11 Clifford Geertz, *Works and Lives: The Anthropologist as Author* (Oxford: Blackwell, Polity Press, 1989), pp.146–147.
12 Sahlins, *Culture in Practice*, p.10.
13 James Clifford, *The Predicament of Culture: Twentieth Century Ethnography, Literature and Art* (Cambridge, MA: Harvard University Press, 1988), p.92, quoted in Kuper, *Culture*, p.212.
14 Kuper, *Culture*, 1999, p.222.
15 www.awid.org/Library/Eradicating-Female-Genital-Mutilation-Sexual

ity-rights-vs.-Cultural-relativism (ccessed 20.08.12). The quoted article was accessed in 2007 and is no longer on the site of the Association for Women's Rights in Development (AWID). The site referenced above, however, raises the same issues and provides a number of other cases that centre on the contemporary issues of the contest between culture and rights.
16 See Chapter 2 in this volume, p. 32.
17 Henrietta L. Moore, *Still Life: Hopes, Desires and Satisfactions* (London: Polity Press, 2011), pp. 37–8.
18 Moore, *Still Life: Hopes, Desires and Satisfactions*, p. 44.
19 Moore, *Still Life: Hopes, Desires and Satisfactions*, p. 46.
20 Benjamin, *The Work of Art in the Age of Mechanical Reproduction*, p. 6.
21 Frederic Jameson, 'Postmodernism, or the Cultural Logic of Late Capitalism', *New Left Review*, 146 (July–August 1984), p. 56.
22 Featherstone, *Consumer Culture*, p. 16.
23 Featherstone, *Consumer Culture*, pp. 16–17.
24 Paul Jeffcutt and Andy C. Pratt, 'Editorial: Managing Creativity in the Cultural Industries', *Creativity and Innovation Management* 11(4) (2002): 225–233, pp. 225–226.
25 See www.hlf.org.uk/Pages/Home.aspx (accessed 22.08.12). The policy implications of using the HLF are discussed in Chapter 6, p. 153.
26 www.artfund.org/what-we-do/art-weve-helped-buy/artwork/8877/madonna-of-the-pinks (accessed 22.08.12).
27 www.telegraph.co.uk/culture/art/3647412/A-lot-of-pounds-for-a-few-pinks.html (accessed 07.06.13).
28 www.nationalgallery.org.uk/paintings/raphael-the-madonna-of-the-pinks-la-madonna-dei-garofani (accessed 07.06.13).
29 Eilean Hooper-Greenhill, Jocelyn Dodd, Lisanne Gibson and Ceri Jones, *Evaluation of the Education and Community Strategy for the Madonna of the Pinks 2004–2007* (Leicester: University of Leicester Research Centre for Museums and Galleries, 2007), www2.le.ac.uk/depart ments/museumstudies/rcmg/projects/madonna-of-the-pinks/MOTP.pdf (accessed 23.08.12).
30 Any connection between this discussion and the 2011–12 scandal over the conduct of journalists at the Murdoch-owned *News of the World* is too complex to address here.
31 James Murdoch, 'The Absence of Trust', Edinburgh International Television Festival MacTaggart Lecture, 28 August 2009, http://image.guardian.co.uk/sys-files/Media/documents/2009/08/28/JamesMurdochMacTaggartLecture.pdf (accessed 07.06.13), p. 5.
32 John Carey, *What Good Are the Arts?* (London: Faber and Faber, 2005), pp. 29–30.

33 Pierre Bourdieu, *The Field of Cultural Production: Essays on Arts and Literature*, ed. R. Johnson (Cambridge: Polity Press, 1993), p.43.
34 Featherstone, *Consumer Culture*, pp.13–51.
35 Frow, *Cultural Studies*, pp.23–24.
36 Featherstone, *Consumer Culture*, p.44.
37 See Chapter 2 in this volume, p.32.
38 Featherstone, *Consumer Culture*, p.15.
39 Nicole Woolsey Biggart, *Readings in Economic Sociology* (Oxford: Blackwell, 2002), p.40.
40 Marshall Sahlins, *Stone Age Economics* (London: Routledge, 2004), p.xiii.
41 Sahlins, *Stone Age Economics*, p.xii For a full discussion of the connection between products, brands and consumers, see below, Chapter 8, pp.221–222.
42 See www.nationaltrust.org.uk/what-we-do/what-we-protect (accessed 14.12.12).
43 Neil MacGregor, *A History of the World in 100 Objects* (London: Viking, 2011).

5

Making 'Shakespeare' culture

In Chapter 4, we described the way that 'culture' functions as an analytical tool, as an expression of commitment to residual aspirations for social coherence, and as a collective term for the vast resources, from the present and the past, available for competitive new markets in symbolic goods. Contests between these definitions, we suggested, structure the supply-side of cultural (re)production, as different agents seek to endorse the combination of knowledge and value that informs their management of the cultural domain. On the reception side, by contrast, consumers are able to take advantage of the huge variety of cultural goods available to them to engage in multiple leisure activities that do not easily fit into the older analytical categories that opposed high and low culture, art objects and a way of life, paying customers and participants in public-sector cultural provision.

This version of culture emphasises the autonomy and agency of consumers: the investment costs and extended levels of technical and organisational work that create the value-chain of supply-side production are invisible at the point of exchange. The choices made by consumers, along with the imaginative and social work that they undertake with those products, constitute 'the expression of the culture' and that work can act as an antidote to the determining force of markets and their tendency to restrict value to the outcome of exchange. Neither the objects chosen, nor the people making the choices, are explicitly constrained by authority or tradition or differentiation based on association with particular social or ethnic groups. Culture, instead, provides a resource for an effective form of adaptation to the restless innovation and global sourcing of exchange markets in the developed world; it also includes social activities that are not limited by, and may even be actively resistant to, the values of markets.

This model of culture and its value is, of course, entirely of its moment. It offers no account of the formal characteristics of individual objects that might make them more or less likely to become the constituents of culture in the twenty-first century, nor of the combination of historical circumstances and institutional interests that bring them into its domain. The content of culture, the particular objects that link the production process and the consumption process, can no longer be the basis for a 'unilateral principle of hierarchisation' and they cannot determine the value of 'a whole way of life'. In the absence of this unilateral principle, it is nonetheless important to identify the different forms of knowledge and work involved in the process that allows the objects whose choice constitutes culture, to have (or not) the potential to be chosen and the effects of different kinds of choices on the forms of culture that they constitute.

'Shakespeare', for the reasons we have already discussed, is a somewhat over-determined example with which to conduct this analysis. However, the plays' continuing significance as a mark of cultural value and the complexity of their role in the work of culture make them an interesting case study with which to explore the possible connections between heritage content and contemporary culture.

Shakespeare and culture

At this point in the twenty-first century, the position of 'Shakespeare' as a valued cultural object continues to appear unassailable. The so-called 'Cultural Olympiad' that accompanied the 2012 London Olympics included the 'Globe to Globe' festival,[1] in which each of the plays were produced by different international companies at the London Globe theatre; the Royal Shakespeare Company (RSC) produced a special series of performances that included new international productions; the BBC launched a Shakespeare season that included new films of the second tetralogy of history plays and broadcast the new Royal Shakespeare Company production of *Julius Caesar*, supported by programmes of commentary and analysis;[2] and the British Museum presented an exhibition entitled 'Shakespeare: Staging the World' that linked objects from its own collections and borrowed from museums and from individuals across the world.[3]

The confidence of these presentations, their high production values and the eclectic diversity of the forms and languages in which 'Shakespeare' appeared suggested that, for their curators and presenters at least, the past century's anxious debates about Shakespeare's position in culture were no longer relevant. The British Museum's exhibition publicity confidently articulated a direct relationship between 'Shakespeare', his theatre and his history, and exemplary material objects from the past:

> The exhibition shows how the playhouse informed, persuaded and provoked thought on the issues of the day; how it shaped national identity, first English, then British; and how the theatre opened a window on the wider world, from Italy to Africa to America, as London's global contacts were expanding through international trade, colonisation and diplomacy ... The exhibition creates a unique dialogue between an extraordinary array of objects – from great paintings and rare manuscripts to modest, everyday items of the time – and the plays and characters that have had a richer cultural legacy than any other in the western world.[4]

Objects that illustrated the world of the court and the day-to-day life of London's population celebrated the co-existence of high and low culture in Shakespeare's time: the portrait of the Moorish Ambasssador and a copy of the First Folio sat side-by-side with everyday objects excavated from the sites of the Globe and the Rose theatre, such as the 'sucket fork' for sweetmeats or the bear's skull that hinted at the practice of bear-baiting. They represented both the craft skills and the mass-production of early modern England and Europe, their 'pricelessness' assured by conservation in museums and their significance refocused by their discursive connection to Shakespeare. 'A series of new digital interventions' allowed visitors 'to encounter Shakespeare's words and characters alongside the objects on display' in readings by celebrated Royal Shakespeare company actors such as Harriet Walter, Antony Sher and Sir Ian McKellan, reprising recent performances.

The extraordinary accumulation of material remains and interpretation from the present and the past, brought together in this and other events in the Shakespeare offerings required a huge deployment of both financial and intellectual resource.[5] It is impossible to identify the exact proportion of the funding allocated to the 'Shakespeare' element of the cultural events surrounding the Olympics, though there were '62 Shakespeare productions, and only 55 non-Shakespeare theatre and performance events'[6] and

85,000 tickets were sold for the Globe festival. Corporate sponsors provided a total of £700 million pounds to offset the £9.3bn budget for the whole event,[7] 16 million people took part in the Cultural Olympiad as volunteers as well as audiences and Arts Council England contributed over £4m. This scale of this financial outlay is insignificant, compared, for example, with the '$450bn annual revenue'[8] of Exxon Mobil, but it is comparable with the cultural outlay of $237m that the Exxon Mobil philanthropic foundation dispenses world wide on projects including science education and the development of opportunities for women.[9] The time spent by academics, curators, administrators, actors and technicians preparing the exhibition and the performances, the costs of travel and insurance for companies and for the objects lent from other museums and companies from overseas, the publicity and marketing that ensured the attendance of thousands of visitors were held in the same economic frame of 'global capitalism' and mass reproduction. They encompassed both producers and consumers since the entrance fees to events and performance provided only a fraction of the exhibition's and the performances' cost and its only explicit forms of exclusion were those applied to the significant numbers of groups whose applications to offer their products as part of the 'Cultural Olympiad' were turned down.

On the supply-side of the cultural economy of the twenty-first century, the combined financial instruments of sponsorship, multiple funders and partnerships between the state, philanthropic trusts and the private sector had become the norm for high-profile events. Their costs are not matched by sales, but rather the combination of the priceless and the priced are linked across the whole process. Museums can draw on collections accumulated over centuries to create differently themed exhibitions, and successful live theatre events are filmed and distributed on DVD as well as in cinemas. The 2009 RSC production of *Hamlet* starring David Tennant and Patrick Stewart, for example, had short theatre runs in Stratford and London, and was filmed and shown on BBC TV in 2010; the film is available in different media forms and David Tennant presented a programme in the 2012 BBC 'Shakespeare Unlocked' season discussing the challenges of the role and comparing his performance with a canon of previous performances, some of which were shown in the TV programme. Knowledge that might once have been regarded as the specialist field of academics or the private intellectual property of a commercial organisation can now be broadcast to an audience of millions, funded by an ingenious, if sometimes controversial, set of bargains struck between corporations, tax-payers and the public sector.

This combination of accumulated assets, knowledge, finance and not-for-profit philanthropy supports the whole of the culture market in developed societies. The levels of intellectual and financial investment that it can deploy, at least on special occasions, allays earlier anxieties about the relations between the value of the cultural offering, the value of the financial resources required to sustain it and the endorsement of its value by the engaged attention of significant numbers of people. In the shift from 'cult value to exhibition value' managed by the British Museum's curators and designers and theatre companies across the world, 'Shakespeare' can become an occasion for high-quality arts events, as well as a symbolic proxy for 'international trade, colonisation and diplomacy' and the new internationalism symbolised by the Olympic games themselves. In a circuit of symbolic meaning, 'Shakespeare' pointed to the historical abstractions that link his time to ours and back to the eclectic collection of objects assembled in his name.

In the preparation for the British Museum exhibition, for example, the plays had been mined for references to objects that could be sourced from the catalogue of extant historical objects and the relevant lines used in turn to transform the objects from their historical origins to a contemporaneous symbolic statement. The cataloguing protocols that in other contexts might have identified historical objects by their material form, provenance and date (e.g. sword; Spanish; sixteenth-century) were now re-animated by Shakespeare words: 'I have another weapon in this chamber/It is a sword of Spain, the ice-brook's temper' (*Othello*, 5.2). There was no crass suggestion that the sword, or the sucket fork or the bear's skull actually belonged to or had even been seen by Shakespeare. Instead Shakespeare's lines gave significance to the objects while the object may have given a sense of tangibility, a physical version of an editorial gloss to the viewer's sense of Shakespeare. The potential existed to make a connection between the object and the viewer that would create the elusive moment of shared meaning that could link producer and consumer, object and viewer, the individual and 'culture', but the outcome was not restricted by this or any other directly determined expectation.

The exhibition's potential for creating cultural value existed at the point of contact. Its funders and curators could create the right conditions through selection and design and they could count on at least the familiarity with Shakespeare assured by over a century of compulsory education. But apart from the enthusiastic advocacy of the publicity, there was no scope for a limited authoritative account of Shakespeare's plays to interpose itself between the show and its viewers. As we show in Chapter 6, the anxious debate about the connection between institutions, funders and public engagement that had preoccupied the Secretary of State in 2004 had not gone away, but it could be overcome by the deployment of resource that exceeded the limited 'taxation pot' and applied techniques of engagement developed in the commercial sector.

Writing on the structures of effective advertising in the mid-twentieth century, Erving Goffmann had explained the importance of 'half finished frames which invite the consumer to participate by filling in the picture':

> the consumer is engaged by his or her own mobility and imagination: Movement and incompleteness energise the imagination; fixity and solidity equally deaden it.[10]

However, creating the dynamic set of connections required to establish and complete the cycle of meaning without '*tyrannically* absolutist' claims to value required more than the imaginative work of the British Museum curators and designers. 'Shakespeare', too, had had to be managed before he could take his place in this configuration of 'culture'.

The object known as 'Shakespeare'

In order to be assimilated into the cultural market of the twenty-first century, the object known as 'Shakespeare' had, as we described in Chapter 3, to be connected to universalising abstractions. By the twenty-first century, he also had to be cleansed of negative associations and redundant forms of authority in order to foster the illusion of the spontaneous and unconstrained engagement that characterised the twenty-first-century vision of culture.

Given the immense range of research and intellectual work that had gone into the preparations for the British Museum exhibition, and the huge resource devoted to Shakespeare in the state school system, it is perhaps paradoxical that one of the key negative associations that inhibited Shakespeare's assimilation into culture was the knowledge associated with the academic study of Shakespeare. As we described in Chapter 1,[11] the education departments of theatre companies had been at pains for some time to distinguish the forms of participative, active and creative forms of learning that they sought to foster in developing children's appreciation of Shakespeare. Both theatre practitioners and policy-makers contrasted the pleasures of theatrical Shakespeare with the misery of an almost comically denigrated 'academic Shakespeare' that had consisted, apparently, of deadly 'learning by rote' and 'reading round the class'. This attention to more direct ways of engaging with Shakespeare were connected to the theatre companies' efforts to build future audiences and sustain their place in the cultural economy, but they also had the effect of assimilating Shakespeare into the free space of culture in which individual perception and spontaneous appreciation could overcome and transcend the 'Shakespeare' associated with difficulty and struggle.

The exclusion of 'academic' Shakespeare knowledge from the purview of 'cultural Shakespeare' was less to do with the intrinsic characteristics of either: it was, rather, the latest phase in a long-running contest over the authority to manage the social relations in which Shakespeare would be assimilated into culture. The value of Shakespeare and, indeed, the importance of extending that value into the cultural life of the nation had been reiterated from the eighteenth century onwards, but older versions of the re-constructions of 'Shakespeare' that were created in the process had to be repudiated and renewed at every stage.

The 'academic' Shakespeare constructed in the early twentieth century had been valued as a gift from serious and principled people to those whose leisure might, they feared, 'be limited to the reading of penny, three penny or even sixpenny newspapers'.[12] Their sense that culture resided in texts and was inherently connected to the cultural capabilities of those who engaged with it made them insist that education in Shakespeare and Renaissance literature must address the 'full comprehension of the utterances of the past' including 'changing meaning in words since the Elizabethan period' in order 'to free it from the dominion of the idols of the marketplace' (p. 220). These high-minded scholars placed themselves in between

Making 'Shakespeare' culture 123

the production and consumption of culture and explicitly separated the discourse of value from the discourse of the market. They stabilised 'Shakespeare' into a formal curriculum that could be valued as a 'real service not only to students but to the community at large'. The knowledge provided by education became, for these advocates, the link between culture as a canon of valued objects and culture as a way of life.

The effect of organising the resistance to the 'idols of the marketplace' in educational institutions, however, was to ossify this version of cultural value. Shakespeare was institutionalised in education, whose formal requirements were aligned with the high levels of skill that education might provide and the social rewards it offered in the form of accreditation and examination success.

Later in the twentieth century, those who had benefitted from the value of those rewards attributed the skills they had developed in education with the intrinsic characteristics of the material they studied but they were not perceived as a gift to the socially excluded. Rather, the skills required to access their particular sources of value were seen as the reason why they had not been more widely appreciated. As John Guillory expressed the problem:

> the intrinsic difficulty of literary language marked the distinction between high cultural artefacts and the mass cultural artefacts and the distinction also defined the social spaces appropriate for the consumption of these artefacts.[13]

Fiske, too, concurs and realigns those skills with the restrictions and divisions of class: 'the difficulty of highbrow texts functions less to ensure or measure the quality of the text itself ... it works to exclude those who do not have the cultural competence to decode it'.[14]

Guillory's and Fiske's observations act as a useful reminder of the work required to realise the potential for engagement that a complex text might contain, but, in their accounts, the value of that work is subsumed within the social circumstances that might facilitate or impede its operation. These views are limited by their assumption both that 'mass cultural artefacts' do not require similar kinds of work (for example, to understand the rules of snooker or the complex relationships involved in a long-running soap-opera) and that 'Shakespeare' can only fully be consumed in 'appropriate social spaces'. The ability to 'decode' texts was associated with the social spaces and the class divisions in which that work took place but it was also presented a product of their 'intrinsic difficulty' rather than the particular social arrangements that had created the difficulty in the first place.

Yet the intrinsic difficulty of Shakespeare as a literary text and the need for special spaces in which to study it may have been overstated. Jonathan Rose's research on *The Intellectual Life of the British Working Class* and Andrew Murphy's work on nineteenth-century artisan readers of Shakespeare have both demonstrated that, by the later years of the nineteenth century, engaging with Shakespeare texts was not limited to those with a privileged education and it was possible, at that time, to engage with Shakespeare in a wide variety of social spaces. Engaging with Shakespeare did require access to cheap print and the publishing industry's pre-selection of already valued texts. However, those conditions of access included free libraries and did not entirely determine the nature of the engagement. In interviews and autobiographies, readers expressed their engagement with Shakespeare's plays in terms of the 'beauty' or 'wisdom' they discovered there. Their experience both recognised, as they saw it, the qualities of the texts and endorsed the prior cultural evaluation conferred by the texts' pre-selection in classic editions or library collections.[15]

These readers also often placed their engagement with Shakespeare within a wider narrative of self-improvement: a story of how coming to understand Shakespeare was part of a process of engaging with a wider world of knowledge that reading and literature had made available to them. The value that they attached to this self-improvement was attributed to 'Shakespeare' rather than their own work as readers or the commercial and cultural work that had made the texts available to them. In the late nineteenth-century division of labour, the work of reading a complex text seemed to be the antithesis of the repetitive and unrewarding labour with which these readers earned their living. To acknowledge the work of engaging with Shakespeare would be in some sense to devalue their own capacity for autonomous and immediate appreciation and with it their own right to inhabit the world of rewarding, creative and 'self-fulfilling' activity.

These alignments between 'Shakespeare', the social relations that structured cultural engagement and the contested relations within the twentieth-century cultural market have all but disappeared in the twenty-first century's philanthropically supported reproduction of 'Shakespeare'. However, they continue to exercise some leverage in the contest between academic Shakespeare and the more diverse commercial forms that use Shakespeare for innovative production in a more strictly commercial market environment. Richard Burt, for example, has denounced the products of what he calls 'Shakespeare after mass media' as 'trash, kitsch, obsolete, trivial, obscure, unknown, forgotten, unarchived, beyond the usual academic purview'.[16] His terms suggest not only dissatisfaction with the formal qualities of the products concerned but also academic frustration at their resistance to the protocols of knowledge management that will allow them to be assimilated – as many other mass produced forms have been[17] – into the value structures of the academy. For Burt and many other academics, the valued outcome of Shakespeare reproduction is its creation of objects for 'difficult' hermeneutic analysis. Products that do not lend themselves to that practice can therefore be relegated to the familiar negative pole in the division of culture that polarises 'the democratisation of high culture through low media' against 'the dumbing down and debasement of Shakespeare for the masses'.[18]

As we suggested in Chapter 4, this division of culture into high and low, elite and mass cannot effectively align the diversity and ingenuity of new cultural forms either with their underpinning economic structures or the social categories of those who engage with them. What Burt's categorisation does reveal is a continuing contest between the value of particular versions of 'Shakespeare' and the value assigned to the status of their assumed or intended audience. 'The masses', unlike 'citizens' or even 'consumers',[19] are never a source of value and so a product assumed to be aimed at them is 'dumbed down' and 'debased'. However, even in productions where the Shakespeare narrative is adapted to the point of disappearance, the value is nonetheless sustained by the value-added of creative work, and the engagement of the audience. When the Oily Cart theatre company, for example, created a 'multi-sensory' show for children with learning disabilities, all that remained of the 'Shakespeare' that they claimed as their source was sheep, a baby, a statue that came to life and 'uncut lines of Shakespeare's *Winter's Tale*'.[20] Talk of 'dumbing down' would have been deeply inappropriate: 'Shakespeare uncut' had entered culture as a resource for the practitioners' creative work, legitimated by grants from Arts Council England and charitable funding and assured by the expectation that

'Shakespeare' as 'an experience of theatre' was as appropriate for 'severely disabled children' as any other social group.

The place of Shakespeare in culture continues to depend on distinctions being made about the value of the audience or the legitimating sources of the finance that makes it possible. Within these distinctions direct engagement with an audience unmediated by profit-seeking technologised production tends to have a higher status. The quality of the creative work and the narratives of direct audience engagement seem to be the critical factors in adding value to 'Shakespeare' rather than the hermeneutically dense, complexly historicised version of Shakespeare that is both the content and the product of advanced work in the academy. In her account of the use of Shakespeare as content for commercial executive training programmes, Mary Polito has observed that the programmes

> are entirely free to read for and utilize the affective potential of the plays and Shakespeare's name as a guarantor of value and ethics. There is no mechanism by which they are compelled to consider the critical tradition of the plays.[21]

Polito is right to observe that these programmes make no acknowledgement of the academic work that has contributed to the continued availability and standing of these texts. The value consists instead of the practitioners' creative management of Shakespeare's ethical authority, which strips it of its associations with formal learning. Value then derives from the apparently unmediated engagement with its 'truth', as an account of the work of the successful management training company Richard Olivier Mythodrama makes clear:

> The idea, says Olivier, is that 'in most of the great Shakespeare plays, there is some wisdom about human nature that's encoded into the story and which can help guide us.' In other words, if something was rotten in Denmark, it's probably rotten in UBS.... Or MoneyGram (MGI). Or the CIA.[22]

The 'wisdom' of Shakespeare in these cases is presented as encoded and in need of expert facilitation in order to be revealed, but that revelation no longer depends upon the detailed (and perhaps tedious) attention to questions of editorial integrity or systems of transmission. It works, rather, by analogy, connecting the Shakespeare narrative to the anxieties and challenges faced by the programmes' consumers. The programmes are then revalidated by narratives of transformation that are structured by the same conversion narratives that we observed Chapter 1.

An interview with an initially sceptical participant who had taken the Mythodrama programme as part of an elite MBA course reported how:

> minutes into the program, as Olivier was explaining the story of the magical duke Prospero, McFarland (a management executive from the IRS) swears Olivier looked right at him. The moment was as 'brief as the lightning in the collied night,' as Shakespeare might have said, but it changed McFarland's life forever ... After he and Olivier locked eyes in Paris, 'Olivier said, "If you're leading a major change, you have to be willing to change yourself. You might have to be willing to *die* for it."' McFarland was stunned. He felt the weight of his job – tens of thousands of employees' lives and careers depended on his success. He had no idea that working for the IRS could be like *The Tempest*.[23]

The revelation that transformed McFarland's view of Shakespeare depended on the interaction between a charismatic trainer and a receptive individual but it was also facilitated by the long-standing critical tradition that had read *The Tempest* as an allegory of 'power' presenting Caliban as the source of resistance to unauthorised and violent colonial oppression.[24] Richard Olivier, however, apparently offered a more straightforward narrative of Prospero's life on the island in order to address the management challenge of organisational change. The effect of his assimilation of Shakespeare to the cultural needs of his audience depended on their ability to apply the allegory to themselves:

> When he talks about the play's most climactic moment – when Prospero relinquishes his power by snapping his magical staff – McFarland sounds as if he's about to cry. 'At the peak of his power he gave it up,' he says. He vowed to conduct himself the same way when he got back to work.

More cynical participants in the programme might have had a different reaction:[25] the managed adaptation of Shakespeare into culture cannot determine reception. However, this attempt to assimilate Shakespeare into culture showed the importance of presenting Shakespeare as a direct source of immediately applicable affective knowledge: a Shakespeare without his footnotes, without any alienating sense of scholarly uncertainty. This Shakespeare is open and available for the diversity of interpretation and application. It does not depend on the endorsement of authoritative specialised knowledge even though, as we described in Chapter 3, its transmission and adaptation has been the result of the long chain of value that stretches from the non-rival value of the texts to the particular moment of reception in which that value is recognised, celebrated and endorsed

Not only does the assimilation of Shakespeare's value into culture require frequent re-endorsement, but that endorsement itself is communicated through narratives that engage different constituencies. The 'dumbed down' mass-media Shakespeare deplored by academic specialists does not carry the hermeneutic potential that characterises their engagement but it often provides the frisson of iconoclasm that has engaged audiences for Shakespeare parody since the plays were first circulated. The conversion of Walt McFarland may have little empathetic impact beyond the readers of *Business Week*. Occasionally, however, narratives of engagement with Shakespeare can be reshaped and managed in a ways that present them as the paradigm confirmation of value. The constituent elements of authority, empathy, memory and commentary that are deployed in that management provide a special insight into the connection between Shakespeare and culture at the present time.

One of the most commented on of the objects displayed in the 2012 British Museum exhibition was a copy of Shakespeare's works, a cheap, mass-produced Collins edition, published world wide since the 1950s. The book, however, was transformed into a significant object because it was the property of Sonny Venkatrathnam, who had been a political prisoner with Nelson Mandela on Robben Island during the apartheid struggle in South Africa. He had circulated the book among the political prisoners, each of whom had marked a passage in the text. Mandela's inscription marked the following lines from *Julius Caesar*,

> Cowards die many times before their deaths
> The valiant never taste of death but once.
> Of all the wonders that I yet have heard.
> It seems to me most strange that men should fear;
> Seeing that death, a necessary end,
> Will come when it will come.
>
> 2.2.32–37.

For anyone who had followed the story of his role in the anti-apartheid struggle, Mandela's choice of passage has an overwhelming resonance. That resonance comes partly from the text's rhetorical distinction between 'the coward and the valiant' and the rhythmical caesura that separates 'me' from 'men', but that commonplace effect is massively amplified by the connection to a reader's particular memory of Mandela's political heroism. The ethical authority of Shakespeare's lines is reinforced by Mandela's own ethical standing, together with the empathetic effect of a voice from the past.

The particular concatenation of recognised authority and empathetic memory had to be carefully managed in order for it to endorse and recreate the role of Shakespeare in culture. The book had been displayed before, in an exhibition of copies of Complete Works mounted by the Shakespeare Birthplace Trust in connection with the RSC's 2007 Complete Works festival. Those small numbers of people who attended that exhibition were very taken with this remarkable exhibit[26] but, in the absence of a marketing budget that would ensure national media coverage, it did not receive the attention of the 2012 display. In 2012, the significance of the lines for press, radio and Internet audiences were reproduced in Greg Doran's resonant readings of Mandela's chosen passage; a play based on the story was performed in the British Museum and featured on the BBC's 'Front Row' review of the show.[27] The book was also claimed as the inspiration for Greg Doran's production of *Julius Caesar*, whose black cast and production setting re-enacted contemporary concerns with the alleged failure of democratic institutions in contemporary Africa. The 'priceless' nature of a significant historical artefact was secured by the information, from the RSC website page: 'Venkatrathnam who still owns the book has, to this day, refused numerous offers from people wanting to buy the priceless piece of history that is the "Robben Island Bible"'.[28] The complex overlayering of association, memory and knowledge, combined with an insistence on value that transcended the market, was able to reassert the enduring value of that particular instance of 'Shakespeare'. Making Shakespeare culture, in this instance, depended on the potential for empathetic effect and the authority both of the original selection of Shakespeare's lines and of the British Museum's and the RSC's re-endorsement of their significance.[29]

Any analysis of the long value-chain that connects the text of a Shakespeare play, through its editorial history to the Collins edition and its circulation in South Africa, comes from a completely different intellectual domain where other knowledge blurs the immediate effect of empathy. Knowledge of the whole play would indicate that Caesar's heroic statement is not only an exemplar of Shakespeare's 'wisdom' but also a device that characterises the speaker in contrast to the timid fearfulness of his wife and involves the same self-presentation of superhuman courage that had been called into question by his political opponents. Knowledge of the whole of Shakespeare's works might cause a cynical reader to reflect that the book might have had a less iconic effect if Mandela's taste for Shakespeare had been exemplified by Falstaff's more iconoclastic reflections on the connection between courage and honour (*1 Henry IV*, 5.1).

The information, from an interview with Venkatrathnam,[30] that Mandela's choice reflected his sense of his Roman destiny, forged by his relatively privileged education,[31] also provided a more politically mediated sense of the complex cultural resonances of Shakespeare in both pre- and post-apartheid South Africa.[32] That knowledge, even when it is shared with enthusiastic advocates of this apparent endorsement of Shakespeare's value, however, plays no role in the primary experience. The cultural significance of the Shakespeare-book depended on the creation and communication of a moment of recognition. That moment of recognition did not depend on specialist knowledge of the object's provenance or the truth of the connection claimed. It was created (or resisted) by a new relationship between an object and an engaged viewer, both of whom are playing role in constructing the present cultural value of Shakespeare.

Work and play

It is perhaps remarkable that the value of Shakespeare in the case of the Robben Island volume was located in a book. It had become commonplace in the late twentieth century to insist that the value of Shakespeare resides primarily in performance and to treat the texts of Shakespeare's plays as 'scripts for performance' or 'textual traces' of their original performances. In part this insistence on the plays in performance was an attempt to reach beyond the editorially contested 'texts' to the historical authenticity of the performance that lay chronologically behind them, closer to the 'lost' Shakespeare manuscripts and closer, it was implied, to the creative genius of Shakespeare himself. The intersection between textual and theatrical Shakespeare structured a contested discursive field in which editors debated a choice between 'a text which is as close as possible to what Shakespeare originally wrote' and 'a text presenting the play as it appeared when performed by the company of which Shakespeare was a principal shareholder in the theatres he helped to control'.[33] Professional editors, however, found it impossible to constrain those whose 'ambitions as a theatre director' might 'easily get in the way of a dispassionate attempt at understanding the theatrical implications of the surviving text in the desire to render it theatrically vivid'.[34]

These scholarly debates, however, took place on the margins of the theatre performances of Shakespeare whose creativity and innovation transformed the experience of Shakespeare in ways that ensured his place in culture. That transformation, once again, required careful management of knowledge about Shakespeare that excludes, or at least does not pursue, other possible forms of knowledge that might confuse or dissipate its potent effects. Contemporary knowledge of Shakespeare depends on the book form of Shakespeare, which provides a cultural object that is 'stable, secure and lasting'.[35] However, the sense that the book did not represent the elusive, original, theatrical Shakespeare also allowed directors and actors to open the potential for interpretative gaps that existed between the written speeches and the imagined world that those speeches gestured towards. In the theatre, the verbal form of the book is turned into the physical experience of seeing and hearing the story unfold in real time and shared space.

The director of a play must replace the reader's imaginary work in order to decide what Macbeth's witches look like or how fat to make Falstaff, and the 'four or five ragged foils' that constitute the English army in *Henry V* can become a heroic 'happy few' or a gang of thuggish neo-fascist invaders. An actor must decide on a tone of voice (dejection or triumph or intrigued curiosity) in which Rosalind will say 'So this is the forest of Arden', and, when Falstaff pleads with Prince Hal not to 'banish plump jack', the future monarch's response – 'I do. I will' can sum up the past and future of their relationship in the regret, determination or mockery that inflects his voice.

The work involved in theatrical reproduction is less concerned with rendering an imagined Shakespeare and is directed instead to creating an experience for the audience. As Robert Shaughnessy describes, the actor's basic task is

> to render the text as meaningful bodily action ... habitually practising physical and also intellectual analogies that animate the archaic by referencing the local, the immediate and the contemporary ... the harnessing of wilfully tendentious or unserious reference points that enable the performer to render action, motivation and behaviour plausible, concrete and specific.[36]

In order to achieve this synergy between text and performance, the theatre work creates a new capacity for emotional communication out of the plays' unfamiliar handling of rhetoric, the formal structures of blank verse and extended commentary.

Led by the legendary Cicely Berry from the RSC, and supported by academically trained directors from Peter Hall onwards, practitioners have developed an enormously influential set of techniques that have allowed actors to make sense of the often complex relationship between the syntax and metrics of the speeches in the text as well as training them in the more difficult task of enunciating the language so that it appears to be the spontaneous utterance of a real human being interacting in a narrative. This allows actors to connect rhetorical commentary to their imagined emotional situation in real time and opens the possibilities of engagement with even the most formal of Shakespeare's speeches. Familiar lines take on new resonances as the connections between character and language are enacted in surprising ways and even minor figures from the plays can be given a psychological depth that is seldom explicit in the text but which connects them to commonplace contemporary social ideas and ensures the connection necessary to turns words into situated and shared experience.

In a 1976 Royal Shakespeare Company production of *King Lear*, for example, Judi Dench gave her Regan a stammer. The device drew attention to her performance, required a reaction from the actor performing Lear, who showed irritation when she did it, and created the potential for a whole new narrative to emerge from the few scenes in which Regan plays a part in Lear's story. In order to make sense of it, viewers, however residually, could have connected the stammer, only present when Lear was on stage, to childhood trauma, or the psychological damage inflicted by their relationship. The dramatisation of Regan could be moved from Shakespeare's cruel woman to a woman victimised by her father and the play's narrative transformed into a psychologically motivated family drama. In a discussion after the performance Dench explained that the device showed 'how Regan came to be as she was':[37] the actor's work of creating a back story for a character out of the gaps in the play's text opened up the possibility of a new narrative that preceded the play's action and created a new field for interpretative engagement. The specific social, political and economic ideas that surrounded Shakespeare's adaptation of the Lear story were of no significance. Instead, they were replaced by the interactions of characters whose behaviour could be understood in contemporary terms.

By offering an explanation for the character's action that could be recognised by a modern audience, Dench's performance suggested a 'truth' in the narrative that became a source of the value of 'Shakespeare' as well as providing opportunities for elaboration into further adaptations that claimed Shakespeare as the source of their cultural significance. This process, described by Douglas Lanier as 'remotivated narrative',[38] informs both new adaptations in a variety of forms and the connections that actors use to create the connection between the plays' texts and the performances that represent Shakespeare as both contemporary and universal.

This connection of speech to interiorised character can be achieved even in single lines when the surprise of a new reading re-animates familiar sequences through changes in setting and design. A 2010 production of *Romeo and Juliet*, performed at the Bristol Tobacco Factory, and renamed *Juliet and her Romeo*, broke the current conventions of emphasising the lovers' youthfulness by setting the play in an old people's home. In the balcony scene, when Juliet calls back Romeo as he tries to leave, the line 'I have forgot why I did call thee back' layered the forgetfulness of an older woman onto the sentimentality of the lovers' impossible parting. It was not a reading that was available in the narrative structures and speeches of the play's text, but the actors and directors' work had overlaid the text with new resonances to create a syncretic resource whose connection to contemporary culture needs no explanation.

By making the words of sixteenth-century plays about the social disruptiveness of love or the difficulties of managing inheritance provide the dialogue for twenty-first-century plays about elderly lovers or dysfunctional families, the interpretative work of the directors and actors could assimilate the historical play into the consensual cultural values about love and the family in the twenty-first century.

This kind of interpretative reworking, however, was most effective in assimilating the plays to the conventions of realism familiar in television and film. In order to insist on the specificity of theatre as a live form that offered a direct sensual engagement with the experience of the plays, some performances of Shakespeare have deployed forms of highly physical acting, adapted from international styles of playing, and enhanced by creative use of design. In his monumental production of *The Histories*, Michael Boyd had the actors trained in army assault techniques and the Latin American dance form *capoeira* to give a new energy and a physical excitement to the whole performance. Actors swarmed down from the roof space on ropes, raced in from entrances all around the auditorium and used palpable and visible physical strength in the combat sequences. The plays were costumed in ways that signified historical periods from the middle ages to the late twentieth century, but specific historical periods and narratives were subsumed within a symbolic world of blood and roses whose colour was part of a design palette contrasting with the brilliant white of royal robes or the streams of fine sand that poured from the flies over the lamenting body of a deposed king in the production of *Richard II*.

The plays' complex narratives of dynastic conflict were presented with great clarity, but the overall effect of sound and colour was of a total theatre that did not depend on interpretative reading. The moments of recognition that connected audience to action came from memorable visual images: Katy Stephens as a black-clad Joan of Arc reincarnated as the tormented and ultimately pathological Queen Margaret; or the chilling development of Jonathan Slinger from limping schoolboy soldier, fooling with a pig's severed head, to the murderous Richard III. Though the plays' texts provided most of the productions' speeches, their theatricalisation used design and physical action to create visual images that gave an emotional resonance to the plays' narrative connections.

At the end of *3 Henry VI*, for example, when the accession of Edward IV and the birth of his son brought an uneasy end to the civil war, the king was crowned in a robe of brilliant white. As he exited the stage, he swept his white robe across the stage and smeared it with blood left there from King Henry's murder in the previous scene. His child had been passed to his brother, the future Richard III, and the final image of the performance is of the figure associated with the worst atrocities of the previous action, cradling the child on whom the hopes for peace and dynastic succession will rest. The final image gave a powerful ironic resonance to the finale in a single visual metaphor. It complicated the narrative communication enough to provide a space in which the spectators' imaginative engagement with suspense and irony could add value and in the context of the production as a whole it extended the range of the theatrical experience in its creative use of light and sound.

The effect of Michael Boyd's creative work in 'The Histories' was to present a narrative that communicated in visual and spatial ways as well as in narrative time. The work of director and performers filled the gap between the text and its implied actions with spectacle. The significance of the action was summed up in powerful images rather than discursive communication of the 'wisdom of Shakespeare'. The historical and social implications of the plays' actions – their potential for analogy with other wars and conflict – were addressed in essays in the programmes, but performance itself communicated ideas more directly through image and action. The shifts in costume and setting from mediaeval to modern, the visual oscillation from the present to the past, dramatised the familiar theme of the continuities of recurring violence and war.

From time to time, the productions included visual effects that linked past and present in less commonplace ways. In the opening sequence of *Richard II*, the figure of the king was presented with white make-up and red hair in an eerie simulacrum of well-known portraits of Elizabeth I. The effect was transitory: there was no extension into a point-for-point comparison with Elizabeth or a reading that allegorised the play's action. The connection to Elizabeth's own identification with Richard II, a commonplace of editorial commentary, was left hanging. The connection was available to informed members of the audience, a reminder that their knowledge was shared by the director and designer, but for others it constituted only a half-heard echo that enhanced the production's resonance without imposing meaning.

This shift from an explicitly discursive or thematic presentation of Shakespeare, to one structured by key images, was remarked on in a review of the RSC *Julius Caesar* at the Roundhouse in January, 2011. *The Times*'s critic Libby Purves admired the way that 'in classical theatre, the director's resistance to pointless modish updating leaves you free to find echoes everywhere. Including now.'[39] Purves's rejection of 'pointless modish updating' indicated a distaste for the tendentious reworking of the plays to illustrate particular, worked-through, 'new readings'. The alternative she proposed is to leave the audience 'free' to hear the 'echoes' and make of them what they will.

In newspaper reviews that necessarily replaced the experience of the play with discursive summary, the echoes sometimes produced idiosyncratic reflections on the contemporary political situation, such as Purves's own startling imaginative leap in her review from 'Elizabethans under an ageing absolute monarch with no clear successor' to the complex politics of fundamentalism in Pakistan.[40] 'Hearing the echoes' does not often make for coherent intellectual analysis. Nevertheless, the openness to any connection that might engage an audience allowed the assimilation of theatrical Shakespeare into any cultural frame of reference that an audience might share.

Antony Holden, reviewing the entire History cycle, remarked:

> There are times it all resembles a superior, Shakespearean Sopranos.[41] The profusion of severed heads, furtive stabbings, litres (literally) of stage blood, punctuated by much power-whispering in posh corners, also evokes potent parallels with our time, from war in Iraq via back-stabbing in the corridors of power to the mini-Falstaff's partying with our fun-loving Prince Harry. There are still real-life Dukes of York, Gloucester etc knocking around, too, as if to say, hey, plus ça change.[42]

Holden's cheerful acceptance of the continuity between mediaeval kings and a contemporary heir to the English throne makes difference disappear, and the plays can be subsumed within the cultural knowledge provided by current affairs and television series.

None of these connections needed to be insisted on in the plays' production. The directors and designers could focus on using their skills to create a shared experience for the whole audience for whom the 'most gripping feature might lie in the scenographic or performative rather than in a scripted or thematic element'.[43] However elusively and however temporarily, the experience of theatre – created by the work of directors and actors and funded by the complex financial instruments of state subsidy, box-office takings and philanthropic trusts – can create the illusion of a synergy between culture as a fulfilling experience and culture as a continued engagement with a venerated object from the past.

This creative attention to the points of recognition through which audiences could connect directly to Shakespeare's characters removed many of the 'difficulties' that had earlier been perceived as markers of the plays' historical value. New styles of performance could render the plays immediately accessible; new settings and new spatial arrangements could emphasise the continuity between the worlds of the plays' narratives and the world of the audience. The value of Shakespeare no longer depended upon its rhetorical articulation of complex ideas and 'difficult' language. Its acclaimed universality depended less on its connection to a specific moment in the past and more on its capacity to create immediately recognisable human experience within the narratives.

These reproductions of Shakespeare in what has become the classic RSC style illustrate the transformation of 'Shakespeare' into a form that combines the physical theatre associated with play rather than work. Moreover, under Michael Boyd's leadership the Stratford venue was used to host performances of less respectful versions of 'Shakespeare', developed by small-scale companies such as Kneehigh, and international collaborations, such as the British Council-sponsored *A Midsummer Night's Dream*, directed by Tim Supple in 2007. These productions explicitly challenged Shakespeare's 'high cultural' status by translating the plays into multiple languages to insist on their universal cultural reach and on occasion mocking their narrative complexity or linguistic density, using techniques of audience engagement pioneered in popular cultural forms. If they outraged some audience members' expectations, or, better still, caused a walk-out, the sense of mischievous iconoclasm would further enhance the pleasure shared with the remaining audience.

This constant innovation and witty disruption of the 'high-culture' Shakespeare, allowed the company to manage concerns both about 'popular' Shakespeare that denied the 'hermeneutic density' of new forms and the requirement for a culture that could engage the whole demographic spectrum. Their creative and organisational work, together with the powerful advocacy and institutional innovation (which we will discuss in Chapters 6 and 7) created a series of vivid theatrical experiences that culminated in the huge artistic as well as commercial success of the World Shakespeare Festival and replaced the venerated 'Shakespeare' of earlier cultural aspiration with one that was live, international, multicultural and of its time. The credit for that transformation, however, was less to do with the intrinsic value of Shakespeare and more to do with the work of reproduction and distribution that produced the added-value in the long and recursive chain from an early modern printed book to a contemporary performance.

The assimilation of this particular version of 'theatrical Shakespeare' into its important position in twenty-first-century culture required creative discursive management as well as creative practice. Writing in *The Stage* about the 'ensemble' that he had proclaimed as an organisational as well as theatrical principle for the RSC,[44] Michael Boyd observed:

> I sometimes talk of theatre as ice sculpture, in that it only lives in the memories of those who 'were there', but even that image is an overstatement of theatre's substance. It only truly exists in the space between the players and between them and the audience held in a moment of trust. A collective encounter hanging in the air between us. Without that embrace, our work is nothing.[45]

As so often with accounts of cultural value, the vivid image communicates through metaphors that appear instantly recognisable. Boyd's invocation of a transient collective encounter emphasises the consensual and communal aspirations that link culture and theatre, and the reference to 'trust' and 'embrace' places the experience of theatre within the emotional frame that depends on the active collaboration of the audience unaffected by the price of tickets or the prior evaluation of the content of the show.

Boyd's articulation of the values that underpinned his idea of theatre said nothing of the scripted content of the performances, or of the chain of funding, and creative work that made the practice possible. He presents theatre as a shared memory, and celebrates rather than regrets the evanescence of a work that leaves not a rack behind. Its imaginative power was that it appeared special to those who had 'been there'. It offered the fantasy of a unique connection between the performance and the audience, a connection that could not be captured by the market and did not depend on knowledge or work. It did not depend for its value on a significant sum of valuers and it did not need to claim the capacity to be scaled up in order to meet the analytically defined requirements of a bureaucratic assessment of value.

Boyd's invocation of the shared moment of memory created by theatrical Shakespeare may seem most resonant to those with an existing commitment to earlier connections between the content of a Shakespeare text and the values of culture as community. However, the historical 'Shakespeare' is not essential to this effect. As Dennis Kennedy has refreshingly explained, 'assisting at the spectacle' as co-operative attendees, can apply as easily to sporting events or lap-dancing displays.[46] The exciting sense of a shared experience depends on the balance between the production values of design and performance and the consumption values that are created by the social circumstances in which the event takes place. The connection between production and consumption can be insisted upon by cultural advocates, and produced by theatrical and artistic work, but its ultimate success depends upon the willingness of the audience to play along.

The 'theatrical Shakespeare' available in contemporary culture is a resource for cultural reproduction whose effects are managed by performance and design to create a space for communal pleasure. That pleasure may come from the high-end style of expensive creative processes but it may as easily be produced by a low-budget amateur show whose primary pleasure relates to a shared experience with friends and family. The experience may involve reasserting consensual ideas about love and the family through representing the familiar narratives, it can generate immediate sensational apprehensions of complex ideas and it can be used as a template for nostalgic evocation of the repertory of past cultural objects to reinforce an audience's sense of their participation in a shared culture.

These cultural effects can be recognised and endorsed because of the plays' open-ended potential for interpretation, the requirement to match speech to narrative that can be exploited in creative reworking. Engaging with a cultural object from the past in that way does not depend upon the particular cultural competency associated with high levels of education or more privileged access to time beyond the leisure to engage with relatively but not prohibitively expensive entertainment. The same 'Shakespeare as resource' is available for multiple reworkings in other media, and, as in the case of other forms of culture, there is no possibility of controlling this unarchived multiplicity of forms into an authoritative hierarchy of valued and disvalued products. Their capacity to be representative of 'culture' is limited by their ephemeral nature, but that ephemeral quality also creates the potential for endless renewal: the ice-sculpture melts and has to be recreated in another form, including the form of academic analysis or the parodic and transgressive forms of mass-media Shakespeare. The plays' entry into culture will depend upon the management of the repertory by brokers and agents and their ability to share with 'Shakespeare' an existence both as heritage objects, conserved and thus out of time, and as new objects, part of whose pleasure and value consists in their capacity to be selectively rediscovered and revived and thus create connections, however temporary or transient, between Shakespeare as cultural object, the lived experience of those who engage with his contemporary forms, and the varied forms of advocacy on behalf of different institutions of culture. 'Shakespeare' thus becomes a free resource for cultural reproduction as well as an open field of knowledge in which individual taste and opinion can have free play.

That free play, of course, depends upon the discursive and fiscal management of supporting resources. In the remaining chapters we will discuss the ways that government and institutions managed those resources as they came under increasing economic pressure and faced the challenges of new forms of technologised distribution.

Notes

1 http://globetoglobe.shakespearesglobe.com (accessed 28.08.12).
2 www.bbc.co.uk/arts/shakespeare (accessed 28.08.12).
3 www.britishmuseum.org/whats_on/exhibitions/shakespeare_staging_the_world.aspx (accessed 24.08.12).
4 www.britishmuseum.org/about_us/news_and_press/press_releases/2012/shakespeare_staging_the_world.aspx (accessed 25.08.12).
5 Further examples are discussed in Chapter 8, pp. 230–232.
6 www.guardian.co.uk/culture/2012/jul/22/critics-notebook-lyn-gardner (accessed 31.08.12).
7 See www.bbc.co.uk/news/magazine-18182541 (accessed 26.08.12). The question of branding in the structures of cultural production will be discussed in Chapter 8.
8 Moses Naim, 'No compromise equals success', review of Steve Coll, *Private Empire and American Power* (London: Penguin, 2012), *The Washington Post*, 11 May 2012.

9 www.exxonmobil.co.uk/UK-English/news_releases_refining_cinema_promo.aspx (accessed 02.17.12); www.exxonmobil.com/Corporate/community_foundation.aspx (accessed 02.07.12).
10 Erving Goffman, *Gender Advertisement* (New York: Harper and Row, 1976), quoted in Richard Sennett, *The Culture of the New Capitalism* (New Haven, CT and London: Yale University Press, 2006), p.149.
11 See p.25 and Chapter 7, p.193.
12 Sir Henry Newbolt, *The Teaching of English in England. Being the Report of the Departmental Committee Appointed by the President of the Board of Education to Inquire into the Position of English in the Educational System of England* (London: HMSO 1921), p.54.
13 John Guillory, *Cultural Capital: The Problem of Literary Canon Formation* (Chicago: The University of Chicago Press, 1993), p.172.
14 John Fiske, 'Popular Discrimination', in James Naremore and Patrick Brantlinger, eds, *Modernity and Mass Culture* (Bloomington and Indianapolis: Indiana University Press, 1991), pp.103–116, p.105.
15 See Jonathan Rose, *The Intellectual Life of the British Working Class* (New Haven, CT and London: Yale University Press, 2001) and Murphy, *Shakespeare for the People*.
16 Richard Burt, 'To E- or not to E-?: Disposing of Schlockspeare in the Age of Digital Media' in Richard Burt, ed., *Shakespeare After Mass Media* (New York: Palgrave, 2002), pp.1–32, p.30.
17 Most notably cinema, whose adoption of Shakespeare as a creative resource has enabled the development of a sub-discipline devoted to analysing both the content of individual films and the role of Shakespeare in the film industry. See Richard Burt, *Shakespeares After Shakespeare: An Encyclopedia of the Bard in Mass and Popular Culture* (Westport, CT: Greenwood Press, 2007).
18 Burt, *Shakespeare After Mass Media*, p.3.
19 The terms implied in Sandel's and James Murdoch's categorisations of the source of value. See p.45 and 100.
20 'From Baa-r-baa-ra the sheep to Shakespeare uncut', *The Guardian*, 22 December 2012, p.14.
21 Mary Polito, '"Warriors for the Working Day": Shakespeare's Professionals', *Shakespeare* 2 (2006), p.18.
22 www.businessweek.com/articles/2012-11-29/shakespeare-in-the-board room (accessed 14.12.12). We are grateful to Scott Newstok for drawing our attention to this latest account of the role of Shakespeare in management training.
23 www.businessweek.com/articles/2012-11-29/shakespeare-in-the-board room.
24 The long history of those readings is discussed in Shankar Raman, *Renaissance Literature and Postcolonial Studies* (Edinburgh: Edinburgh

University Press, 2011), pp. 56–57. On the development of 'historical allegory' within modernist discussions of Shakespeare, see Halpern, *Shakespeare Among the Moderns*, pp. 6–10.

25 In a private conversation, a member of the Mythodrama team indicated that the most resistant audiences for the programme were a group of Italian lawyers.

26 Including David Schalkwyk, who has taken the book into mainstream academic discourse. See *Hamlet's Dreams: The Robben Island Shakespeare*, Shakespeare Now Series (London: Bloomsbury Academic, 2013).

27 http://robbenislandbible.blogspot.co.uk (accessed 12.12.12).

28 www.rsc.org.uk/whats-on/julius-caesar/julius-caesar-and-nelson-mandela.aspx? (accessed 11.06.13).

29 The particular role of institutions in managing those objects as part of culture is addressed in Chapter 7.

30 http://news.bbc.co.uk/today/hi/today/newsid_9738000/9738782.stm (accessed 27.08.12).

31 See Karin Barber, *Africa's Hidden Histories: Everyday Literacy and Making the Self* (Bloomington: Indiana University Press. 2006).

32 See Natasha Distiller, *Shakespeare and the Coconuts* (Johannesburg: Witswatersrand University Press, 2012).

33 Stanley Wells, 'General Introduction', in *William Shakespeare: The Complete Works*, ed. Stanley Well, Gary Taylor, John Jowett and William Montgomery (Oxford: Clarendon Press, 1988), p. xxxv.

34 Richard Proudfoot, 'New Conservatism and the Theatrical Text: Editing Shakespeare for the Third Millennium', in William R. Elton and John M. Mucciolo, eds, *The Shakespeare International Yearbook, 2: Where Are We Now in Shakespeare Studies* (Aldershot: Ashgate, 2002), pp. 127–142, p. 135.

35 George Sarton, *Six Wings: Men of Science in the Renaissance* (London: Bodley Head, 1958), discussed in Elizabeth Eisenstein, *The Printing Press as an Agent of Change* (Cambridge: Cambridge University Press), p. 507.

36 Robert Shaughnessy, 'Falstaff's Belly: Pathos, Prosthetics and Performance', *Shakespeare Survey* 63 (2010): 63–77, p. 70.

37 Stanley Wells, *Shakespeare: A Dramatic Life* (London: Sinclair Stevenson, 1994), p. 26.

38 Douglas Lanier, 'Recasting the Plays: Homage, Adaptation, Parody' in *Shakespeare and Modern Popular Culture* (Oxford: Oxford University Press, 2002), pp. 82–109.

39 Libby Purves, review of *Julius Caesar* at The Roundhouse, *The Times*, 12.01.11, p. 13.

40 See, 'Salmaan Taseer: Murder in an Extremist Climate', *The Guardian*, 5 January 2011.

41 A popular US TV series featuring a mafia family from New Jersey.
42 Antony Holden, 'Kings of a Great Long Weekend', *The Observer*, 28 May 2008, www.guardian.co.uk/stage/2008/may/18/rsc.theatre (accessed 02.11.11).
43 Dennis Kennedy, *The Spectator and the Spectacle: Audiences in Modernity and Postmodernity* (Cambridge: Cambridge University Press, 2009), p. 13.
44 Evaluated in Robert Hewison, John Holden and Samuel Jones, *All Together Now: A Creative Approach to Organisational Change* (London: Demos, 2010).
45 Michael Boyd, 'Building Relationships', *The Stage*, 02.04.09, pp. 10–11, p. 10.
46 Kennedy, *The Spectator and the Spectacle*, p. 95.

6
Government and the values of culture

In the first part of this book, we observed the widespread public consensus that 'culture' is valuable. The shared ideal of a value that 'transcends individual preferences and facilitates collective endeavour' (see Chapter 2, p. 34) is a powerful one. This kind of value seems to get above the discord of divergent individual opinion, to exist beyond particular social and historical circumstances while staying relevant to new contexts, and even to transcend conflicting beliefs, offering a unifying set of values for a diverse society to hold in common. Unfortunately, it is also very difficult to sustain in practice.

Governments and their associated funding bodies will almost inevitably fail to reconcile the appealing language of shared consensus with the vexed task of cultural decision-making:

> if we consider that to support one person's or group's culture is also to make a decision not to support another's, on what bases do we make these decisions?[1]

Allocating funding to culture effectively means choosing, as Lisanne Gibson here suggests, to support or not to support: deciding not only between different cultural organisations but between 'one person's or group's culture' and another's. With limited resources to draw on, government-funded culture – as vividly demonstrated in the 2011 announcement of Arts Council England (ACE) funding and cuts, in which 638 applications for funding were turned down, 206 of them formerly regularly funded by ACE – can more closely resemble a competition than a consensus.

In this competitive climate, it is easy to assume that the state's investment in culture is merely 'instrumental', with governments choosing to use their limited funds to support only those activities and organisations that bring demonstrable economic and social benefits to a nation. Some critics place this ends-driven vision of 'cultural value' in binary opposition to the 'intrinsic' value of culture. The reality, of course, is much more complex, not least because of the multiple roles that governments simultaneously have to play in relation to culture. Governments navigate the paradoxes of whether their role is to manage the democratic mass distribution of culture, or to protect the arts from the encroachments of mass production; to act as a bulwark against market failure, or to provide the arts as social goods, like health and education. Government departments responsible for culture such as the Department for Culture, Media and Sport (DCMS) also have to prove their legitimacy to at least two different audiences at once, negotiating with Treasury for financial support while conveying to the tax-paying public their authority to implement effective funding decisions about art, theatre, music and dance. This complexity creates particular analytical challenges for understanding the role of public policy in sustaining cultural value. As this chapter will show, though, the powerful influence of policy discourse on the concept of cultural value makes this analysis all the more urgent.

Government-funded culture might not necessarily be reductively instrumental. However, the discourse of government funding has nonetheless profoundly shaped the perceived meaning and purpose of culture and value. The way that governments articulate the value of culture has changed significantly over time, particularly under economic and social pressure, and the first decade of the twenty-first century alone saw a major shift in government discourse from New Labour's attempt to establish a new vocabulary with which to value culture on its own terms at its beginning, to the more pragmatic rationales for valuing culture that accompanied a severe economic downturn and the arrival of a Conservative–Liberal Democrat coalition at its end. Within the decade flourished the notion of maximising the 'public value' of culture, not just in terms of its social and economic benefits, but in terms of its effects on the people who encountered it.

The neglected upshot of such changes is the way that they drastically relocate and redefine the very notion of 'value', and the knock-on effects of that relocation for all those working in – and engaging with – cultural organisations and institutions. In the twenty-first century, government discourse has increasingly relocated value away from cultural objects and events, and towards people's experiences of them. Tessa Jowell's *Government and the Value of Culture*, first encountered at the beginning of this book, is a key document in this relocation process. Jowell made the inevitably limited attempt to cast off the purely instrumental role of government and find a new language of cultural value that was founded in people's positive experiences; as will be discussed below, she sidestepped instrumentalism by suggesting that benefitting people is an intrinsic property of culture. Yet while Jowell's larger aim was to foster public engagement, the effect was to change the knowledge base of cultural decision-making, referring value outwards from cultural objects, and from the knowledge and expertise of cultural intermediaries that had traditionally ascribed such value to them, to the public's sense of what culture 'does' for them.

Some criticised Jowell and the 'public value'-oriented approaches to culture that followed hers for undermining expert cultural knowledge and putting too much judgement in the hands of the people. Such moral panic is predictable, but misses the point: the real implications of this value relocation are troubling for rather different reasons. The first implication of any attempt to base cultural decisions more firmly in the experiences and wishes of the wider public is practical. 'Public value' techniques, as the central part of this chapter will show, struggle to measure the value of culture, and the challenge of developing new forms of measurement has occupied everyone from think-tanks to funding bodies, to the extent that it has become a primary focus of discussion about cultural value. Over the course of the first decade of the twenty-first century, new government narratives continued to refer value outwards, while seeking to develop ever more complex ways of capturing and anatomising that value.

The second implication, then, is the increasing pressure this puts on cultural organisations to demonstrate to central government the value of what they do. In that decade alone, funded cultural organisations were successively mandated to provide 'access' to culture, to proffer powerful 'experiences' of culture for their visitors, and, latterly, to promote 'creativity' in their visitors. Shakespeare is a high-status cultural object whose leading theatrical institution is in receipt of regular, major government funding via ACE: the support of the Royal Shakespeare Company has been revalued in all of the above terms in the last decade. Each seemingly innocuous linguistic shift demands ever more inventive measurement mechanisms as the locus of value moves further from the object under the institution's control, and into the (equally) subjective realms of the visitor experience and the lifelong benefits that flow from it. But as value has been relocated, so has responsibility: while the chapter begins with an example of government seeking a new language with which to justify its cultural spending to the tax-paying public, it ends with a vision of cultural organisations seeking ever more effective tools with which to justify themselves to government agencies – a shift acutely resonant of corresponding changes in the funding of higher education. As the burden of measuring and demonstrating cultural value moves from governments to organisations, and becomes more financially urgent, the question of the value of culture itself seems to disappear from the debate; proving – and thus survival – is all.

However, the most significant, and least observed, implication of the increased impetus to venerate the public's experience of culture is, ironically, the disservice that this does to the public. Previous critiques of the public-value movement in government policy have focussed on its failure to make measurement widely representative, as if the optimum result would be achieved by asking everyone in the country about their experiences of culture. What has not yet been fully taken into account is that focussing on the public's experience might undermine the public's authority. The language of public value can ultimately disempower the public, offering them limited opportunities to talk about their responses, and, often, a ready-made language with which to do so. It does not necessarily equip them with the critical tools and skills with which to evaluate their experiences and understand their significance – skills that would put them in more productive conversation with practitioners and policy-makers. It also entangles the public in the central confusion about whether members of the public should speak for themselves as individual consumers, or speculate, as citizens, about what is good for others. Successive languages of value seem to have brought neither the public, nor governments and practitioners any closer to being able to explain how culture works in the twenty-first century; rather, they have created a climate in which the primary business is to adapt in order to survive.

The 'cultural value' moment

At the turn of the twenty-first century, Tony Blair's New Labour government set out to reject what it regarded as the excessively instrumental approaches to culture of previous governments. The phrase 'cultural value' encapsulated a way of talking about culture that focussed less on its social and economic benefits, and more on its 'essential' qualities. Central to this movement was the 2004 paper in which the then Secretary of State, Tessa Jowell, launched a search for a new language of value.

> Too often politicians have been forced to debate culture in terms only of its instrumental benefits to other agendas – education, the reduction of crime, improvements in wellbeing – explaining – or in some instances almost apologising for – our investment in culture only in terms of something else.[2]

Instead of agreeing to talk about culture 'only in terms of something else', or for 'other agendas', Jowell posed the challenge of 'investigating, questioning and celebrating what culture actually does in and of itself'.[3] She aspired to free the New Labour government from the social and economic constraints under which politicians – thanks, it was implied, to the previous Conservative administration – have been 'forced to' value culture in the past. She appeared to advocate a return to valuing the 'intrinsic' merits of culture; and was instantly applauded by some (and critiqued by others) for championing arts for art's sake in the face of growing instrumentality.[4]

For all that, Jowell's vision is still an instrumental one at heart. She laments that politicians have to debate culture 'in terms *only* of its instrumental benefits' (emphasis added), but she does not dismiss the instrumental value of culture altogether. Eight words – 'what culture actually does in and of itself' – belie Jowell's dual concern not only with what culture *is* 'in and of itself', but what it '*does*': its effects on people as much as its essential qualities. Culture is still supposed to be *doing* something for the benefit of the tax-paying public. To make this mission sound less instrumental, though, Jowell intimates that these benefits are themselves an intrinsic property of culture.

This persistent instrumentalism is, in many ways, understandable. First, it is driven by the continued need to justify the spending of public money. The precise nature and distribution of the government's public 'investment in culture', as Jowell's mention of 'explaining' and 'apologising' suggests, requires tough decisions and a comprehensible rationale. Sometimes, these decisions have already been made, and part of Jowell's challenge is to justify the government's continued investment in flagship cultural organisations like the Royal Opera House, English National Opera and the Royal Shakespeare Company, whose relevance to a diverse nation might not necessarily be obvious. The need for justification becomes more pressing when cultural funding comes more directly from public subscription, via (since 1994) the Heritage Lottery Fund.[5]

Second, that a government should value culture for its contribution to the public good – that is, for its *effects* on people as much as its content – is not a new phenomenon. Lisanne Gibson argues, in response to criticism of recent governmental agendas, that there is 'nothing remotely new about instrumentalism in cultural policy', giving examples of cultural organisations such as museums and galleries founded in the nineteenth century for the benefit of people's health and education, and of the nation's industry.[6] The post-war establishment of the Council for the Encouragement of Music and the Arts (CEMA), and, latterly, the Arts Council of Great Britain, was linked to the beginnings of the welfare state.[7] In this sense, the state funding of culture has parallels with the provision of other social goods such as free healthcare and compulsory education, and, as Gibson observes, UK cultural institutions and programmes 'have had an instrumental dimension since before the Thatcher or New Labour Governments'.[8] Yet in the twenty-first century, culture's instrumental role has been amplified, rather than minimised, by its place in New Labour's larger programme of public service reform. This is despite the claim that, where the previous Conservative government's 'New Public Management' had stressed the need for accountability and performance measurement in the public sector, the new administration set out to create a 'greater role for the public in the design and delivery of public services'.[9]

New Labour's attitude to public services was informed by the theory of 'public value', which originated in the United States in the 1990s, and recommended that the public be given an equivalent decision-making role in the public sector to shareholders in the private sector.[10] These principles were adopted in the Prime Minister's Strategy Unit's 2002 paper *Creating Public Value: An Analytical Framework for Public Service Reform*, which emphasized the importance of citizen consultation in decisions around public services.[11] Subsequently, the Work Foundation specified that 'people who receive public services – whether a benefit, an education, a GP appointment or a TV programme – should not be seen as passive consumers, but citizens with democratic rights';[12] and these principles were tested at organisations such as the BBC.[13] Applied to cultural policy, these principles not only afforded greater significance to the public's sense of the good of the nation, but also led to the greater prioritisation of the individual's personal experience of culture.

Jowell's concept of 'cultural value', then, simply revivifies the persistent political question of what culture 'does' for a nation: the only difference is that she now articulates these benefits not in the broad terms of social and economic impact, but in terms of their effects on individuals:

> Yes, we will need to keep proving that engagement with culture can improve educational attainment, and can help reduce crime. But we should also stand up for what culture can do for individuals in a way that nothing else can. Culture alone can give people the means better to understand and engage with life, and as such is a key part in reducing inequality of opportunity, and which can help us slay the sixth giant of modern times – poverty of aspiration. This must be the next priority in the mission at the core of this Government: to transform our society into a place of justice, talent and ambition where individuals can fulfil their true potential.[14]

The social goals of boosting 'educational attainment' and reducing 'crime' are still present in Jowell's account, alongside other instrumental benefits: culture apparently enables people 'to understand and engage with life', reduces 'inequality of opportunity', raises aspirations, and creates a society where individuals can 'fulfil their true potential'. Now, though, Jowell presents these benefits in the language of personal growth, focussing on 'what culture can do for individuals'. Of Shakespeare, she says that we need to be able to explain in objective, rather than subjective, terms why it is right to 'allocate millions' to the Royal Shakespeare Company: her justification is the '*personal* value added which comes from engagement with complex art' (emphasis added).[15] When she refers to 'intrinsic value' it is to speak of 'the intrinsic value of culture, in the lives of citizens'.[16]

The point of this chapter is not to reinforce historical perceptions of the great gulf between the 'instrumental' and 'intrinsic' value of culture, when those values, and many others, are so obviously entwined. But it is clear that, by playing down the instrumentality of her agenda, Jowell overemphasised the significance of the individual experience in a way that would not be wholly beneficial either to government or to the public. To critique Jowell in this way seems counter-intuitive when the individual experience of culture makes for such a compelling message:

> I'm a politician, not a cultural theorist or practitioner. I can't express this unique power with the eloquence of a Neil MacGregor, a Nicholas Serota or a Christopher Frayling. But I have experienced it, both in my own life and seeing the lives of others as a politician.[17]

Jowell might not share the expert knowledge of the directors of major arts institutions like the British Museum, the Tate and ACE respectively, but by asserting that 'I have experienced it', she suggests that their cultural capital is unnecessary to appreciate the true 'power' of culture. While the MacGregors, Serotas and Fraylings of this world might be able to 'express' that power more eloquently and intellectually, everyone, she implies, can 'experience' it, regardless of education and class (and even race and gender – her chosen directors are all white men). Jowell's notion of 'experience' attempts to level these distinctions; she implies that culture speaks directly to the essential nature not just of the UK citizen, but of the human.

Yet by choosing 'power' as a synonym for 'value', and casting people's responses to culture as instinctive rather than intellectual, Jowell neatly avoids the vexed – and potentially elitist – issue of professional evaluation. 'Power' appears here not as historically or politically contingent, but as an inherent and enduring quality of culture. The eloquence of the cultural brokers named above seems almost unnecessary to that force: their words might 'express' the power of culture in especially articulate ways, but, crucially, they do not *determine* it. Jowell effectively denies the critical processes by which value has been ascribed to cultural objects, and celebrates instead the apparently natural propensity of culture to affect people. This might not be a deliberately deceitful manoeuvre, but, by obscuring the evaluative processes that ascribe value to some objects and events and not to others, it potentially excludes the public from participating in these critical processes, and restricts them to merely reacting.

Even Jowell, though, cannot entirely cast off the importance of acquired cultural skills in her reassuringly democratic vision of cultural experience. She promotes the rewards of learning to 'grapple' with 'complex culture', and claims, for example, that there is no point in the state funding opera if it does not provide musical training for its audiences. Yet Jowell deliberately sidesteps any possible exclusivity by proposing that this training can be fairly distributed through music lessons in state education. By choosing opera, like Shakespeare, as an example of a high cultural experience for which all state-educated school children can easily be equipped, Jowell attempts to deflate the complaint made of the subsidised arts that the bulk of funding goes to flagship national companies to 'provide the "cultured" wealthy with a night out cheaper than it might be'.[18] Jowell obscures, of course, the other kinds of social capital – from knowing what to wear to knowing when to clap – that are entwined with the enjoyment of these high-culture productions, and overlooks those 'psychological' barriers to accessing culture that are more restrictive than financial ones.[19]

The public, even in this vision of a nation 'grappling' with 'complex culture', still remains confined to reaction. Jowell hopes that through early training, responding to culture will *become* a 'sixth sense' for all people.[20] She recasts even acquired cultural skills as primary senses or reactions, rather than secondary, analytical and exclusive, practices of evaluation. Jowell's focus on the natural power of culture resonates most closely in recent literary studies with what Andy Mousley has described as the rise of the 'literary humanists' who have challenged the increasing exclusion of the personal and the experiential response to Shakespeare as criticism has become increasingly professionalised in the twentieth century, and championed the particular ethical force of Shakespeare's work for all.[21] Of course, this kind of criticism is still produced by professionals with abundant cultural capital, each attempting to imagine the experiential responses of a different kind of reader through their own – and potentially excluding that kind of reader from more complex kinds of evaluation.

Jowell's 'complex culture' is not about criticism, either: it conveniently skips past old distinctions of high and low, creating demand for the existing recipients of regular state funding, and generating a new set of terms for the mass consumption of culture which incorporates the most appealing aspects of the language of the market:

choice, value for money and 'personal value-added'. In the process, it denies the role of evaluation and attribution of value in culture, and confines the public to the role of cultural consumer rather than critic.

These major issues were, however, often overlooked in subsequent years: Jowell's paper was enormously influential, and people's personal experiences of culture went on to be increasingly prioritised in cultural policy, accelerated by the growing presence of the corporate principles of 'public value' in government policy. In 2006, Demos think-tank analyst John Holden devised a triangular model to distinguish between what he saw as the three different values of culture: 'instrumental value', 'institutional value' and 'intrinsic value'.[22] He separated 'instrumental' values, associated with governments, from 'institutional' values, associated with cultural organisations, in order to liberate institutions from the dutiful fulfilment of government agendas, and to encourage them to fashion their own, mutually beneficial relationships with their visitors: 'creating trust and mutual respect among citizens, enhancing the public realm, and providing a context for sociability and the enjoyment of shared experiences'.[23]

It was the visitors, though, that came out on top. In Holden's model, 'intrinsic' value referred not to the inherent qualities of a cultural event or object, but to the public, and their estimation and experience of that event or object.[24] Holden and Robert Hewison would apply this model to the heritage industry when they scrutinised the value of the Heritage Lottery Fund; and, in that context, 'intrinsic' value was said to refer to:

> the value of heritage in itself, its intrinsic value in terms of the individual's experience of heritage intellectually, emotionally and spiritually[25]

Holden goes further than Jowell to redefine 'intrinsic' value as something that occurs in the experiences of members of the public. Indeed, he declares that his mission is to 'debunk the old "art for art's sake" idea that culture could have some value "in and of itself"', and to argue instead that 'value is located in the encounter or interaction between individuals (who will have all sorts of pre-existing attitudes, beliefs and levels of knowledge) on the one hand, and an object or experience on the other'.[26]

This triangular model of cultural value was, like Jowell's paper, heavily cited in the first decade of the century, each repetition reinforcing the association of intrinsic value and personal experience. If the implications were problematic, Holden and Hewison's aims, at least, were admirable. They shared a long-standing concern to give the public a greater sense of ownership of the cultural objects and events that their taxes fund. Hewison had argued in 1995 that, by making public culture for 'everyone', it had been emptied of meaning so as to come to mean nothing to anyone. He urged that public culture needed to be connected once more with what people think and feel.[27] It is unsurprising, then, that a decade later he would endorse the notion of locating meaningful 'intrinsic value' in people's experiences, in what they think and feel about culture.

Governments and think-tanks appear to find 'experience' an extremely useful levelling term. It is assumed to be available to everyone, but need not be the same for everyone, since it evidently need not be articulated or described. It connects high and low culture, expert and public, actor and audience, producer and consumer, in an imagined, 'magic' moment of positive engagement. It unites very different kinds of art, and embraces both cultural preservation and cultural production. It provides a category large enough to value existing cultural objects and flagship institutions, and to appreciate new work; to encompass design as well as heritage, street festivals as well as Shakespeare, creativity as well as conservation. It recalls earlier meanings of the word 'culture' – that is, more anthropological descriptions of the practices and behaviours people hold in common – before 'culture' crystallised into referring to a set of prized objects, and it borrows some of the naturalness of that earlier meaning to imagine people's ideal relationships with those objects. Furthermore, unlike more overtly instrumental terms of social impact, 'experience' does not seem to be imposed upon people from above.

'Experience' is not, however, a benign term, for it drastically changes the perceived location of value. For policy-makers and analysts to assert that 'intrinsic value' is created anew in the moment of encounter[28] is rhetorically to shift value away from the object. Individuals' positive experiences of culture become not merely the measure, but the site, of intrinsic value. 'Intrinsic value' is a slippery term, and to argue that it can be traced to a particular cultural object is not straightforward. Yet to conflate it with people's enjoyable experiences is equally problematic. As Noah Lemos has argued, 'it is reasonable for us to hold that the state of affairs *something's being intrinsically valuable* is not identical with *something's being pleasant or approved or desired*'.[29] Furthermore, the equation of experience and intrinsic value seems to suppose that intrinsic cultural value can be optimised by giving more people the opportunity to experience the arts. This, too, is at odds with Lemos's observation that, philosophically speaking, intrinsic value cannot decrease or increase in favourable conditions.

Very often, discussion of 'intrinsic value' can mask the acts of judgement and criticism that have ascribed value to a certain object or event. While, as Lemos notes, 'Traditionally, a variety of things have been thought to be intrinsically good: pleasure, morally good emotions, the satisfaction of desire, correct judgment, knowledge, understanding, consciousness itself, beauty, and, in at least some cases, the flourishing of nonsentient life', cultural theorists (as mentioned in Chapter 2) have suggested that such value is, in fact, the product of a prior act of evaluation:

> The values that we prize come into being because of acts of energetic, painful appraisal; values are the sedimental deposits of the imperative to value. But all values must remain continually vulnerable to appraisal[30]

If, as in Steven Connor's view, 'values are the sedimental deposits of the imperative to value', then passed-down culture and heritage are the products of inherited, residual valuations. Cultural institutions are traditionally the places where such prior acts of valuation have been performed: places that both maintain value judgements and facilitate new cultural experiences for their visitors. By focussing exclusively on people's cultural experiences, and locating value primarily in the moment of encounter, policy-makers and analysts occlude the decision-making that has often already determined what constitutes 'culture', and ascribed value to it, before the encounter takes place. Indeed, as Connor less positively observes, 'the institutions and procedures which we employ to actualise the evaluation of values ... are always likely to become fixated by the desire to conserve and reproduce particular values'.[31]

Holden and Hewison are committed to promoting the role of the institution in creating cultural value. It is ironic, then, that, by reifying people's personal experiences of culture, they could obscure the fundamental evaluative work of the institution and, through future adoption of their model, inadvertently promote relationship-building and even customer-pleasing as the institution's primary task. The resonances between the situation of cultural and higher education institutions – where increased fees, a more competitive admissions environment and the publicly visible results of the National Student Survey have heightened student concern for 'value for money', and in turn increased universities' anxious concern to enhance the perceived quality of the 'student experience' – are difficult to ignore; and the shared focus on the consumer, their pleasures and their rewards are similarly challenging.

Yet while it seems to flatter the public with the role of all-powerful customer who must be satisfied at all costs, 'experience' is not necessarily empowering for visitors, either. It can deny people access to the evaluative processes that have enshrined certain cultural objects when they most appear to extend it. Intended to promote a more active engagement with culture than mere 'access', the notion of 'experience' can make visitors passive consumers of objects and events whose importance has been pre-determined for them. (Though we should note that Holden and Hewison do not themselves preclude analysis: the public can respond 'intellectually' to culture as well as 'emotionally' and 'spiritually'.)

The implications of this model for the public recall Raymond Williams's much earlier anxieties about the public's exclusion from the 'democratic and pluralistic participation in the institutions and practices of culture, a "common" evaluation-in-process of an undecided future'.[32] His lecture, 'Communications and Community', was directed against the welfare provision of a handed-out Arnoldian culture to the poor and struggling, at a time when 'a minority culture, received and continuing, would be diffused to an ever-widening audience' and 'Culture – "the best that is known and thought in the world", would now, literally, be "broad-cast"'.[33] Where T. S. Eliot had feared that the free dissemination of culture would dilute its quality, Williams saw it instead as an imposition that prevented the public from speaking for themselves.

In the twenty-first century, the language of cultural engagement has shifted from broadcasting and delivering culture to all, to encouraging more active engagement, yet some troubling issues persist. When the *The Madonna of the Pinks* went on national tour, it was surrounded by a host of cultural engagement activities, including working with young people from less privileged areas. As we showed in Chapter 4, invoking a direct experience of work of art explicitly excludes the prior knowledge of the cultural brokers who not only provide access to the work but also articulate the terms in which engagement can be expressed. As the researchers gauging the impact of the tour noticed, the artists recruited to work with teenage mothers from the Rhondda Valley who were unaccustomed to visiting museums and galleries, 'talked a great deal about being mothers' in order to engage them with the subject of the painting, 'but they did not discuss the <u>representation</u> of motherhood (either secular or religious)'.[34] The researchers saw this as a missed opportunity to extend beyond merely addressing the young women's own self-definition as mothers, and challenging them to engage with the painting in new ways. This twenty-first-century version of the welfare provision of culture is troubling not because it merely hands culture to people, but because, through 'experience', it purports to give them an active role in engaging with culture, but then merely provides the public with a self-confirming language with which to value it. For all the encouraging focus on their 'experience', without access to the intellectual and evaluative processes that first enshrined a particular object or event, the public might still be in danger of being handed an unchallenging language that substitutes for their own experience.

Measuring the 'public value' of culture

In addition to relocating value and drastically changing the role and authority of both institutions and their audiences, another, very practical challenge presented by 'experience' in government policy is that of measurement. As John Carey observes, 'the inaccessibility of other people's consciousness, and the variability of personal responses to artworks, makes all statements about art's emotional effects suspect'.[35] It also makes suspect all general statements about what 'people' want from culture. How can governments first capture individual experiences, and then extrapolate from those myriad responses a fair and meaningful cultural policy for all, upon which funding decisions can be based?

Cultural funders have increasingly come to rely on personal narratives for evidence. For example, the booklet summarising the results of 'The Arts Debate', ACE's 2007 survey into public attitudes towards the arts, featured headline testimonials from individuals involved in the consultation process:

Relaxation, enjoyment, inspiration, all them things, if you didn't have that access to art, you'd do a full day's work, you'd go and get pissed and you'd go home and go to bed. [Parent, high arts engagement, urban][36]

In this personal testimony about the value of the arts, the speaker gestures at the importance of a hinterland of culture around the mechanical daily routine of work. More importantly, though, the ungrammatical language of 'all them things' (not to mention the colloquial 'go and get pissed') performs a valuable rhetorical function for ACE, suggesting with seemingly unpolished sincerity the wide social reach of the arts (and, indeed, the survey) beyond the educated and privileged elite; the repeated word 'you' suggests the applicability of the ACE's work to all.

Arts Council England seem deliberately to have selected and presented such idiosyncratic voices not only to show the reach of their work, but also to contrast the broadbrush language of social and economic impact that characterised the previous government's approach to culture. Their survey does not write these large-scale benefits out of its conclusions. Rather, it recasts them in more personal language, suggesting that they are the *consequence* of powerful, individual encounters with the arts. According to the survey, the three key ways in which the arts are important to people are:

- **'capacity for life'** – bringing understanding, expression, and others' perspectives,
- **'experience of life'** – giving pleasure, entertainment, relaxation, or solace,
- **'powerful applications'** – providing an outlet for emotions, and thus health, self-confidence, and social cohesion.[37]

The most instrumental-sounding item, 'powerful *applications*', follows only after the more person-centred benefits of 'capacity for life' and 'experience of life'. The arts provide 'an outlet for emotions, *and thus* health, self-confidence, and social cohesion' (emphasis added): the syntax suggests that large-scale effects proceed from individual rewards. The same sense of causation is evident in the summary report: '*Because* the arts can have these effects on people as individuals, they are *also* seen to have some wider outcomes or applications, such as bringing people together, creating links between different communities and encouraging people to feel a sense of pride and belonging in their local area' (emphasis added)[38] ACE do not altogether reject the social or economic impact of culture, but imply that it is a result of individual engagement.

But is the individual really an individual in government-funded culture? The words 'and thus' in the paragraph above could denote two very different relationships between the individual's experience of culture, and the benefits of culture in wider society. Does a person's positive experience of culture, and the 'outlet for emotions' it provides, radiate outwards to benefit directly the people around them? Or are these individual experiences, categorised as 'parent, highly engaged, urban', instead representative, needing only to be multiplied to calculate the benefits of culture to a nation? Both ideas seem to be in play at once: the large-print testimonials celebrate the value of culture to individuals, and also require those individuals to function as synecdoche that encourage the reader to imaginarily multiply this kind of positive story on a national scale.

This brings us to a central tension in the survey. In the social sciences, qualitative research is prized for its ability to access the voices of diverse individuals, including those normally excluded or marginalised from debate in the public sphere:

> There are and must be different experiences of the world and different bases of experience. We must not do away with them by taking advantage of our privileged speaking to construct a sociological version which we then impose on them as their normality. We may not rewrite the other's world or impose upon it a conceptual framework which extracts from it what fits with ours. Our conceptual procedures should be capable of explicating and analysing the properties of their experienced world rather than administering it. Their reality, their varieties of experience must be an unconditional datum.[39]

These qualitative methods are intended not to shape experience but to observe it: to capture the voice of often little-heard groups without determining what they mean, and to observe their difference and idiosyncrasies without forcing them into assumed categories.

At the same time, though, these techniques for engaging with individual perspectives are in tension with a larger desire for those individuals to be representative:

news stories appear to bridge the gap between fact and emotion by providing 'authentic' accounts from ordinary people forced to confront puzzling events ...

Given this representational milieu, it is hardly surprising that many qualitative researchers, in search of foundations for their practice, buy into this vocabulary. So the media's question 'How was it for you?' has become for many their very own qualitative research instrument and unique selling proposition. For the claim to 'get closer' to 'the individual's point of view' appears to differentiate qualitative research beautifully from those benighted number-crunchers whose concern for mere 'facts' precludes a proper understanding of authentic experience.[40]

This criticism, which goes on to proffer a more pragmatic approach to research methodology, points to the temptation, and the difficulty, of extrapolating out from vividly compelling, individual, qualitative accounts of infinite 'varieties of experience' to larger patterns, and wider human experience. In twenty-first-century cultural policy, this methodological tension is exacerbated by the reified status of the individual's experience of culture in a policy environment informed by the principles of public value.

Adding to this tension, an urgent part of the work of cultural policy-makers is not just to satisfy, but to create, public demand for existing cultural products. As well as designing new research, ACE have conducted more advocacy-oriented 'segmentation research' into patterns of arts consumption, and suggested new ways in which institutions can engage with (i.e. sell to) people in each of the thirteen segments, from multi-ticket offers labelled 'Dinner and a show' to tempt infrequent attenders, to 'in-venue marketing' to attract 'Traditional culture vultures', to new kinds of cultural event.[41] Research into public attitudes inevitably comprises both social analysis, which attempts (albeit with limitations) dispassionately to observe and understand people's behaviours and preferences, and market research, which uses those social-science tools to gather and interpret information about the consumption patterns of individuals and groups, with a view to better targeting their needs and desires.

The Arts Debate, ACE's first ever attempt to measure the 'public value' of the arts, did not simply poll the public on their attitudes and reactions to culture, but brought them into sustained and, it was hoped, mutually informing, conversation with cultural practitioners and organisations, in the spirit of 'deliberative democracy':[42]

Government and the values of culture 161

> Much of the inquiry will be based on deliberation, so that participants are provided with relevant information and evidence from a wide range of perspectives and given time to explore and debate the issues before coming to a reasoned opinion.[43]

The debate therefore comprised separate focus groups with members of the public and arts professionals, an online public consultation, and 'deliberative events' where the initial responses of each of the constituent groups were further debated and discussed.

Predictably, the online debate attracted anxious concern about the public's lack of qualification to pass judgement on culture:

> Well ... I need a double hernia operation ... shall I call in the local tyre fitter to give his opinion or shall we just stay with the surgeon? (tom.cunliffe, 14 February)
>
> Members of the public should no more be consulted about arts funding decisions than they be about which part of a brain a brain surgeon operates on. (Tony Clifton, 9 April)
>
> I'm a writer, but when it comes to visual art I wouldn't trust my decisions as far as I could throw me, so what value would my opinion have? You may as well ask me my opinion on how to perform brain surgery. (Darren Ross, 19 April)

This recurring analogy of the tyre fitter and the surgeon shows how firmly held is the belief that only trained expertise should inform cultural decision-making. The analogy belies all sorts of additional assumptions about class, professionalism, education and intellectual ability, and the cultural authority these qualities bestow. The anxiety held by some quarters is that the public will dilute – even dangerously – the quality of cultural decisions.

Other critics, however, were, conversely, more concerned about the inevitably limited scale, and thus representativeness, of the project's 'measurements' of public opinion, given the numbers of individuals that can physically take part in a sustained, face-to-face discussion about the value of the arts; they recommended that ACE should simply have asked more people what they thought.[44] Stage One of the debate saw 20 discussion groups and 10 interviews conducted with 170 members of the general public across England.[45] The less restricted online forum attracted 1,251 responses, 819 comments on the website and 432 in writing.[46] While the numbers involved are encouraging in themselves, they seem small on a national scale, and lack the reach and simplicity of democratic consultation techniques like voting, even if it is a 'blunt tool for the expression of complex opinions and detailed preferences'.[47] Even some culturally engaged individuals expressed their nervousness about contributing to the online forum, and imagined the millions who would not feel able to do so at all.

The public part of the debate was followed by consultation with practitioners,[48] and then by 'deliberative events' that brought these constituencies together to discuss what emerged as shared concerns.[49] People's 'top-of-mind' or initial responses to questions about the importance of culture were distinguished in the results from the answers they gave after plenty of discussion and helpful information:

> In many cases people's opinions shifted as a result of their exposure to the experiences of others, particularly during the deliberative stage. This appears to reflect a strong desire and capability among most people to put individual interests and concerns aside and to consider wider issues and the collective good.[50]

The deliberative process encouraged people to move from a reflex response to a more considered position about the value of culture. Yet if the 'intrinsic' value of culture is, according to Holden and Hewison's model, located in the experience of culture, then the deliberative process surely took people further from their immediate, apparently intrinsically valuable, responses.

Even as it invites and celebrates the public's opinions, then, the Arts Debate almost inadvertently challenges the rhetorical primacy of the individual experience in public value. The 'deliberative' emphasis of the Arts Debate suggests that the public's opinions are being not just captured and measured, but informed and changed, by the process. For example, one of the chief 'priorities' that emerges from the debate by public and practitioner consensus was 'innovation': that 'a failure of innovation in the arts is also a failure of public funding', and that ACE should in future prioritise 'innovation and public engagement'.[51] Yet innovation was a matter on which the different constituents of the debate had initially been divided, and while artists and managers saw it as 'an inherent part of the creative process' and 'a self-evident goal',

> Members of the public were cautious at first. They felt that artists, arts organisations and arts funders need to take risks and were comfortable with the idea that not every project or idea will 'work'.

At the same time, members of the public – and indeed a number of arts professionals and other stakeholders – were concerned that very groundbreaking work can be inaccessible or alienating. However, as participants deliberated on these issues further, they developed a broad consensus that innovation matters – and a clear understanding of why.[52]

Initially 'cautious' about the value of innovative and conceptual art, the public participants in the debate, through the deliberative process, came to see artistic innovation as 'essential'.[53] They had its value explained to them in terms of their own personal experience, and, from fearing that it would be 'inaccessible or alienating', came to appreciate that it was 'a means of heightening the overall experience of the arts – even if that experience is sometimes difficult or disturbing'.[54] While this 'broad consensus' achieved by the end of the debate might allay fears about public involvement leading to 'safe' decisions, it does, however, suggest that the deliberative process of public value, applied to the arts, can tend towards the education of the public by experts, bringing them to 'clear understanding' of how the arts world works, rather than effecting the mutual refinement of preferences.[55]

The role of the individual's experience, so reified in public value, is further complicated by the contradictory revelation that, for some participants, instrumental thinking can be more of a knee-jerk reaction than talking about their own experiences of culture. This is particularly the case with those participants categorised as 'low-engaged', who declared that culture is 'not for me', talked very easily about its social and economic value (or lack of same), and had to be nudged to see how it related to them personally; that they eventually did so was billed as one of the triumphs of the debate. The public-value model relies on the public to speak for themselves, but the Arts Debate showed them to be capable of speaking and thinking from multiple perspectives. While Holden and Hewison's values, intrinsic, institutional and instrumental, are respectively aligned with the public, professionals and government, the more fluid trio of values that emerged from the Arts Debate (capacity for life, experience, application) is not associated with three distinct groups. All participants moved between personal and practical applications in their discussions, and the final report acknowledged that multiple, even contradictory values of culture can, and must, co-exist.[56] The Arts Debate, and the complex individual and collective responses it attracted, showed the limitations of public value when applied to culture; and the false dichotomy of instrumental government agendas and 'public value'.

Finally, these complex and even resistant reactions from members of the public challenge the assumption that the 'experience' of culture is something naturally, and readily, available to all. The report declared that 'empowerment came to be seen as equal to, if not more important than, that of access'.[57] As mentioned above, ACE have observed that the barriers to attending arts events tend to be psychological rather than financial or practical; and thus 'empowering' people to feel that they could legitimately attend a cultural event is an important goal for a funding body committed to bringing 'great art to all'. Yet even more important than access and empowerment, and more frequently overlooked, is the work of training people to register – and, crucially, to articulate – that they have had a cultural 'experience'. If, as anthropologist Clifford Geertz observed, 'For human beings … all experience is construed experience, and the symbolic forms in terms of which it is construed thus determine … its intrinsic nature',[58] then these 'symbolic forms' can all too easily be articulated and imposed from the outside, and people's 'experience' determined for them by those keenest to capture and understand it. The ideal work of the 'deliberative' process would be to develop a shared vocabulary for talking about cultural experiences, events and objects. Its least ideal form would be the imposition of a remote and pre-determined cultural vocabulary on new and inexperienced audiences.

The issues with using public-value techniques to measure the value of culture, and with the reification by government of the individual's experience of culture, are not the expected moral panic about the public's lack of authority to judge cultural matters. Rather, it is that the focus on the individual's immediate experience of culture is not sustainable in practice. Deliberative events, with their residual focus on knowledge and education, tend to move participants from their immediate reaction to a more considered (and potentially externally determined) response. The public, like institutions and government representatives, resist categorisation in the multiple ways they think about culture, and it can take some effort to persuade members of the public that their own experience of culture has any significance or value. Finally, there is a danger that, while the process gives the impression of a voice to the public, it only hands them a limiting language with which to talk about their personal experiences, rather than helping them genuinely to develop a vocabulary to reflect on their own encounters with culture. Simply asking more people what they think, as the ACE have been urged to do by critics, will be of limited value if their questions comes with a pre-determined set of responses.

The public-value debate is ultimately less a precise form of measurement than a model for producing consensus, or, at least, understanding from all parties that the issues it raises can never be resolved. The ACE's online debate, like the Arts Debate more broadly, started from the assumption that culture is valuable: it asks 'what do you value about the arts?', rather than 'do you value the arts?', and the resulting sense of constructive co-operation that it promoted between the public and arts professionals in determining not whether, but *how* that culture should be valued becomes somehow even more significant than 'culture' itself.

While the individuals consulted might represent slices of the population, distinguished by their level of engagement with the arts ('low', 'medium' or 'high engaged'), as well as gender, family circumstances, home and working status, the aim of the survey is not to foreground these differences. More often, they were grouped in the report as 'people', whether talking warmly of the value of culture for 'bringing people together, creating links between different communities and encouraging people to feel a sense of pride and belonging in their local area', or observing how 'People's opinions shifted' in the course of the debate.[59] If the word 'experience' overrides judgement and evaluation, then the word 'people' seems to override other kinds of difference for governments and practitioners. It occludes divisions of class, gender, race and even interest group, and looks beyond cultural difference to the practices a nation has in common.

The use of the word 'people' in the context of government cultural policy bespeaks the desire for 'culture' to stand in for a common humanity, and for individuals' positive 'experiences' of culture to be widely, and constructively, shared. As one Arts Debate testimonial declares,

> 'I think when you've been to something, you also feel that you're communicating with everybody else that's been there, you're part and

parcel with them, it's cohesive again, isn't it?' [Retired, medium arts engagement, urban][60]

This image of the 'cohesive' audience is increasingly familiar from the marketing of live theatre. Where early twentieth-century critics' visions of a utopian culture had expressly excluded the consumption – and, by extension, the consumers – of mass commercial culture,[61] this utopian language has a more democratic embrace, used by funders, organisations and – perhaps influenced by their language – individual visitors themselves to tell a different story of inclusion and equality. In this widespread account, people, rather than culture, are the espoused site of intrinsic value. This only leaves the persistent question of how these 'people' come to inherit the language of value that they speak, to such compelling effect, when asked what they value about culture. Williams observed that 'the making of culture is the finding of common meanings and directions and its growth is an active debate and amendment under the pressure of experience, contact, and discovery, writing themselves into the land'.[62] Governments and cultural brokers in the public sector, albeit in all good faith, appropriate the notion of 'finding common meanings and directions' to understand better the concerns of the public and to create and sustain demand for their existing cultural products, legitimating the government funding of a common 'culture' that will be valuable to everyone. In the research process, however, they can often give back to the public the 'common meanings' they find, determining, for good or ill, their past and future experiences.

New narratives of value

Following Tessa Jowell's report, and ACE's first attempt to measure the value of culture through a 'public value' survey, the first decade of the twenty-first century saw rapid transformation in the government discourse of cultural value. Accelerated by pressures of economic crisis and political change, these changes encompassed a swing from public value to expert judgement; from articulating people's experiences of culture to capturing the creativity it inspires in them; and from privileging narrative impressions of the benefits of culture, to seeking 'hard', numerical evidence of its contribution to the nation's economy. At the same time, the burden of responsibility shifted: where government once defended its cultural decisions to the public, now institutions demonstrate to the government the value of what they do. What seems to be taken for granted in the process is the question of whether culture is valuable.

The language of public value was enthusiastically applied to culture for most of the first decade of the twenty-first century. As the above analysis has shown, though, applying the model in practice challenges the albeit attractive simplicity of the model's association of 'intrinsic' value with the public, and throws open again the question of cultural value. Nonetheless, it is a rather unappealing prospect to revert from the attempt at public engagement that the Arts Debate represented, to the reassertion of the value of expert judgement that took place almost immediately after the results of the debate emerged. Sir Brian McMaster's report, 'Supporting Excellence in the Arts: From Measurement to Judgement', seemed from its subtitle alone to promise an outright rebuttal of the social sciences techniques of ACE's Arts Debate, and a return from capturing a nation's estimation of the value of culture, to reinstating expert evaluation.[63]

The report seemed driven by underlying anxieties about the public's ultimate authority to judge. McMaster had been commissioned by James Purnell, then Secretary of State for Culture, to undertake a review that would report on:

- how the system of public sector support for the arts can encourage excellence, risk-taking and innovation
- how artistic excellence can encourage wider and deeper engagement with the arts by audiences
- how to establish a light touch and non-bureaucratic method to judge the quality of the arts in the future. (p.6)

McMaster, drawing on his previous experience as director of the Edinburgh International Festival, consulted directly with a wide range of arts professionals to answer these questions. He also offered a month-long period in which the public could write in to say what they believed constituted 'excellent' art (it attracted a total of 183 responses (p.29)). McMaster saw his report as working in 'synergy' with the Arts Debate, and endorsed its key findings that public funding should support 'innovation', and enhance the quality of the artistic 'experience' (p.5) (findings that, as discussed above, were achieved with the public after a substantial period of deliberation). Yet despite this nod to a more democratic mode of valuation, McMaster still demonstrated that the people he believed were best qualified to act as cultural arbiters were arts professionals themselves. Funding bodies, he advised, should institute a system of 'self assessment and peer review that focuses on objective judgements about excellence, innovation and risk-taking and is made up of people with the confidence and authority to take tough decisions' (p.6); and cultural organisations should have on their governing bodies at least several artists and practitioners (p.12). The qualities of 'confidence', 'authority' and 'objective judgement' are not intended to be exclusive: they reflect a desire to see decisions informed by people with practical experience of how culture works, and not just by remote committees. Nonetheless, these terms promote the importance of knowledge, education and specialist training, and reinstate the role of the expert in ascribing value to culture, to the potential exclusion of others. Even if the public have a say, ultimate responsibility for cultural decisions lies, in McMaster's vision, with the arts community.

However, the challenge of managing the democratic distribution of the benefits of culture was still present in McMaster's brief to 'encourage wider and deeper engagement with the arts by audiences'. The government minister who commissioned the report, James Purnell, stressed the democratic potential of 'excellence', proposing in the Foreword that 'The time has come to reclaim the word "excellence" from its historic, elitist undertones and to recognise that the very best art and culture is for everyone; that it has the power to change people's lives, regardless of class, education or ethnicity' (p.4). Accordingly, even in this expert-oriented vision, the value of culture is still referred outwards from the object to people's experience of culture. As McMaster observed:

> The best definition of excellence I have heard is that excellence in culture occurs when an experience affects and changes an individual. An excellent cultural experience goes to the root of living. (p.9)

McMaster has much in common here with the 'public value'-informed projects discussed above, locating value in the moment 'when an experience affects and changes an individual', and dealing in universals like 'the root of living'. He seems to combine the expert- and experience-oriented models of value available in cultural policy to suggest that the higher the quality, the better the experience. Innovation and excellence are, for McMaster, an institution's responsibility to their audience, and he recommends that 'cultural organisations stop exploiting the tendency of many audiences to accept a superficial experience and foster a relationship founded on innovative, exciting and challenging work' (p.18). While the measure of this kind of value, were measurement possible, would be in audiences' experience of culture, the judgement of the value remains firmly in the hands of professionals.[64] He refers the moment of value out to the public, but exacerbates the problem of public value models that the public's valuation of culture is responsibility-free.

The 'tough decisions' mentioned by McMaster would still be strongly felt by those arts organisations reeling from what was described by the *Guardian* as the 'bloodiest cull in half a century', just weeks before its publication:[65]

> The Arts Council admitted the pre-Christmas timing was bad, but said 'tough decisions' had to be made. Its spokeswoman, Louise Wylie, said the criteria on which it was taking the funding decisions included access and breadth of audiences, and the excellence of work. The council has been taking decisions in tandem with a national review into excellence in the arts by Brian McMaster, former director of the Edinburgh International Festival. The government is expected to publish his report in January.[66]

Arts Council England's decision-making process shares with McMaster's report a dual focus on the access and breadth of audiences, and the 'excellence' of the cultural product. It did not make the inevitable cuts more palatable for organisations like Exeter's Northcott Theatre, which was told that it would lose its annual funding almost as soon as it opened after expensive redevelopment; limited funds seemed necessarily to override all previous discussions and aspirations (even if the theatre later got a reprieve[67]).

The rapidly changing financial climate for the arts would also have major effects on the government's language of cultural value. In the face of economic downturn, the Labour government placed increasing emphasis on culture's capacity to regenerate a tottering UK economy. In the same year that McMaster's findings were published, the UK government's *Creative Britain* report envisaged Britain becoming 'a hub of creative endeavour, innovation and excellence', in which the arts are central to a strong 'creative economy'.[68] The economic value of the arts is newly prominent here: not, now, in terms of their direct (and necessarily limited) contribution to the nation's GDP, but, rather, in terms of their potential to nurture the national creativity that might make a limitless contribution to that GDP in future. Just as Jowell re-energised traditional cultural organisations like museums and theatres by suggesting that they could be the source of powerful *experiences*, the *Creative Britain* report recasts experiences of traditional culture as a formative breeding ground for the more obviously money-spinning mass production of creative industries like advertising, computer games and design. The Royal Shakespeare Company is listed in the report as one of a number of members of the 'creative industries' willing to enable the DCMS to offer 5,000 formal apprenticeships a year,[69] transforming theatre arts into transferable skills and expertise.

This new emphasis on creativity would complicate the perceived roles of traditional organisations. The portmanteau title alone of ACE's 2005–11 'museumaker' project – a project that sought to 'unlock the creative potential of museum collections' – demonstrates the fusion of conservation and creative activities that were increasingly encouraged in their work. Each of the sixteen museums involved 'commissioned one or more outstanding makers to create intriguing new work in response to the venue, its associations and collections'. As well as offering 'new experiences for existing museum visitors', and attracting new audiences, the project set out to stimulate creativity, encouraging museums and makers to 'draw on each other's rich resources, take creative risks and trial new ideas'.[70] In the wake of the *Creative Britain* report, institutions would be strongly encouraged to foster creativity not only in artists connected with their work, but in their audiences, too. Stimulating as this might be – and as the many testimonials of visitors' creative experiences attest – it also presents a significant challenge to museums and theatres who are charged both with facilitating the kinds of encounters that will lead audiences to go on to produce their own creative work, and, crucially, with proving to their funders that the institution is the source of a cultural value that is generated outside their walls, and after the event.

This burden of proof is a particular challenge. In the first decade of the twenty-first century, the responsibility for proving the value of culture seems to move from governments themselves to the institutions that seek funding. As the perceived location of value shifted from the object, to the experience of that object, to the creative endeavours that resulted from that encounter, the onus has increasingly been placed on arts organisations to collect the testimonials that proved that something valuable had taken place during a visit. Cultural brokers now devote time to helping organisations to fulfil this duty while accruing maximum benefits to themselves and their visitors. The September 2011 'Culture Shock!' conference in Newcastle, entitled 'Community Engagement through Digital Storytelling', showcased the work of 'one of the largest digital storytelling projects in the world' that 'has engaged with nearly 600 participants, who have created their own digital stories inspired by museum and gallery collections'. The conference used Culture Shock as an example of best practice, training cultural workers in how to use this 'ideal method of engagement and participation' to 'unlock and showcase stories from people who are not recognised as having a voice in history making' and 'achieve real impact for individuals and communities'.[71] Such digital interventions not only give communities more opportunities to engage creatively with the museums and galleries in their towns, and help institutions to refresh their offer. In a climate where 'stories' and 'storytelling' – narratives of value – take on a new economic value, this cache of community stories would also constitute an organisation's representative batch of evidence that they deserve funding.

As fears of global financial crisis and UK recession were realised towards the end of the first decade of the twenty-first century, the pressure to demonstrate the economic value of culture only increased. The 'Culture and Sport evidence programme' or 'CASE' study, a strategic collaborative research programme led by the DCMS along with ACE, English Heritage, the Museums, Libraries and Archives Council and Sport England, seemed to confirm the return of the economic measures of culture that Jowell had sought to replace in the early years of the decade. Now, though, the question of 'What is the economic value of engaging in sport and culture?'[72] drew on a panoply of other 'interdisciplinary' values of engagement (including 'achievement', 'diversion', 'escape', 'expression', 'health', 'income', 'self-esteem', 'skills/competency', 'employment', 'productivity' and 'citizenship'[73]), and attempted to link the short-term individual benefits of 'subjective wellbeing', and the long-term economic benefits in terms of healthcare and prosperity, thus drastically broadening out the language of value. As befits a government department whose responsibilities range from the theatre to the running track, these measures encompass (sometimes uneasily) the benefits that come from engaging in sporting events or activities. What unifies 'culture and sport' in this account is the value of the experience of them – what people, and thus nations, get out of them. Far less central to the research – perhaps inevitably – is the question of what 'culture' actually means.

The transition from a Labour government to a Conservative–Liberal Democrat coalition in 2010, and the threat of severely reduced funding for the arts after the first comprehensive spending review, threw the focus even more squarely on the economic value of culture, and on the urgent need to prove it in order to survive swingeing spending reviews. The 2010 'Measuring Cultural Value' report, in an AHRC collaboration with the DCMS, restored both the language of measurement, and the emphasis on the economic benefits that accrue to the country from the arts. Dave O'Brien's chief recommendations were that:

1. DCMS, in consultation with the cultural sector, should create clear guidance on how to use the **economic valuation (rather than economic impact) techniques** already deployed across central government and recommended by HM Treasury.
2. DCMS should develop closer links with academics working in the area of **cultural economics**, to use existing and future studies as best practice guidance on the use of economic valuation for the cultural sector.
3. DCMS should use existing work in this area to explore the possibility of developing a **multi-criteria analysis** for cultural decisions, of the type recommended in DCLG's [Department for Communities and Local Government] Multi-criteria Analysis: a manual.[74]

There was a 'needs must' quality to the document that suggested that only being able to express the value of culture in tougher, more numerical terms – 'in a way that can be understood by decision-makers', and 'using methods which fit in with central government's decision-making' – would guarantee its future.[75] The report placed particular emphasis on how to make a convincing case for the value of culture when appealing to a limited pot of central funding. It urged the DCMS to draw on economic valuation techniques, and on the findings of cultural economists, in order to offer to the Treasury a more rigorous and compelling valuation of culture.

In a firm departure from the currency of personal and creative 'stories' discussed above, O'Brien expressly noted that 'narrative accounts of cultural value' were no longer sufficient in their own right. They might 'provide a framework for our understanding' as part of 'multi-criteria analysis', but they 'fail to represent the benefits of culture in a manner that is commensurable with other calls on the public purse'.[76] To redress this potential failure, he proposed instead that more use be made of the existing measures of the social benefit of public spending set out in HM Treasury's *Green Book* – that is, the central 'framework for the appraisal and evaluation of all policies, programmes and projects', putting culture on the same footing as any other request for government investment.[77]

Now, just as government departments like the DCMS have had to make a better case to central government, the onus was on would-be recipients to prove their value to their funders. With its budget reduced, ACE's funding announcements of March 2011 were heralded with bleak anticipation.[78] In actuality, they comprised a 'reduced grant in aid budget (down 14.9%) in context of wider public sector cuts': a 'National portfolio of 695 organisations replaces previous regularly funded portfolio of 849', with '110 new organisations brought into the mix', and '206 regularly funded organisations turned down'.[79] The biggest change was that 'the portfolio of funded organisations has been created through an open-application process': 'We received 1,333 applications and have offered National portfolio funding to 695 organisations'. This more equitable-sounding 'open and transparent' process perhaps reduces the need for the government to re-energise and re-justify value statements to support older, long-funded institutions, but it most certainly increases the competitive work required of institutions themselves.

By the end of the first decade of the century, then, Tessa Jowell's urgent sense that 'we need to be able to explain' and 'we need to find a way to demonstrate' the value of spending on culture seems to have been relocated from government to the organisations who seek government support. A recent report commissioned by the ACE appeared to offer cultural organisations the 'toolkit' they needed to prove themselves. BOP Consulting's paper, 'Measuring the Economic Benefits of Arts and Culture', might echo many cultural policy publications of the previous decade, but its subtitle is more pragmatic: 'Practical Guidance on Research Methodologies for Arts and Cultural Organisations'.[80] The report outlines four different practical approaches to measuring the value of culture, two of them 'measures of spending', and two of them 'valuations of wider benefits', but all of them resolving into a monetary figure that can be expressed to funders or stakeholders. The approaches include 'economic impact assessment', which gauges the amount of money spent in the local economy as a result of the 'pulling power' of the arts organisation in question; 'economic footprint analysis', which measures the size of an organisation's activities, 'comparing it with the national economy as a whole' (p.14); 'contingent valuation', which 'aims to estimate the extent to which consumers benefit from a product or service, over and above the price they pay for it (p.19) (a measure attempted by Bolton Libraries and the British Library); and 'social return on investment', which measures the 'value of an organisation's activities based on their effects on the organisation's stakeholders and audiences'.

While all of these approaches result in economic figures, there seems to be considerable choice for organisations, depending on their particular circumstances:

> Whichever method you choose, though, the analysis needs to be credible. Partly because there have been a number of economic impact assessments in particular that have made grandiose claims, there is scepticism in some quarters towards the claims made by arts and culture representatives for the economic benefits of their work. If you are commissioning work of this kind, it is imperative that your figures be believed.[81]

The range of options and the helpful caveats about believability underscore the shift in responsibility for demonstrating the value of culture. The friendly repetition of 'you' – 'you choose', 'your figures' – only exaggerates the sense that the tasks of articulating one's value, and of convincing others that one is telling the truth, lies with the organisations themselves. Just as in the higher education sector, where the 'assessment outcomes' or the measure of the research outputs produced by universities now 'inform the selective allocation of their [funding bodies'] research funding to HEIs', and government funding for research and teaching is not guaranteed,[82] the responsibility to prove the value of one's cultural organisation leads to a new kind of competition. Such requirements seem typically to have been presented to the cultural sector some years before they reach higher education; how cultural organisations have responded to this challenge, and its serious implications for the nature of cultural value, is explored in the next chapter.

One can observe a circularity in the changing language of value in the first decade of the twenty-first century. In a recent document, Dave O'Brien has asked 'what is missing from economic valuations?' – that is, what are the 'essential qualities of cultural artefacts and activity, such as aesthetic or symbolic values' that are absent from economists' assessment of culture?[83] He seems to reinvigorate the power of stories: 'The arts and cultural sector are, to some extent, founded on narratives and are at their most powerful when presenting qualitative evidence of impact, whether cultural or social'. But now, instead of functioning as heart-warming testimonials that gesture in the direction of consensus, these narratives need a new precision: 'How can we develop rich and detailed descriptions of the values associated with the arts and cultural sector in ways that can be useful for central government?' O'Brien is now concerned with how to combine the 'inherent appeal' of this qualitative evidence with 'Green Book-compliant decisions'. His 'toolkit' for the 'sector' is not primarily concerned with justifying itself to the public, but rather, now directs itself, as persuasively as possible, at the Treasury. The public might have been disempowered by the language of public value and personal experience, but, now, their estimation of culture is no longer at the centre of the picture. With the DCMS's budget now proposed to be cut by £12 million in 2013–14, and £22 million in 2014–15,[84] it seems unlikely that their views will return to the centre in the foreseeable future.

The first decade of the twenty-first century saw a fascinating shift in the language of cultural value, from one founded in the discourse of public value, which sought to privilege the public's estimation of culture and draw them into consensus about its significance, to a more competitive cultural environment, and a language of value that seeks to convince the government to fund one's organisation (and the Treasury to fund one's culture department). The responsibility to prove that value has shifted from governments to the organisations that seek their support. In the process, 'cultural value' can become tautologous: it is valuable because we value it and have positive experiences of it. As the examples in this chapter show, the 'aesthetic qualities' of culture that O'Brien seeks to reinstate, the formal qualities of their artistic structure that make them, as we discussed in Chapter 3, specific and particular, are rarely discussed, and preferences are paramount. 'What culture does' might be described with more and more accurate detail, but the question of what culture is, and whether it is valuable, is assumed and accepted: what it does *is*, in great part, what it is.

Amidst these changing languages of value, the perceived importance of Shakespeare persists. But is it still the same 'Shakespeare' that was upheld even at the beginning of the twenty-first century? Because of the dramatic medium in which the playwright worked, 'Shakespeare' has been more readily able than some cultural figures to adapt to each new discourse of funded culture. 'Shakespeare' is able to make an especially smooth transfer from a valued *object* (a body of work, a First Folio, a birthplace, a theatre) to an *experience* (live theatrical performance, emotional engagement). Indeed, the image of the audience united around a stage in a live theatrical experience has been a compelling one in the new language of government funding, modelling the collaborative generation of value in the figures of the closely proximate actor and audience. Going beyond 'experience', though, Shakespeare himself can be appropriated as a role model of successful, even competitive, 'creativity', and the fact that his plays can be raw material for new acts of artistic endeavour – from acting and directing his existing plays to adapting and reworking them into films, musicals, novels, television programmes and comic books – lends him readily to newer narratives of value, in which value resides not just in the experience of culture, but in what people go on to do with it. As later chapters will show, even the resurgence of economic valuations of culture does not necessarily challenge Shakespeare's cultural status; instead, new emphasis is placed on the market dominance of his global 'brand', and even on his own, apparently exemplary, commercial savvy as an early modern playwright, now distilled into managerial self-help. As this book goes to press, the economic impact and 'legacy' of the 2012 Cultural Olympiad, of which the World Shakespeare Festival was a centrepiece, is being calculated and celebrated.

Whether 'Shakespeare' in government-funded organisations is really an enabling source of creativity, or, rather, a familiar but adaptable face through which governments can endlessly legitimate new discourses of funding, deserves further consideration. The impression of Shakespeare's comprehensiveness and knowledge of human nature, first established in the eighteenth century, underpins an ongoing belief in his endless adaptability and relevance to new generations, and this perception makes him seem all the more responsive to the changing language of government culture in the twenty-first. His supreme adaptability makes him, of course, a special case, and masks the difficulties that other kinds of cultural organisations might face in responding to this changing language. What appears to be the 'transcendent' value of Shakespeare might rather be, as noted in earlier chapters, a result of 'dynamic potential for continual negotiation and adjustment to different historical circumstances' – or, in this case, to a rapid succession of different rhetorics of value. More than this, though, Shakespeare's seemingly endless ability to be revalued in new terms is coupled with a pervasive sense of responsibility to make sure that he continues to be revalued. The persistent assumption of, and commitment to, his value seems to underpin every attempt to generate new kinds of value in his name. That commitment, and the work that comes with it, is the subject of the next chapter.

Notes

1 Lisanne Gibson, 'In Defence of Instrumentality', *Cultural Trends* 17(4) (2008): 247–257, p.255.
2 Jowell, *Government and the Value of Culture*, p.8.
3 Jowell, *Government and the Value of Culture*, p.8.
4 James Fenton, 'Down with this Access Pottiness', *The Guardian*, May 29.05.04, www.guardian.co.uk/artanddesign/2004/may/29/artspolicy (accessed 11.06.13).
5 Heritage Lottery Fund, 'About Us', www.hlf.org.uk/aboutus/Pages/AboutUs.aspx (accessed 11.06.13).
6 Gibson, 'In Defence of Instrumentality', p.248.
7 See e.g. Francis Mulhern, *Culture/Metaculture* (Abingdon: Routledge, 2000), pp.49–60, and Robert Hewison, *Culture and Consensus: England, Art and Politics since 1940* (London: Methuen, 1995), pp.22–49.
8 Gibson, 'In Defence of Instrumentality', p.248.
9 Emily Keaney, *Public Value and the Arts: Literature Review* (London: Arts Council England, 2006), p.6.
10 Mark Moore, *Creating Public Value: Strategic Management in Government* (Cambridge, MA: Harvard University Press, 1995).

11 Gavin Kelly, Geoff Mulgan and Stephen Muers, *Creating Public Value: An Analytical Framework for Public Service Reform* (London: Cabinet Office, 2002).
12 The Work Foundation, *Public Value in Culture, the Arts and Broadcasting: A Background Presentation* (London: The Work Foundation, 2006).
13 BBC Press Office, 'BBC Launches its Vision of the Future and Manifesto for Action', 29.06.04, www.bbc.co.uk/pressoffice/pressreleases/stories/2004/06_june/29/bpv.shtml (accessed 11.06.13); Richard Collins, *Public Value and the BBC: A Report Prepared for The Work Foundation's Public Value Consortium* (London: Work Foundation, 2007).
14 Jowell, *Government and the Value of Culture*, p.17.
15 Jowell, *Government and the Value of Culture*, p.5.
16 Jowell, *Government and the Value of Culture*, p.13.
17 Jowell, *Government and the Value of Culture*, p.18.
18 Jowell, *Government and the Value of Culture*, p.6.
19 Creative Research, *The Arts Debate: Findings of Research Among the General Public* (London: Creative Research, 2007), pp.50–58.
20 Jowell, *Government and the Value of Culture*, p.6.
21 Andy Mousley, *Re-Humanising Shakespeare: Literary Humanism, Wisdom and Modernity* (Edinburgh: Edinburgh University Press, 2007), p.8.
22 John Holden, *Cultural Value and the Crisis of Legitimacy* (London: Demos, 2006), p.15.
23 Holden, *Cultural Value*, p.18.
24 Holden, *Cultural Value*, p.31.
25 Robert Hewison and John Holden, 'Public Value as a Framework for Analysing the Value of Heritage: The Ideas', in Kate Clark, ed., *Capturing the Public Value of Heritage: The Proceedings of the London Conference*, 25–26.01.06 (Swindon: English Heritage 2006), pp.14–18, p.15.
26 Holden, *Cultural Value*, pp.14–15.
27 Hewison, *Culture and Consensus*, p.306.
28 See also Eleonora Belfiore, 'Determinants of Impact: Towards a Better Understanding of Encounters with the Arts', *Cultural Trends* 16(3) (2007): 225–275 for an exploration of the range of approaches that suggest that 'aesthetic experiences' are the product of the interaction of the individual and the artwork', rather than the property of one or the other of these participants.
29 Noah M. Lemos, *Intrinsic Value: Concept and Warrant* (Cambridge: Cambridge University Press, 1994), p.115.
30 Connor, *Theory and Cultural Value*, p.3.

31 Connor, *Theory and Cultural Value*, p. 4.
32 Raymond Williams, *Resources of Hope: Culture, Democracy, Socialism*, ed. R. Gable (London: Verso, 1989), pp. 23–31, quoted in Mulhern, *Culture/Metaculture*, p. 73.
33 Mulhern, *Culture/Metaculture*, p. 50.
34 Hooper-Greenhill et al., *Evaluation of the Education and Community Strategy*, p. 84.
35 Carey, *What Good Are the Arts?*, p. 48.
36 Arts Council England, *What People Want From the Arts* (London: Arts Council England, 2008), p. 7.
37 Catherine Bunting, *Public Value and the Arts in England: Discussion and Conclusions of the Arts Debate* (London: Arts Council England, 2007), p. 14.
38 Arts Council England, *What People Want From the Arts*, p. 7.
39 Dorothy E. Smith, *The Conceptual Practices of Power: A Feminist Sociology of Knowledge* (Toronto: University of Toronto Press, 1990, repr. 1995), p. 25.
40 Clive Seale, Giampietro Gobo, Jaber F. Gubrium and David Silverman, 'Introduction: Inside Qualitative Research', in Clive Seale, Giampietro Gobo, Jaber F. Gubrium and David Silverman, eds, *Qualitative Research Practice* (London: SAGE Publications, 2004), pp. 1–11, p. 3.
41 Arts Council England, 'Arts-Based Segmentation Research', www.artscouncil.org.uk/what-we-do/research-and-data/arts-audiences/arts-based-segmentation-research (accessed 11.06.13).
42 See Louise Horner, Rohit Lekhi and Ricardo Blaug, *Deliberative Democracy and the Role of Public Managers: Final Report of The Work Foundation's Public Value Consortium – November 2006* (London: The Work Foundation, 2006).
43 Catherine Bunting, *The Arts Debate – Arts Council England's First-Ever Public Value Inquiry: Overview and Design* (London: Arts Council England, 2006), p. 3.
44 Clive Gray, 'Arts Council England and Public Value: A Critical Review', *International Journal of Cultural Policy* 14(2) (2008): 209–214, pp. 212–213.
45 Creative Research, *The Arts Debate: Findings of Research among the General Public* (London: Creative Research, 2007), www.artscouncil.org.uk/media/uploads/ArtsDebate_public_findings_report.pdf (accessed 21.06.13), p. 1.
46 Arts Debate findings, www.artscouncil.org.uk/what-we-do/research-and-data/public-value-programme/arts-debate-findings (accessed 06.07.12).
47 Keaney, *Public Value and the Arts*, p. 6.
48 'Qualitative research' agency Cragg Ross Dawson interviewed 49 artists and arts managers, 6 umbrella organisations, and 24 partners,

funders and representative bodies, from a variety of arts activities, regions and funding situations, and invited these arts professionals to discuss the definitions of art, the perceived barriers to engagement, and the priorities of funding; their chief concerns, it emerged, were the need to achieve a balance between privileging the tangible and intangible benefits of the arts, the process and function of arts funding, and the dangers of conservative, risk-averse public involvement in arts funding decisions. See Cragg Ross Dawson, *The Arts Debate: Research among Stakeholders, Umbrella Groups and Members of the Arts Community* (London: Cragg Ross Dawson, 2007) and Emily Keaney, *The Arts Debate: Arts Community and Stakeholder Findings* (London: Arts Council England, 2007).

49 See Opinion Leader, *Arts Council England: Public Value Deliberative Research* (London: Opinion Leader, 2007).
50 Bunting, *Public Value and the Arts in England*, p. 7.
51 Bunting, *Public Value and the Arts in England*, pp. 18 and 28.
52 Bunting, *Public Value and the Arts in England*, p. 17.
53 Bunting, *Public Value and the Arts in England*, p. 17.
54 Bunting, *Public Value and the Arts in England*, p. 17.
55 Even if Bunting stressed that the Arts Debate was a research process rather than an 'advocacy initiative' (Bunting, *The Arts Debate*, p. 4).
56 These include the tensions observed between the 'right to artistic expression' and 'the desire to engage and connect with others'; between 'creativity' and 'accountability'; and between 'expert judgement' and 'inclusive consultation'.
57 Bunting, *Public Value and the Arts in England*, p. 19.
58 Clifford Geertz, *The Interpretation of Cultures* (London: Fontana Press, 1993), p. 405. See also C. Jason Throop, 'Articulating Experience', *Anthropological Theory* 3(2) (2003): 219–241, on the complexity of articulating others' experiences. It has been noted that the experience or reception of a painting, as verbalised by an individual, can be drastically shaped by giving it a new title (M. B. Franklin, R. C. Becklen and C. L. Doyle, 'The Influence of Titles on How Paintings Are Seen', *Leonardo* 26(2) (1993): 39–52), and that audiences respond to the theatre in ways shaped by 'culturally and aesthetically constituted interpretive processes' (Susan Bennett, *Theatre Audiences: A Theory of Production and Reception* (London: Routledge, 1997), p. 86, both quoted in Belfiore, 'Determinants of Impact', pp. 236 and 245.
59 See Arts Council England, *What People Want from the Arts*.
60 Arts Council England, *What People Want From the Arts*, p. 7.
61 See Chapter 5, 'Intercultural Shakespeare: Innovation or Utopian Primitive', in Linnemann, *The Value of Shakespeare in Twenty-First-Century Publicly-Funded Theatre in England*, pp. 186–233.

62 Raymond Williams, 'Culture is Ordinary' (1958), in Imre Szeman and Timothy Kaposy, eds, *Cultural Theory: An Anthology* (Chichester: Wiley Blackwell, 2010), p. 54.

63 Brian McMaster, *Supporting Excellence in the Arts: From Measurement to Judgement* (London: Department for Culture, Media and Sport, 2008).

64 Gibson, 'In Defence of Instrumentality', sees it as a return to the very 'simplistic' 'provide excellence and they will come' discourse, especially in the suggestion of offering free access to cultural institutions for the general public for a week each year, as if there were no other barriers to access beyond financial ones (p. 250).

65 Mark Brown, 'England's Arts Face Bloodiest Cull in Half a Century as Funds Are Cut for 200 Groups', *The Guardian*, 17.12.07, www.guardian.co.uk/uk/2007/dec/17/theatrenews.artsfunding (accessed 22.08.12).

66 Brown, 'England's Arts Face Bloodiest Cull in Half a Century'.

67 'Northcott Saved – For Now', www.bbc.co.uk/devon/content/articles/2007/12/12/northcott_threat_feature.shtml (accessed 11.06.13).

68 Department for Culture, Media and Sport, with the Department for Business, Enterprise and Regulatory Reform and the Department for Innovation, Universities and Skills, *Creative Britain: New Talents for the New Economy* (London: Department for Culture, Media and Sport, 2008), www.culture.gov.uk/images/publications/CEPFeb2008.pdf (accessed 01.12.12), p. 1.

69 Department for Culture, Media and Sport, *Creative Britain*, p. 13.

70 Arts Council England, 'museummaker', www.artscouncil.org.uk/funding/funded-projects/case-studies/museumaker (accessed 19.06.13).

71 Culture Shock! Conference, www.cultureshock.org.uk/culture-shock-conference-2011.html (accessed 25.08.12). The organisation's site has the subtitle 'Digital stories by people in the North East: Inspired by museums and galleries'.

72 CASE, *Understanding the Value of Engagement in Culture and Sport: Summary Report* (London: Department for Culture, Media and Sport, 2010), www.gov.uk/government/uploads/system/uploads/attachment_data/file/88449/CASE-value-summary-report-July10.pdf (accessed 19.06.13), p. 22.

73 CASE, *Understanding the Value of Engagement in Culture and Sport*, p. 9.

74 Department for Culture, Media and Sport, *Measuring the Value of Culture: A Report to the Department for Culture Media and Sport'*, www.gov.uk/government/publications/measuring-the-value-of-culture-a-report-to-the-department-for-culture-media-and-sport (accessed 11.06.13).

75 Dave O'Brien, *Measuring the Value of Culture: A Report to the*

Department for Culture Media and Sport (London: Department for Culture, Media and Sport, 2010), p. 4, www.culture.gov.uk/images/pub lications/measuring-the-value-culture-report.pdf (accessed 11.06.13).
76 O'Brien, *Measuring the Value of Culture*, p. 9.
77 HM Treasury, *The Green Book: Appraisal and Evaluation in Central Government*, www.hm-treasury.gov.uk/data_greenbook_index. htm (accessed 11.06.13).
78 Mark Brown, 'Arts Council Funding Decision Day: As It Happened', *The Guardian*, 30.03.11, www.guardian.co.uk/culture/culture-cuts-blog/ 2011/mar/30/arts-council-funding-decision-day-cuts (accessed 11.06.13).
79 'Arts Council England Announces Funding Decisions and New National Portfolio of Arts Organisations', 30.03.11, http://press.arts council.org.uk/content/Detail.aspx?ReleaseID=1219&NewsAreaID=2 (accessed 19.06.13).
80 BOP Consulting for Arts Council England, 'Measuring the Economic Benefits of Arts and Culture: Practical Guidance on Research Methodologies for Arts and Cultural Organisations' (London: Arts Council England, 2012), www.artscouncil.org.uk/media/uploads/pdf/ Final_economic_benefits_of_arts.pdf (accessed 11.06.13).
81 BOP Consulting, 'Measuring the Economic Benefits of Arts and Culture', p. 32.
82 'Research Excellence Framework', *REF 2014*, www.ref.ac.uk.
83 Dave O'Brien, *Measuring the Value of Culture: An AHRC Briefing Paper*, in AHRC workshop, 'Valuing Culture: Developing a Toolkit and Evidence to Meet Policy Needs', 2011.
84 Charlotte Higgins, 'What the Chancellor's Autumn Statement Means for the Arts', *The Guardian*, 05.12.12, www.guardian.co.uk/culture/ charlottehigginsblog/2012/dec/05/autumn-statement-2012-arts-funding (accessed 11.06.13).

7

Value in Shakespeare institutions

In 2007, on the verge of resigning from his role as Prime Minister, Tony Blair looked back on a 'golden age' of culture in Britain: not, as his audience might have assumed, the Renaissance period but, rather, the last ten years of Labour governance. Addressing an audience of arts leaders in the turbine hall of Tate Modern, he reflected with pre-emptive nostalgia on the achievements of a decade of government investment in the arts: 'box office numbers in the seven major regional theatres have risen by nearly 40% on five years ago. ... the RSC sold more than half a million tickets for its shows in London and Stratford-upon-Avon; and visits to national museums have risen by almost 30 million'.[1] The latter achievement was due in great part to the government's removal of entry charges for many galleries and museums, which boosted visitor numbers, even if it did not necessarily widen the range of visitors. Nonetheless, Blair credited much of this success to the professionals in front of him.

More audaciously, however, Blair claimed to have resolved the gulf between 'two important conceptions of culture – that it should be of the highest quality, on the one hand, and that it should reach as many people as possible on the other'. To illustrate the significance of this hitherto insurmountable divide, he led his audience on a tour through two centuries of cultural policy and theory:

> Ever since Matthew Arnold this distinction has been central to arguments about culture. Culture, it was said, could either be excellent or popular but not both. It could be high – meaning good – or low – meaning bad.
>
> The post-war history of arts policy in this country tended to reproduce these distinctions. In its early years, the Arts Council operated as if the elite art forms needed to be preserved against encroaching popular idioms.

Jennie Lee, as Arts Minister, did start to change this but a lot of her good work was undone as, during the 1980s, some art forms became unaffordable for all but the rich. Community arts projects were scaled back. The critical balance – box office and subsidy – was upset. The funding squeeze persisted through the early 1990s and cemented the spurious distinction between excellence on the one hand and broad access on the other.

The reductive use of Arnoldian language aside, this rapid-fire guide was by way of building to Blair's ultimate claim that:

> The great virtue of what we have managed to achieve in this country is that we have clearly got the best of both. We have deepened our culture, extended its reach, with at the same time no compromise on quality, indeed rather the opposite.[2]

Blair boldly declares that he has resolved a persistent paradox of cultural policy: the challenge of promoting and supporting the quality of 'great' (or as Jowell had put it a few years before, 'complex') art, while simultaneously ensuring that it is available to the whole nation. In Blair's eyes, solving this paradox is not, as it was for Jowell, an aspiration, but, rather, a past success: 'the best of both' has been achieved; the 'spurious distinction' between 'excellence' and 'access' dismissed; and 'compromise' not countenanced (even if the word remains hovering in the wings). The audience of arts professionals is invited to reflect with Blair that 'This is an enormous achievement. One that we have done together.' This is a compelling declaration of a mission collaboratively accomplished, its persuasive force only slightly diminished by the fact that this was the Prime Minister's first ever public speech on culture.

Practitioners at the helm of major cultural institutions echoed Blair's claim to have solved the divide between 'great' culture and culture that is for 'everyone'. In a foreword to John Holden's essay *Democratic Culture*, Nicholas Hytner, artistic director of the National Theatre, applauds Holden for 'identifying the false dichotomy between excellence and access, and then … demolishing it'. He takes an example from his own experience of theatre-making:

> Take a play. For the sake of argument, take a play by Shakespeare. You've been thinking about it for several years. You spend the best part of a year bringing actors together for it, creating a stage world for it, rehearsing it. You examine every line in it, every thought. … At no point during the process does it occur to you that you may want to

trade in quality for popularity. You assume that the years of thought and experience and the months of investigation have been deployed to produce the best possible Hamlet, and you hope that the best possible Hamlet will be the most popular possible Hamlet.[3]

Hytner is suggesting that the 'false dichotomy' between 'access' and 'excellence' is counter-intuitive: that those actually engaged in the work, physical and intellectual, of putting on theatre and bringing Shakespeare to life, instinctively know (or at least always hope) that 'the best possible Hamlet will be the most popular possible Hamlet'. That Hytner speaks from the practical perspective of one experienced in producing plays supports the impression that balancing quality and popularity is not an external imposition, but something that all cultural professionals recognise is at the heart of what they do. His conviction is matched by Blair's confidently catchy phrase, 'best of both'. This balancing act is also writ large in ACE's former slogan, which declared the organisation's mission to get 'great art to everyone'; and in Sir Brian McMaster's report on the value of culture, which stressed the importance of balancing 'excellence' and 'access'. All four of these cultural brokers readily promote the notion of an optimal 'cultural value' that comprises both high quality and wide reach.

Such ambitious ideals are not uncommon in cultural policy, but putting them into practice is a different matter. The task of optimising cultural value falls not necessarily to governments, but rather to cultural institutions. As hinted when Blair evidenced the success of his mission by reference to regional theatres, museums and the RSC, it is institutions, particularly if they are in receipt of government funding, that are required to work simultaneously to preserve and produce 'great' art, and to bring it to as many people as possible. Hytner's vision of the 'best possible Hamlet' being 'the most popular Hamlet' is not one that happens without work: to achieve it, he says, 'cultural professionals' must 'acknowledge their responsibilities as educators and public servants. It is not enough merely to hope that a good Hamlet will be a popular Hamlet: our education system and our cultural institutions have to work to extend the cultural franchise so that the discussion of Hamlet can be universal.'[4] Being 'for everyone' is, of course, not necessarily at odds with being 'great', even if Blair's insistence that there is 'no compromise on quality, indeed rather the opposite', and Hytner's assertion that culture is not 'debased', hint at widely held anxieties to that effect.

However, the very fact that they are still being discussed suggests that the 'spurious distinction' between 'great' and 'everyone', dismissed out of hand by Blair, has not been fully resolved, and that (as in Hytner's phrase) the 'work' of – and, crucially, the 'responsibilities' for – holding together these two competing conceptions of cultural value will continue to be charged to cultural institutions in the foreseeable future.

In one definition, 'cultural value' can be pegged precisely to artistic merit. Writing in the twentieth century, Bourdieu (as discussed in Chapters 4 and 5) felt that the value of a cultural object increased with its complexity and difficulty, and decreased as its popular audience grew. In his estimation, intellectual, exclusive poetry had a higher value than bourgeois theatre; and, even within Parisian theatre, left-bank, intellectual work was deemed to be of higher value than more commercial right-bank productions.[5] In another sense, however, rather more familiar to cultural policy-makers than to Parisian intellectuals, the value of culture – its benefits to a nation – ostensibly increases with the number of people who experience its impact, directly or indirectly. Both of these notions are, or have been, available to funders. Bourdieu suggested that market failure was a mark of artistic quality, and subsidy thus a symbol of artistic value, enabling 'great' art to be produced when it might otherwise flounder in the mass market; his was in many ways a restatement of the *Kulturkritik* position, but one that has provided a less and less precise analogy for the cultural landscape of the UK. More recently, and partly because of the addition of new directly publicly funded support structures like the Heritage Lottery Fund, the award of subsidy has increasingly placed the onus on institutions to maximise the benefit of government investment in culture for as many people as possible, delivering culture, as the last chapter suggested, as if it were a public service.

'Great art for everyone' is just one of a number of perceived binary oppositions that cultural institutions navigate in their daily work. Some of these tensions are inherent in the act of becoming an institution, and the mixed purposes for which they have been established: the competing but simultaneous claims of 'preservation' and 'access', for example, of keeping objects in fine condition while letting as many people as possible benefit from proximity to them, and of honouring both what culture 'is' and what culture 'does'. As we noted in Chapter 6, Gibson has shown that nineteenth-century institutions such as the South Kensington Museum (now the V&A), which installed gas lighting to enable evening opening and encourage evening visits as a healthy alternative to frequenting London gin palaces, and set out to educate skilled workers to boost the flagging lace industry, are 'constitutively instrumental'.[6] These founding beliefs in public service mean that tensions between quality and access are built, however deliberately, into the fabric of long-established cultural institutions.

In the twenty-first century, though, these tensions have been exaggerated by the new ways in which traditional institutions have been asked by governments, funders, and even audiences, to present themselves to the world. The growing rhetoric of 'experience' and 'creativity', as critiqued in the previous chapter, has complicated the primary institutional activities of access and preservation, and re-animated persistent ambiguities in the meanings of 'value' and even of 'culture'. Critical and anthropological definitions of culture have co-existed at least since the almost contemporaneous publication of Arnold's *Culture and Anarchy* and Tylor's *Primitive Culture* (see Chapter 4),[7] and they persist in the contemporary discourse of institutional work. The abstract to John Holden's *Democratic Culture* declares that 'Culture should be something that we all own and make, not something given, offered or delivered by one section of "us" to another': an anthropological view of culture, in which institutions promote the shared practices, behaviours and even creative products of their communities and visitors. Yet the subtitle of Holden's paper is 'opening up the arts to everyone' – a phrase which more readily evokes the 'access' model of facilitating encounters with already prized cultural objects. Such conflations in the discourse leave institutions grappling with multiple roles.

In this environment, the taxonomy of cultural institutions that Bourdieu articulated in passing in his work no longer holds firm. His distinction between 'institutions for conservation' (e.g. museums), 'institutions for diffusion' (e.g. 'publishers and theatrical impresarios') and 'institutions for reproduction of agents who can value culture' (e.g. the educational system) begins to break down even within his own text, and collapses entirely when applied to the work of twenty-first-century organisations. Even without the complex network of auxiliary activities that surround many organisations – the shop, the restaurant, the archive, outreach and marketing – even traditional institutions combine the roles of 'conservation', 'diffusion' and 'education' to varying degrees.

Institutions also have to navigate the tensions between the roles of public service and business, a duality that will be explored in greater detail in the next chapter on the 'Shakespeare brand'. Far from being insulated from the risk of market failure by public money, no organisation in the UK's twenty-first-century cultural economy necessarily works with a single source of funding, and even flagship publicly funded institutions are only partially supported by the state. The RSC and British Library both receive public subsidy from the UK government, the former awarded £15.2m in 2008–9 via the arm's-length development agency Arts Council England and regional distribution body Advantage West Midlands, and the latter £106.9m directly from the government's Department for Culture, Media and Sport, in both cases amounting to about 30–40% of their operating budgets.[8] By contrast, Shakespeare's Globe Theatre and Shakespeare Birthplace Trust (SBT) are not publicly funded in the sense of receiving taxpayers' money: The Globe Trust, established by Sam Wanamaker, supplements its box-office revenue with the support of Friends, corporate sponsorship, trusts and foundations, as well as income from its exhibition and educational events. The SBT similarly relies on income from visitors, Friends and donations, as well as the less visible support of gift aid. Both address themselves directly to the purse-strings of the public: visitors to the SBT website are urged that the charity 'depends entirely upon the public for support', and visitors to the Globe website that 'Your support is vital to enable the Globe to grow and flourish',[9] as if the public's help is all the more necessary for these independent organisations.

There is, however, considerable overlap in the way these state-funded and non-state-funded operations work. The RSC is a registered charity, and, like the Globe and SBT, appeals to its visitors for financial support, as well as raising revenue through its gift shop and public events. Conversely, as a publicly funded organisation, it does not have the monopoly on public service. Founded in 1847 to purchase Shakespeare's birthplace for the nation, the SBT is concerned with caring for 'Shakespeare's heritage' and 'promoting Shakespeare across the world'. The Globe claims to embrace 'the most democratic audience in the world', and stresses, in its appeal for funding, that new donors would be supporting 'one of the most prestigious and important arts and education centres in the country'. All of these organisations balance the imperatives of public support and market success, and work to connect the language of public service – of providing citizens with what is 'good for you' – with that of the service economy, and of offering consumers a great experience.

These tensions have been exacerbated by the influence of new technology and business on cultural policy. The government's changing language of cultural value has, over recent decades, drastically reshaped the work of the institution through a series of roles in turn: from fostering access to culture and conveying the prior value of that culture to an audience, to facilitating creativity, and serving as a resource for the generation of new value in future. The major implications of these seemingly minor linguistic shifts are analysed below.

From access to creativity

Historically, 'access' to cultural objects has long been held to be the most valuable thing that an institution could provide: a founding imperative for many museums and galleries. The National Gallery, established in a nineteenth-century mission for public improvement, was deliberately located in Trafalgar Square 'so that the poor could walk to it from the east and the rich drive to it from the west'.[10] The word 'access' implies shared ownership or rights to the materials: the British Library rests upon 'foundation collections' of important texts, based on the King's Library of King George III, that were donated to the nation; the SBT was established to 'preserve and maintain' Shakespeare's houses, also for the nation; and the RSC chartered to 'conserve, advance, and disseminate the dramatic heritage of Shakespeare'. The mandate to provide 'access' also confers the impression of 'intrinsic' value on the objects contained within the institution. Despite attracting criticism for the passive role it affords to audiences and visitors, the term has persisted in cultural policy, from the post-war establishment of the Council for the Encouragement of Music and the Arts[11] to the provision of free entry to national museums and galleries in 2001.

In some ways, 'Shakespeare' suits the 'access' model very well. He offers, in the form of copies of his plays, a material object whose perceived *a priori* value can be conveyed to new readers and audiences. Historically and linguistically distant, 'Shakespeare' seems to require the institutions that bear his name to remove obstacles – of language, understanding, or even interest – to full engagement with his work. The notion of 'making Shakespeare accessible' – or, in the case of the RSC, keeping 'modern audiences in touch with Shakespeare as our contemporary' – remains a compelling one for institutions from theatre companies to publishers. As we discussed in Chapter 4, cultural organisations can trade, often profitably, off the perceived difficulty widely associated with Shakespeare through his presence in compulsory education, and profess to offer a more engagingly direct 'access' to his works – through opportunities to watch or participate in performance, or to admire objects associated with his life – than the tedious act of 'sitting at desks and reading the plays'.[12]

Yet when institutions devise lively educational programmes to engage disenchanted pupils, or plan exhibitions that convince older visitors of the relevance of Shakespeare to modern life, it raises the question of whether they are, indeed, making Shakespeare more accessible – that is, finding new ways to put audiences in contact with his intrinsic value – or whether they are in fact constituting that value, by constructing 'Shakespeare' as important, engaging and relevant, and collaborating with exclusively educational institutions to train new audiences in the vocabulary needed to ascribe value to his work. It has been argued that institutions do not simply *convey* cultural objects to a new generation, but bring them into existence. As Randal Johnson observes with reference to Bourdieu, 'works of art exist only for those who have the means of understanding them', and to decode and value an object is 'not a universally shared natural talent, since it involves much more than the direct and immediate apprehension of the work'.[13] Bourdieu himself suggests that the seemingly '"pure" gaze' of aesthetic apprehension and understanding is constructed by the 'institution of the work of art as an object of contemplation', both physically (in the building itself) and professionally (in the team of experts assembled to conserve it).[14]

Shakespeare-based institutions continually work to construct Shakespeare as valuable, and, in turn, use 'Shakespeare' to help constitute the value of new work: the RSC promoted Greg Doran's 2011 production of *Cardenio* as 'Shakespeare's lost play',[15] and the Globe advertised their experiment to host thirty-seven foreign-language productions of Shakespeare's plays with the words that 'Shakespeare is the language which brings us together better than any other'.[16] Proponents of 'cultural institutions studies' are especially interested in the shaping influence institutions have on a new cultural good before that good comes into existence. Where some might lament the way that artistic talent is compromised by mass production, these critics argue that 'the economic and social dimensions are intrinsic to' cultural goods because they are present from the outset, not distorting existing work but subtly shaping it into what it will ultimately become.[17] Thus, new writing at the RSC, a specially commissioned play by a company participating in the 2012 Globe to Globe Festival, or even a Shakespeare-focussed research funding application that responds directly to a current 'theme' of the AHRC such as 'Science in Culture' or 'Translating Cultures',[18] are all instances where institutions are constitutive of value, creating the conditions that determine what cultural goods come into existence, and what they come to mean.

For all their commitment to the unquantifiable complexity of the forces that shape 'culture', cultural institutions theorists still focus on the way these forces affect the 'production, distribution and reception' of a cultural good: a neat triplet that suggests that these analysts are beholden to the sequential imagery of cultural production. Their primary example is the individual artist, whose cultural outputs are inevitably pre-shaped because he or she positions him- or herself in the art world, self-regulates, or writes for a certain kind of publisher. The 'case of Shakespeare' quickly shows the limitations of this temporal or sequential explanation for how value accrues to a cultural good. Shakespeare organisations, and theatres and heritage organisations more widely, continually raise the question of who the artist is (Shakespeare, or his adaptors, actors, directors, and producers?), when the moment of creation is (in the work of the early modern dramatist or the twenty-first-century ensemble or audience?), and who ultimately shapes and determines its significance and value (see also Chapter 3).

This kind of institutional work is occluded by the twenty-first-century discourse of 'experience', which rhetorically locates the value of culture in the immediate response of the 'magic moment' of encounter. The application of public-value principles to decisions about culture, as discussed in the previous chapter, has meant that institutions are increasingly prized for their ability not to convey, or even to constitute value, but rather to facilitate valuable experiences. In this view, the value of culture is not just *evidenced* by visitors' positive experiences of prized cultural objects and events, but generated in that experience.

Shakespeare institutions have evidently responded to the 'experience' agenda by adapting their operations in significant ways. The auditorium of the Royal Shakespeare Theatre was extensively redesigned so that, when it officially reopened in 2011, rather than watching the performance from in front of a proscenium arch, audiences would now be ranged around three sides of a thrust stage. The RSC claims that this facilitates a better experience:

> The aim is to improve the relationship between the audience and the actor by bringing them closer together and creating a more intimate theatre experience. The furthest seat will be reduced from 27–15 metres.[19]

Physical proximity to the actors, the RSC asserts, 'improves the relationship' and enhances the 'experience' of attending a theatre performance. Since no one is technically relegated to the furthest reaches of the theatre, this is not only an 'intimate theatre experience', but a more inclusive one, too. 'Experience' was the key selling point of this redesign project, and, promoting the 'transformation' to the public, the RSC invited visitors to 'Experience a new kind of theatre', even if some commentators have suggested that the somewhat Globe-style structure of the Royal Shakespeare Theatre is a historical cliché, and asked whether spectacle, rather than actor proximity, might in fact more successfully engage new audiences.

Theatres, unlike more static collections of art and heritage objects that need constantly to be repackaged, can respond relatively swiftly to the 'experience' challenge by promoting and enhancing the collective experience of live performance. But even more object-based organisations can be seen to tweak their marketing accordingly. The 2012 poster campaign of SBT invited visitors to 'Discover your Shakespeare', emphasising the enjoyable – and, crucially, personalised – experience that awaited visitors within their walls; the larger-scale structural changes the SBT has made in the name of improving the 'experience' of Shakespeare are discussed below. Experiences have become the quasi-commercial products of all kinds of cultural institutions.

Fuelled by the growth of user-generated technology, and by a drive by the previous Labour government for regeneration in the face of global recession, cultural policy in the first decade of the century has encouraged cultural organisations to prioritise not only 'participation' or 'experience', but also 'creativity'. Increasingly, the focus of the government rhetoric of cultural value is not just on people's experiences of culture, but on what they go on to do with those experiences. In previous decades, organisations such as museums, galleries and theatres were somewhat uneasily situated in the category of 'cultural industries', a grouping that better suited the large-scale production of music, advertising and TV than the 'preservation' of objects and practices.[20] The twenty-first-century emphasis on creativity has reinvigorated this association between 'traditional' organisations and mass producers of culture, this time giving traditional organisations the imperative not simply to create new cultural products, but to facilitate creativity in their visitors.

The government's existing public subsidy of the arts was rewritten, in publications like the *Creative Britain* report discussed in the last chapter, as investment in cultural experiences that would foster future creativity in visitors, and, by so doing, enable Britain to become 'a hub of creative endeavour, innovation and excellence'.[21] Through associated schemes like 'Find Your Talent', which proposed that school children be provided with five hours of 'culture' per week, cultural organisations are in turn repackaged as 'the key that unlocks their [young people's] creative talents, opening them up to the possibility of a future career in the creative industries':

> Within those five hours – in and outside school – the aim is for every young person in England to have the chance to:
> - attend top quality live performances
> - visit exhibitions, galleries and museums
> - visit heritage sites
> - use library and archive services
> - learn a musical instrument
> - play music or sing
> - take part in theatre and dance performances
> - produce creative writing, or listen to authors
> - learn about and make films, digital or new media art
> - make a piece of visual arts or crafts.[22]

This list of activities deals in increasingly active verbs, from 'attend' and 'visit', which evoke 'access' to culture, via the more participatory language of 'learn' and 'take part', to 'produce' and 'make', words that betoken creativity, in both traditional and digital media.

Read as a sequence, this list enacts the recent discourse shift in policy from 'access' to 'creativity', and presents it as a developmental learning process. Early, passive experiences of 'top quality live performances', we are encouraged to believe, lead quite naturally to future acts of creativity, in the classroom and, it is implied, throughout people's lives; the benefits for the individual, and for Britain's economy, seem to come at no additional cost to the nation.

Analysts of cultural policy have already pointed out the banality of this upbeat, globalist devotion to a doctrine of 'creativity'.[23] Conveniently, it needs no specified output to be valuable, and is elastic enough to link the arts with science and technology and, as shown above, positive audience experiences of building-based culture with recession-busting new growth industries. Hitherto uninspected, however, are the pressures it places on the funded arts organisations now celebrated for their capacity to stimulate creativity in others, and its appropriation of 'Shakespeare', who is variously called upon to symbolise enduring value and entrepreneurial creativity by organisations and individuals alike.

Cultural organisations have quickly attempted to adapt once again to the newest discourse of value. In 2006, Executive Director Vikki Heywood had celebrated the RSC's value in terms both of its £57 million contribution to the economy, and its staggering effect on the people present:

> in many ways, the excitement of a child completely wowed by their first trip to the theatre, or the play that made you question your perception of humanity, is just as good a measure of what we do.[24]

Heywood offered the child 'completely wowed' as a symbol of a positive experience of the theatre, and a good 'measure' of the value of the RSC's work. The child who appeared among the diverse 'Voices' of actors, designers and audiences presented in the 2008–9 Annual Report, however, was impressed by his experience of the theatre in a rather different way:

> I came to the Open Day last year and had my photo taken for a *Hamlet* poster, it was great fun. Open Day was fantastic, I made a video of the day's events which I edited to music. It was shown to David Tennant and he was impressed, which made me feel very proud.[25]

Far from being simply 'wowed' by the theatre, the child in this testimonial turns his experience of visiting Stratford into the new, creative product of a video edited to music. The contrasting images of children and young people presented in these two reports reveal the RSC's responsiveness to shifting narratives of cultural value. Where the 'child ... wowed by their first trip to the theatre' connotes the unfeigned enjoyment of a young person early in their education, unfettered by cultural capital, it remains an essentially passive experience, and one reported by the RSC. The second, creative child, by contrast, ostensibly speaks in his own 'voice', and with a confidence – the RSC experience having made him feel 'very proud' – that evidently augurs well for his future creativity. The 'child ... wowed' is an abstraction, whereas the creative child, 'Nat Barber, 15', is an individual who functions as metonymy for the value of the creativity generated by the RSC, and in defiance of the faceless passivity of Adorno and Horkheimer's 'hypodermic' mass culture. It is testament to the intriguing expectation that artistic acts of collaboration and creativity will engender effortlessly those same qualities in the wider world, via the audiences with which they come into contact.

This expectation is supported by a belief in the potential of digital technology, and, accordingly, the activities in which 'Nat Barber' engages, including videoing, editing, and sharing his work, are, while very limited in scale, suitably hi-tech. Nat Barber might have come to the RSC to have this improving digital experience, but the Internet, and in particular Web 2.0, has the capacity to change, at least symbolically, how built institutions interact with their audiences and visitors. 'Tate Online', for example, is a virtual addition to the collection of art galleries that bear that name. It not only provides 'access' to a repository of images taken from the holdings of the built institutions, but also a more 'participatory' experience of 'curating' a virtual gallery that is normally reserved for expert staff, as well as a place to research school projects and to shop for original, design-oriented presents from the comfort of one's own home. As the website has grown, it has become a resource to stimulate future creativity, not only playfully, as for school-age children, who can 'Play games, watch films, upload your art online and create new masterpieces' at 'Tate Kids', but, more seriously, for current and future artists or 'young creatives', for whom 'Tate Collectives' is intended as a place 'to discover, share and discuss art', with the assumption that this kind of conversation will promote the creation of exciting new work.[26]

User-oriented virtual activities like this expand the reach of the institution far beyond its physical 'footprint', enabling and encouraging people all around the world to engage with the contents of the Tate galleries without having to enter the buildings. At the same time, however, they significantly challenge the distinctiveness of that institutional footprint:

> digitization of these artefacts allied with increasing amounts of born-digital material has diminished the distinction between the institutions, at least as perceived by Web users. ... Institutional distinctions are of little concern to those who make use of or contribute from outside the organizations to the repositories of digital objects.[27]

The enhanced virtual activity of cultural institutions, whether in the name of marketing, or of enabling more people to engage with its resources, can, ironically, efface the identifying walls of the institution. As Middleton and Lee later observe, Internet visitors 'are happy to grab the content without questioning the provenance'.[28] The challenge for institutions is not just that, because of 'Tate Online', one does not necessarily need to go to the Tate to enjoy a particular painting such as Millais's 'Ophelia', or that, because of the numerous facsimile copies searchable in the British Library's 'Shakespeare in Quarto' webpages, one does not need to visit the physical site of the British Library, and provide the necessary credentials for a reader pass, in order to explore the library's holdings of Shakespeare's plays in quarto.[29] The difficulty is rather that, if one searched for 'Millais's "Ophelia"' or 'Shakespeare Quartos' through a search engine such as Google, and arrived at these sites, one might not necessarily realise that one had been to the Tate or the British Library at all.

This permeability or institutional indistinctness is a challenge that many businesses already face in a world where 'the balance of shareholder value has shifted irrevocably from tangible assets to intangible assets', and 'corporate performance and profitability are driven more and more by the exchange and exploitation of ideas, information, expertise and service, and less and less by control over physical resources'. As Hamish Pringle observes, the Internet offers a significant challenge to 'the protection and monetization of intellectual property', and poses a serious threat to certain kinds of organisation: 'producers of IP [intellectual property] such as music, newspapers, magazines, and book publishers are already in crisis because of the piracy of their content'.[30] The challenge for many organisations is to remonetise this more ethereal, freely accessible, content. The *Times Online* newspaper began to remonetise its online materials by charging for access to the main bulk of the publication, and other content providers have considered developing a less overtly demanding form of 'micropayment' that would allow users to click on an item of interest and pay only pence for it.

While the music and publishing industries are developing new stratagems to protect the monetary value of their intellectual property, cultural institutions are, for now, presented with a different kind of challenge from the Internet. While digital technology has already significantly affected the way music, and, increasingly, books, are purchased and owned, it is still said to have a relatively limited physical effect on the ways people engage with museums, theatres and galleries. Arts Council England's latest survey of the digital offerings of their own regularly funded organisations declared that, for 94% of these organisations, their online presence was a (more or less sophisticated) marketing tool for the live experience of the theatre, gallery or museum. In the 4% of organisations where their website stands up as a destination in its own right – say, mixing your own music at the Philharmonia Orchestra, or curating your own virtual exhibition at the Tate Gallery, as mentioned above – they suggest that the virtual dimension is 'complementary' to the live experience,[31] and more likely to 'enhance' the experience of those who already engage with culture than to attract a new audience altogether.[32] Websites attached to museums or theatres or libraries are considerably less likely to be visited for their own sake than for secondary information (opening times, box office details, educational add-ons); it would take longer in a theatre than in, say, a newspaper for what was originally intended to be their advertising to supplant the product. Unlike many major retail organisations, the digital content produced by the institutions (the 'clicks') currently retains its secondary status to their building-based work (the 'mortar').

This might not always be the case, but, at present, the challenge facing these heritage-focused, building-based institutions is not so much to remonetise a product that the Internet has turned into free content, as to reassert their cultural ownership of that content, at the same time as making it more widely accessible. Since value has been relocated from the object housed by the institution to the experience that the institution facilitates, and, further still, to what people go on to do with that experience, institutions have had to grapple with the difficulty of recording and measuring these more intangible experiences to demonstrate to funders the value of their work. As Dennis Kennedy notes,

> Experience is hard to commodify. Visits can be structured as in safaris and cruises, but the touristic site is only the occasion for the adventure: seeing the Acropolis, touching its stones, is ultimately a prompt for an event that occurs in the mind of the visitor, as the meaning of a performance occurs in the mind of the spectator.[33]

Institutions are here figured as the 'occasion', or 'prompt' of value, doing the structural work that facilitates or triggers the experience. They are not, in this view, completely in control of the meaning and value subsequently produced in the mind of the visitor, or what they do with it in the future. In terms of cultural funding, however, they are responsible for this experience, and need as much as ever to be able to reclaim the cultural value that the discourse of new media has ostensibly shifted outside their walls.

Close inspection of their own Internet discourse suggests that cultural institutions make strategic moves simultaneously to celebrate the potential value that can be realised by their visitors, and to recoup their control over that value: to at once efface and assert the presence of their institutional walls. For example, the British Library's online Shakespeare quartos are freely available for all to access, but they are also carefully branded with the library's logo: the project opens up the British Library's holdings, but also visibly marks them as belonging to the Library. In other parts of its work, the Library has devoted considerable energy both to demonstrating that it generates creativity in others, and to capturing the value of that creativity for itself. In May 2009 the Library emailed its readers with the question 'How has the British Library helped you?'.[34] This was intended to help the Library 'understand more about the value that we add to your research or work': had the Library, for example, helped you to complete a postgraduate qualification, write a book, or start a business? The email included two examples of people who had created original, commercially successful products from the raw materials of the library: the author of an award-winning murder mystery novel and the designer of a new 'superfood' fruit juice. The message both celebrated their commercial success, and reclaimed the value of their success for the library: both projects were researched exhaustively (and in the case of the novel, 'entirely') within the walls of the St Pancras site in London, the fruit juice in both the Science Reading Rooms and Business & IP Centre.

In these testimonials, the Library acts as both a primary resource for future work, and as a value-adding customer service that improves visitors' creative output: it helps visitors both to develop and to enhance their own intellectual property, and then, crucially, claims a kind of ownership over their products, if only anecdotally. Such anecdotes also encourage more typical, academic users to view their research outputs as creative products of the library's raw materials and customer service, and, in turn, these readers are invited to 'send us your stories', transforming that creative output into a narrative that can be rewritten into the building. The library does not simply annex user-generated content for commercial gain, as other online platforms might do, but collects 'stories' – that latest currency of user-generated value – in order to display to the public, and to its funders, the value of what it does.

From experience to objects

For all their ready adaptation, cultural institutions have also reacted to the dominance of the discourse of experience and creativity by reasserting all the more vehemently what is more traditionally considered to be valuable about their work. In one sense, the major redesign of the exhibition space of the SBT seems to give the building over entirely to 'experience'. With the support of £250,000 from Advantage West Midlands, the SBT recruited 'creative design and audiovisual installation company' Sarner to transform its existing exhibition of artefacts into a more 'experiential' space for visitors. 'Life, Love & Legacy', launched in April 2009, offers 'a new introduction to William Shakespeare' in the form of 'a fascinating and immersive journey'. Far from trudging round a static display of artefacts and information, visitors, according to the SBT's website, are promised 'an enthralling *experience* that interweaves theatre with Shakespearian magic' (italics in original).[35]

This promised experience is built into the very structure of the space. The exhibition, at the entrance to the Birthplace, comprises five rooms or 'zones', from 'Pre-Show' to 'Hall of Fame', through which visitors progress, via sets of Tudor Stratford and London, in timed groups. Each zone centres on an audio-visual display, in which actors narrate the story of Shakespeare's life over film and television footage of his plays. It is tempting to read this transformation – with its 'five act' structure, actors and 'sets' – as an attempt by a heritage organisation to 'remediate' (in Bolter and Grusin's term for the appropriation and refashioning of earlier forms by new media[36]) the emotive immediacy of live theatre, as in another recent SBT innovation, 'Shakespeare ALOUD!', which recruited costumed actors to regale Birthplace visitors with Shakespearean speeches. 'Immersive', though, is a word that comes from the discourse of digital technology, and the SBT enlists not only that technology's perceived relevance, but also its capacity to give the impression of unmediated experience. Ironically, the 'authenticity' of an author's birthplace – which relies, as Nicola Watson has shown, on an always-tenuous connection between writing career and long-departed place of origin[37] – is rearticulated as a virtual 'experience', in order to make it more real.

But by focussing on experience, cultural institutions can find themselves straying into territory that, since the 1990s, has increasingly been staked out by business. Pine and Gilmore asserted that the 'experience economy' was of a higher order than the agrarian, industrial or, more recently, service economies that had successively characterised previous centuries, and exhorted companies from shoe shops to airlines to think of themselves as selling not goods or services, but memorable experiences:

> When a person buys a service, he purchases a set of intangible activities carried out on his behalf. But when he buys an experience, he pays to spend time enjoying a series of memorable events that a company stages – as in a theatrical play – to engage him in a personal way.[38]

Businesses are encouraged to borrow the appeal of a theatrical event for which people are willing to pay for its own sake. When Shakespeare organisations, for whom the appeal of a theatrical event should supposedly come more naturally, choose to adopt this discourse, they can find themselves in competition not just with one another, but with more straightforwardly commercial leisure activities, from 'the original live experience' of *Mamma Mia: The Musical* in a different kind of cultural institution in London's West End, to the follow-up SMS text message from local hairdressers Toni & Guy saying 'we hope you had a great experience', and the host of other 'soft' retail experiences and 'first-order experience providers' from free street festivals and concerts to travel agents and even masseurs.[39]

The comparability of the SBT with other leisure 'experiences' was observed by a local newspaper reviewer, who described the exhibition as

> a ten-minute celebration of the Bard's life, using the kind of mixture of props, scenery, music and voice-overs that you might have seen at other local attractions like Cadbury World or Blenheim Palace.[40]

That Shakespeare's Houses and Gardens were named 'Best Tourist Experience', jointly with the Severn Valley Railway and the Ludlow Food and Drink Festival, in the 'Heart of England Tourism Excellence Awards 2009', underscores this comparability. The SBT is not compelled by public funding to use this experiential language, choosing instead to deploy it as part of their marketing strategy. Yet while it might help them to find a rewarding place in the UK leisure economy, it also increases the challenge of demonstrating that the positive effects their 'experience' offers – pleasure, socialisation, entertainment, education, understanding of Shakespeare's heritage – are unique to them.

To demonstrate its uniqueness, then, the SBT, within its experiential space, celebrates the special objects that, it asserts, mark it out from its competitors:

> This enthralling experience interweaves theatre with Shakespearian magic and you will see real treasures and artefacts, associated with the man himself, including Shakespeare's First Folio, brought to life!

The 'real treasures and artefacts' of the SBT – the books and objects that were once the mainstays of its static exhibition – are now 'brought to life!', an intriguing existential claim that, in practice, means they are illuminated, behind gauze or glass, in turn as they are referred to in the film. (Their display cabinet is, however, to the side of the room, so the viewer's gaze might more naturally fall on their digital projection on the large, central screen, rather than on the objects themselves.) The exhibition builds towards what is described as a

> powerful finale – the reveal of Shakespeare's actual First Folio. As the real book is illuminated, the screen above it shows a cgi animation sequence of the pages turning, and from this emerges the wonderful legacy of Shakespeare. Produced as a 30-second collage, the production uses images taken from the pages of the Folio itself and is set to the haunting music of Mendelssohn.[41]

The high point of the SBT's multimedia 'experience' is an invocation of the seemingly intrinsic value of that 'real book', the *actual* First Folio' from which 'emerges the wonderful legacy of Shakespeare'. By tracing back all subsequent value and creativity to the First Folio, the SBT makes a powerful and even retrograde claim for the significance and value of the cultural object. In this exhibition, the object is not supplanted by 'experience' and 'creativity', but is the parent of them.

It is not only the SBT that, in housing what Sarner calls 'a national treasure' in an armour-plated case, resorts to the symbolic value of the 'real' object in the midst of its newest 'experience'. The British Library's 'Shakespeare in Quarto' site reasserts the value of its material holdings, 'our only source for what [Shakespeare] originally wrote', and the library exhibition invites visitors virtually to 'turn the pages' of his plays. The Globe Theatre has advertised the fact that the John Wolfson Library will house the collection of rare books, including Shakespeare quartos and folios, bequeathed to it by Wolfson, now the Globe's Honorary Rare Book Curator. The RSC doubly emphasised the bookish materiality of Shakespeare's 'Complete Works' in a dedicated, year-long festival theatre season by that name in 2006–7, and in a collaboratively produced, First-Folio-based edition. Once a new medium for Shakespeare, the First Folio now functions, in multiple institutions, as a rare 'original'. All of these institutions have responded to the pressure to foster positive experiences and nurture future creativity by reasserting (or even, as the SBT's dramatic 'reveal' above suggests, refetishising) the value of the cultural objects that they own, as anchors for a unique visitor experience. The glow surrounding the SBT's Folio in their web marketing suggests that, in doing so, these organisations might recourse to an older, and, in Walter Benjamin's terms, auratic, language of value.

The ultimate reassertion of the value of the cultural object, as we discussed in Chapter 5, is surely represented in the British Museum's 'Shakespeare: Staging the World' exhibition, a centrepiece of the 2012 World Shakespeare Festival. The exhibition presented Shakespeare's First Folio as an anchor for the diverse array of objects and images from Shakespeare's 'world' that followed, stretching not just through Stratford and London but around the globe, both east and west. Its auratic qualities depended on there being no mention of the other 221 copies world wide; it authorised the ongoing 'dialogue' between objects and text that characterised the exhibition. If the First Folio started the show, the so-called 'Robben Island Bible', discussed earlier in the book, closed it. The two books together stood in for Shakespeare's place in early modern and contemporary culture, movingly representing both the intrinsic value of Shakespeare's texts, and the worldwide value that had subsequently sprung from them. The British Museum partook of both these values.

The newly revived power of the material object extends outwards to the walls of the building: increasingly, these cultural institutions present not just their contents but themselves as objects of intrinsic value. The new, more participatory design of the Royal Shakespeare Theatre was intended to be 'A landmark building instantly recognizable the world over and that Stratford can be proud of. A destination in itself': that is, an object of value in its own right. The invitation to 'Experience a new kind of theatre' elided innovative stage practices with the physical building, bundling together its productions and its rooftop restaurant. (Indeed, at the point of advertising, the theatre was some way from producing its first show, so the invitation rested entirely on the surrounding attractions of the building.) The RSC's iconic, London-based competitor, the Globe, declares that it has no subsidy other than 'the uniqueness of its building and the abiding enthusiasm of its audience'.[42] The BL and SBT's innovative digital exhibitions confer value on their physical buildings, necessitating visits to Henley Street and Euston Road respectively. The institution becomes a reassuring focal point that connotes and contains myriad experiences and ideas. Their incorporated shops, cafes and restaurants take on a more than auxiliary role when they become not just tools for 'porousness',[43] as in the new architectural plans designed to tempt passers-by into the National Theatre, but destinations in their own right.

The value of the physical sites of the institutions is declared almost in defiance of new technology. When Greg Doran's RSC *Hamlet* was filmed for broadcast, the event, despite the play's being filmed 'on location', and remediated into high-definition film for BBC television and DVD consumption, was regarded by Michael Boyd, then Artistic Director, as an amplification of the live theatre performance: 'the screen version of Shakespeare's great tragedy will retain the quality and tone of the critically acclaimed stage production'.[44] Similarly, the Globe Theatre's agreement with arts distributor Opus Arte to 'film, screen and distribute' selected plays from the 2009 season in cinemas and on DVD was articulated as a 'partnership' that will 'record highlights of the season in exceptional quality and share these with even more theatre-lovers around the world'.[45] Note 'theatre-lovers' rather than 'Shakespeare-lovers': the Globe 'is beloved around the world for its iconic architecture and vibrant theatre productions', and this new distribution will take not just Shakespeare, but the Globe itself, to a worldwide audience. The Globe's sense of 'partnership' with Opus Arte contradicts Philip Auslander's observation that 'theatre (and live performance generally) and the mass media are rivals, not partners'.[46] Both the Globe and the RSC present the remediation of their work by other, newer media forms as their own, deliberate appropriation of broadcast technology to extend and promote the physical space of the stage.

However, the urgency with which institutions underscore the importance of their own buildings ultimately reveals their attenuated grasp on the cultural value that supposedly resides within their walls. New technology, and its associated discourses, reinvigorates the institutional challenge of place-making, or ascribing value to a particular location. It exacerbates the notion that tourists can have an authentic experience anywhere, exposes the equally contingent relationship of the 'authentic' Birthplace and the constructed Globe Theatre to Shakespeare's value, and reveals the arbitrariness with which institutions lay claim to particular cultural content. Ownership is particularly difficult to assert in the case of Shakespeare: new media only exaggerate the institutional challenge of, as Diana Owen of SBT put it, 'getting your arms round Shakespeare',[47] when, because of his manifestations in performance, text and cultural heritage, 'Shakespeare' can only be partially contained by an institution that dedicates itself to any one of these aspects. As the next chapter on branding shows, Shakespeare institutions can appear to be his owners when they are really competing to offer the best 'value-added' to his name.

The idea of institutional cultural ownership has been thoroughly challenged by the discourses of user-generated creativity, sharing and co-creation that have sprung from new technology:

> As more of us turn to the web for news, information, entertainment and conversation, for example, we turn away from newspapers, television, film, libraries, bookshops. That may liberate us from the

control of a cultural elite, editors and publishers, critics and commentators who used to oversee what we read and thought. Yet the orgy of user created content the web has attracted might also rob us of high quality journalism and literature, film and music.[48]

Charles Leadbetter here re-rehearses, without resolving, the familiar debate between 'quality' and expertise and the 'liberation' and freedom from 'control' that the Internet might bring. Despite the anxiety about loss of quality, though, Leadbetter ultimately sides with the creative potential of collaboration, whatever it might produce: he describes a societal move from the 'economy of things' in which you are identified by what you own, to the 'economy of ideas', where 'you are what you share', and builds to the enthusiastic assertion that 'the more ideas are shared the more they breed, mutate and multiply, and that process is the ultimate source of our creativity, innovation and well being'.[49] The question that remains is whether the traditional institution has a place in this kind of economy. Leadbetter's celebration of 'what we hold in common' might be a fitting-sounding aspiration for a national institution such as the British Museum, described by its director as a 'private collection for every citizen' and a lending library for other nations and cultures, but it is still somewhat at odds with their struggle to be the definitive place to encounter a certain cultural good. Whether organisations like museums continue to assert so heavily their institutional identity in future, or embrace the potential of the Internet to hold objects and ideas in common by sharing metadata and developing large-scale, online connectivity with other organisations, remains to be seen.

This chapter has shown how very readily different cultural institutions have adapted themselves to the changing discourses of value in the twenty-first century: often by making major physical changes to the way their buildings work, sometimes with very mixed results, and always with implications for the organisation's relationship to the value of culture. In an ideal world, institutions might conceivably break their cycle of responsiveness to every new discourse that comes to them – such as the assumption that performing creative work makes one inherently able to inspire creativity in others – by being more self-conscious about the language with which they articulate the value of the work they do. It is primarily the expediencies of winning funding that keep institutions (including those in higher education) so responsive to new, prized languages of value; yet it is unlikely that a decrease in government funding will result in greater freedom from these languages, since, as the behaviour of non-government-funded organisations above suggests, the imperatives of government can quickly be replaced by the imperatives of business and sponsorship.

Nonetheless, the most valuable recommendation for cultural institutions might be that they reinvigorate their own role as generators not just of content or experiences, but of the language of value itself. The most obscured role of the cultural institution in twenty-first-century culture is that of *constituting* value, and one can see how they might usefully reclaim and make more visible their traditional work of evaluating and attributing value which has, in many ways, been parlayed into their marketing departments. Such critical activities, in which institutions actively shape the language in which culture is discussed, could be carried out in collaboration with researchers in higher education, responding to Lisanne Gibson's call for 'critical engagement that is grounded in the practicalities of culture's administration',[50] and might, in turn, promote in audiences a more evaluative, rather than passively experiential, approach to culture.

The landscape of cultural institutions, however, continues to evolve, and the next chapter shows how 'Shakespeare' is constructed in the twenty-first century in a complex interaction between culture and commerce; and how organisations working in his name simultaneously eschew and assert their own identity in order to profit from the impression of a larger, overarching Shakespeare 'brand'. In this environment, what have seemed throughout this chapter to be unsolvable tensions in Shakespeare institutions' work, such as between high and low, between public service and business, and between access and excellence, are raw material for new media appropriations from advertising to film. In conversation with the market, these perceived, often long-outdated, but still enduring oppositions at the centre of what institutions do can become productive tensions. As the next chapter will show, these tensions, however surprisingly, come to function as a stimulus for large-scale creativity, and a genuine source of potential value for Shakespeare in the twenty-first century.

Notes

1 'Blair's Speech on the Arts in Full', *The Guardian*, Tuesday, 6 March 2007 www.guardian.co.uk/politics/2007/mar/06/politicsandthearts.uk1 (accessed 14.06.2013).
2 'Blair's Speech on the Arts in Full'; see the introduction to this book for discussion of the temptations of 'completing' histories.
3 Nicholas Hytner, 'Foreword', in John Holden, *Democratic Culture: Opening up the Arts to Everyone* (London: Demos, 2008), p. 7.
4 Holden, *Democratic Culture*, p. 7.
5 Pierre Bourdieu, 'The Field of Cultural Production', in *The Field of Cultural Production*, pp. 29–73.
6 Gibson, 'In Defence of Instrumentality', p. 249.
7 For further discussion of these connected but contrasting approaches, see Connor, *Theory and Cultural Value*, p. 232.
8 'Finance Director's Report', RSC Annual Report 2008–9, www.rsc.org.uk/downloads/annualreport2009.pdf (accessed 21.06.13), p. 42; 'Trustee's Annual Report 2008/9', British Library Annual Accounts 2008/09, www.bl.uk/about/annual/2008to2009/accounts.pdf (accessed 14.06.13), p. 40.
9 'Supporting the SBT', *Shakespeare Birthplace Trust*, www.shakespeare.org.uk/index.php?option=com_content&view=article&id=43& Itemid=43 (accessed 01.09.12); 'Support Us', Shakespeare's Globe, www.shakespearesglobe.org/support-us (accessed 14.06.13).
10 Carey, *What Good Are the Arts?*, p. 98.
11 Clive Gray, *The Politics of the Arts in Britain* (Basingstoke: Palgrave Macmillan, 2000); Hewison, *Culture and Consensus*.
12 Royal Shakespeare Company, *Stand up for Shakespeare: A Manifesto for Shakespeare in Schools*, www.rsc.org.uk/downloads/stand-up-for-shakespeare-manifesto.pdf (accessed 14.06.13).
13 Richard Nice, 'Editor's Introduction', in Bourdieu, *Distinction*, p. 22.
14 Bourdieu, *Distinction*, p. 36.
15 'Cardenio', *Royal Shakespeare Company* www.rsc.org.uk/explore/other-writers/cardenio.aspx (accessed 10.09.12).
16 'O for a Muse of Fire…', *Shakespeare's Globe Theatre* http://globetoglobe.shakespearesglobe.com (accessed 10.09.12).
17 Werner Hasitschkaa, Peter Goldslegera and Tasos Zembylas, 'Cultural Institutions Studies: Investigating the Transformation of Cultural Goods', *The Journal of Arts Management, Law, and Society* 35(2) (2005): 147–158.
18 'The AHRC's themes provide a funding focus for emerging areas of interest to arts and humanities researchers': 'Themes', *Arts and Humanities Research Council*, www.ahrc.ac.uk/Funding-Opportunities/Research-funding/Themes/Pages/Themes.aspx. (accessed 10.09.12).

19 'The Vision', *Royal Shakespeare Company*, www.rsc.org.uk/transformation/vision/default.asp (accessed 14.06.13).
20 See David Hesmondhalgh, *The Cultural Industries* 2nd edition (London: Sage Publications, 2007; first edition 2002).
21 Department for Culture, Media and Sport, with the Department for Business, Enterprise and Regulatory Reform and the Department for Innovation, Universities and Skills, *Creative Britain: New Talents for the New Economy*, p.1.
22 Department for Culture, Media and Sport, *Creative Britain*, p.7.
23 Philip Schlesinger, 'Creativity: From Discourse to Doctrine?', *Screen* 48(3) (Autumn 2007): 377–387; Kate Oakley, 'The Disappearing Arts: Creativity and Innovation after the Creative Industries', *International Journal of Cultural Policy* 15(4) (2009): 403–413.
24 Royal Shakespeare Company, 'Annual Report and Accounts, 2005–6', p.9, www.rsc.org.uk/downloads/annualreport2006.pdf (accessed 21.06.13).
25 Royal Shakespeare Company, 'Annual Report and Accounts, 2008–9', p.11, www.rsc.org.uk/downloads/annualreport2009.pdf accessed 21.06.13).
26 Tate, 'Learn', *Tate*, www.tate.org.uk/learn (accessed 14.06.13).
27 Michael R. Middleton and Julie M. Lee, 'Cultural Institutions and Web 2.0.', Fourth Seminar on Research Applications in Information and Library Studies (RAILS 4) (Melbourne: RMIT University, 2007), p.16.
28 Middleton and Lee, 'Cultural Institutions', p.20.
29 *Treasures in Full: Shakespeare in Quarto*, www.bl.uk/treasures/shakespeare/homepage.html (accessed 14.06.13). Furthermore, the British Library is just one of the sources of the digital facsimiles of the online *Shakespeare Quartos Archive*, alongside the Folger and Huntington libraries. *The Shakespeare Quartos Archive*, www.quartos.org.
30 Hamish Pringle, 'Creative Britain', in Shelagh Wright, John Newbigin, John Kieffer, John Holden and Tom Bewick, eds, *After The Crunch* (London: British Council, 2009), pp.56–57.
31 MTM London, 'Final Report: Arts Council England – Digital Content Snapshot', 15.05.09, www.artscouncil.org.uk/media/uploads/downloads/MTM-snapshot.pdf (accessed 14.06.13), pp.14, 18.
32 Synovate, *Consuming Digital Arts: Understanding of and Engagement with Arts in the Digital Arena amongst the General Public. Qualitative Research Report* (Synovate: London, April 2009), p.33.
33 Dennis Kennedy, 'Shakespeare and Cultural Tourism', *Theatre Journal* 50(2) (1998): 175–188, p.175.
34 'How Has the British Library Helped You?', British Library Reader Bulletin, 14.05.09 (by email).

35 'Life, Love and Legacy Exhibition now open!', *Shakespeare Birthplace Trust*, http://houses.shakespeare.org.uk/visitor_centre (accessed 01.05.10).
36 Jay David Bolter and Richard Grusin, *Remediation: Understanding New Media* (Cambridge, MA: The MIT Press, 2000).
37 Nicola Watson, *The Literary Tourist* (Basingstoke: Palgrave Macmillan, 2006), pp. 56–89.
38 B. Joseph Pine II and James H. Gilmore, *The Experience Economy: Work is Theater and Every Business is a Stage* (Boston, MA: Harvard Business Press, 1999), p. 2.
39 See Jon Sundbo, 'Innovation in the Experience Economy: A Taxonomy of Innovation Organisations', *The Service Industries Journal* 29(4) (2009): 431–455.
40 Graham Young, 'Stratford-upon-Avon brings Shakespeare to life with new exhibition', *Birmingham Mail*, 10.04.09, http://www.birminghammail.co.uk/whats-on/things-to-do/stratford-upon-avon-brings-shakespeare-to-life-with-new-89903 (accessed 11.06.13).
41 'Themed Design: Sarner brings Shakespeare to Life', *Blooloop*, www.blooloop.com/PressReleases/Themed-Design-Sarner-brings-Shakespeare-to-Life/1431 (accessed 14.06.13).
42 Shakespeare Globe Trust, *Annual Review 2007–8*, www.shakespearesglobe.com/uploads.ffiles/2011/02/131482.pdf (accessed 21.06.13), p. 6.
43 Robert Butler, 'Inside the Fortress of the National Theatre', *Intelligent Life* (Winter 2008), http://moreintelligentlife.com/story/national-theatre (accessed 14.06.13).
44 'David Tennant reprises role in RSC Hamlet for BBC Two', Royal Shakespeare Company, 29.05.09, www.rsc.org.uk/home/8455.aspx (accessed 01.05.10).
45 'On Film', *Shakespeare's Globe*, www.shakespearesglobe.org/onfilm (accessed 01.05.10).
46 Philip Auslander, *Liveness: Performance in a Mediatised Culture*, 2nd edition (Abingdon: Routledge, 2008), p. 1.
47 Interview with author, 10.3.08.
48 Charles Leadbetter, *We-Think: Mass Innovation, not Mass Production: The Power of Mass Creativity* (London: Profile Books, 2008), pp. 2–3.
49 Leadbetter, *We-Think*, p. 6.
50 Gibson, 'In Defence of Instrumentality', p. 255.

8

Branding Shakespeare

In March 2012, Shakespeare was declared 'one of the strongest brands in the world'.[1] Estimated at $600 million, Shakespeare's monetary value was said by brand valuation consultancy Brand Finance to outstrip easily that of Elvis Presley, Marilyn Monroe and J. K. Rowling, and to warrant the label of 'AAA brand'. Brand Finance's estimate was based on the value of the numerous, diverse products that continue to be sold in his name long after his lifetime. Other marketers have attributed this long-term commercial success to the early modern playwright himself, treating him as an aspirational business figure and drawing out practical lessons for modern-day business by examining 'how he divided his customer base' effectively or how 'he used the Globe theatre itself as a kind of frame' to create a satisfying environment for audiences in a messy media world.[2]

In recent years, 'the Shakespeare brand' has offered scholars, as well as marketers, a compelling language with which to try to explain Shakespeare's value in the twenty-first century. Douglas Lanier titled Shakespeare 'the Coca-Cola of canonical culture',[3] and he and other scholars of Shakespeare's reception have observed that 'Shakespeare', like any successful brand name, is attached to a seemingly endless series of new products, from stage and film adaptations to the tourist-industry staples of souvenir moneyboxes, medallions and tea-towels,[4] and the ironic, academic kitsch of 'the Shakespeare beanie baby, the Shakespeare bobble-head, the Shakespeare action figure, or the Shakespeare celebriduck'.[5] The brand stretches further, too, to unrelated products adorned with his image or 'trademark': 'bank cards, £20 notes (from 1970–93), beer, crockery, fishing tackle, book publishing, cigars, pubs, and breath mints'.[6] In Lanier's case, wry amusement at this array of kitsch products is followed with more serious reflections on the way that Shakespeare lends value as an 'other' to pop culture.

'Brand' is, in many ways, a helpful term with which to explain Shakespeare's commercial and cultural value. With it, scholars can acknowledge that 'Shakespeare' has a symbolic function in the world separate from (if rooted in) the content of his plays. Indeed, as will be discussed below, it is so separable from the historical figure of Shakespeare that the notion of the 'Shakespeare brand' is something of a magnet for those who believe that 'Shakespeare' was the front for, rather than the author of, the Complete Works. It also enables scholars to consider how the range of associations 'Shakespeare' bears – from excellence to Englishness – are deployed in new, commercially profitable, ways, from the gift-shop goodies mentioned above to the worlds of academic publishing, employment and student recruitment. At the same time, though, the frisson of 'otherness' that Shakespeare scholars can find in the idea of the 'brand' can obscure the limitations of the term in understanding how Shakespeare's value is conferred and created in a fascinating collaboration between institutions and the market.

First, 'Shakespeare' is not, in fact, a brand. The word 'Shakespeare' might appear to be a locus of commercial activity, and of a wide range of perceptions, but it is not 'a trade or proprietary name'.[7] Despite Professor of Marketing Philip Kotler's expansive pronouncement that 'Everything is a brand: Coca-Cola, FedEx, Porsche, New York City, the United States, Madonna, and you – yes, you! A brand is any label that carries meaning and associations',[8] 'Shakespeare' still eludes this definition: while the name 'carries meaning and associations', 'Shakespeare', unlike 'Coca-Cola', 'Madonna', and even 'you', is neither a corporation, nor an individual, with any control over the presentation of those associations to the world.

No single organisation or individual (as Lanier acknowledges) is in control of the name 'Shakespeare', its products, or the revenue made from it. As such, 'Shakespeare' cannot properly be described as a brand, in the same way that, say, Coca-Cola, Nike or Apple can. Brand Finance's estimation that Shakespeare is worth $600 million treats 'book sales and downloads, paid attendance at theatre productions, box office and TV receipts from film productions, sale of Shakespeare branded goods, tourism revenue and the Shakespeare brand's contribution to the value of First Folios'[9] as if all the profits from these diverse products accrue to the same company, of which Shakespeare is the figurehead. The YouTube video 'The Shakespeare Brand and what it teaches marketers' similarly ascribes to 'Shakespeare' the agency of a coherent, decision-making commercial playwright, rather than a figure whose free-floating name is used in many and various ways by individuals and organisations for their own gain. While Leslie de Chernatony might proffer fourteen different interpretations of the word 'brand' (including 'logo', 'legal instrument' and 'cluster of values'), all of them concern the deliberate construction by an organisation of its identity. Even if, as de Chernatony acknowledges, some of the associations that later accrue to a brand are partly beyond organisational control (including consumers' images of, and relationships with, the brand), the organisation is in charge of establishing the brand image at the outset.[10]

The phrase 'Shakespeare brand' is, then, primarily metaphorical: to speak of 'the Coca-Cola of canonical culture' is more to draw a compelling analogy from the commercial realm than to suggest a precise equivalent for Shakespeare's annual turnover. (Indeed, it hints at wishful thinking: in the same year that Shakespeare's value was estimated at $600 million, Coca-Cola's was estimated at $31,082 million, a figure that still placed the corporation only eighth in the 2012 brand league tables behind Apple ($70,605 million), Google ($47,463 million) and Microsoft ($45,812 million.[11]) John Frow notes that, while the reproduced signature of an author might have much in common with a brand – not least because the dead canonical author represents in the present 'the state of quality assurance that defines the successful brand' – brand remains a 'corporate rather than a personal' signature, the result of a company marshalling the semiotics of its advertising, more intensely than in even the most commercialised use of authors' names.[12] 'Shakespeare' is indeed frequently 'marshalled' as a guarantee of 'quality' (or, as in the examples noted by Lanier above, in a form of jokey iconoclasm that pits Shakespeare's perceived quality against the cheap plastic 'celebriduck'), but by numerous separate organisations and individuals: it remains a name, and a set of associations, rather than a brand in its own right. Even within his essay, though, Lanier moves quickly from *comparison* of author name and brand ('interesting *affiliations with* the phenomenon of branding') to self-conscious *conflation* of the terms ('the face of Shakespeare' has 'become' the 'trademark' of canonical culture).[13] Shakespeare is not literally a trademark, yet the name evidently enacts this function in a very compelling way.

At stake in the notion of the 'Shakespeare brand' is the question of how Shakespeare's value is constructed and conferred in commercial settings. The notion of the Shakespeare brand can tempt its analysts to see only the value that Shakespeare's name confers on other organisations and products. In doing so, it is easy to overlook the values that accrue to Shakespeare when his name is associated with a diverse range of new products. To question the notion of the Shakespeare brand, then, is not to suggest that Shakespeare is above all commercial concerns; nor is it to deny that 'brand' has a metaphorical function in business (where the word's literal meaning of a mark of ownership has become an abstraction). Rather, it is to observe that the use of the Shakespeare brand as a metaphor can mask the complex, interesting ways in which 'Shakespeare' functions and accrues value in the marketplace. This chapter argues that commercial organisations do not simply borrow value from Shakespeare and trade profitably on his name, but also 'co-produce' new kinds of meaning and value for Shakespeare in the market.

This two-way relationship is one that the critical language of reception and adaptation can struggle fully to describe. Reception studies are founded in key metaphors, from the passive image of 'reception' itself to the more politicised sense of seizure or 'hostile takeover'[14] in 'appropriation'. Julie Sanders has explored the potential of some alternative metaphors – such as, via Genette, the world of horticulture and its images of 'grafting', and of other natural phenomena such as 'filtration' and 'cross-pollination'.[15] With such terms she seeks to get past the 'linear and reductive' relationship between the source and the 'secondary, belated' response that some existing metaphors promote.[16] She eschews such linearity with borrowings from musicology (base and improvisation) and science (genetic inheritance and environmental adaptation), fully aware that these are metaphorical images, rather than literal descriptions:

> the Mendel–Darwin synthesis offers a useful way of thinking about the happy combination of influence and creativity, of tradition and the individual talent, and of parental influence and offspring, in appropriative literature, perhaps in all literature.[17]

What emerges from Sanders' call for a more 'dynamic', 'kinetic' and 'diverse' vocabulary is a strong sense of multiplicity: the need for a language that can encompass influence *and* creativity, tradition *and* the individual talent, rather than a mono-directional line of influence or appropriation; this desire is also visible in Christy Desmet's suggestion of a language of mutual 'donation' or dialogue.[18]

As a metaphor, 'brand' holds out the possibility of such doubleness: seeing Shakespeare as marker and mark, exploited and all-conquering, at once already meaningful, and made meaningful by his deployment. 'Brand' is particularly illuminating as a metaphor if it helps us not simply to describe new instances of Shakespeare's presence in the marketplace, but also to see productive tensions within his name that can in turn generate what Sanders calls a desirable 'tension of expectation and surprise'[19] in his appropriations. Furthermore, the doubleness of 'brand' as a metaphor can usefully complicate the simple linearity of the 'value chain' – in which cultural products pass through a commodity stage and into consumption – and gesture towards a more intricate relationship between the cultural good and the market, in which value is produced.

Ultimately, though, to speak of a 'Shakespeare brand', rather than of the range of organisations that deploy the word 'Shakespeare' in their own corporate identities, is often to occlude unwittingly the work that those organisations do to generate the valuable *impression* of a Shakespeare brand. The brand valuation research that resulted in the declaration that Shakespeare was worth $600 million was, in fact, commissioned by Sony to promote the release of the film *Anonymous*, in order to make the thrilling conjecture that Shakespeare's impressive value might have shaky foundations.

> This value could be based on a falsehood. If it were proven that William Shakespeare was not the author of the works that have been credited to him, the value of the Shakespeare brand would decline.[20]

Sony asserts that the inauthenticity of the author is a threat to his brand value, even as his products, including films by Sony, have travelled far beyond his authorial control, both in time and around the world. The box-office success of their film paradoxically depends both on the possibility of his inauthenticity, and on the continued 'value of the brand'. This is just one, very literal, example of how it materially benefits a company to talk of the 'Shakespeare brand', but the phenomenon is widespread. 'Shakespeare' might not be controlled by one commercial organisation, but it has served a range of organisations well – from the Tonson publishing cartel in the eighteenth century to the RSC in the twenty-first – to seem as if they are desirable products of an overarching Shakespeare brand, even as they developed their own commercial identities. The next part of this chapter shows how organisations have generated, to their own benefit, the powerful impression of a Shakespeare brand, downplaying to a certain extent their *own* identity in order to work in the name of Shakespeare.

Co-producing the 'Shakespeare brand'

There might be no such thing as a 'Shakespeare brand', but what we can observe at work in the marketplace is the powerful *idea* of such a brand. This impression is generated by the organisations that treat 'Shakespeare' as a guarantor of the quality of their own products. This next part of the chapter argues that the Shakespeare brand is an impression retrospectively constructed by the organisations that appropriate and deploy Shakespeare's name for their own purposes.

This impression of a 'Shakespeare' brand has a long history. His commercial deployment has often not only contributed to the success of a new enterprise, but simultaneously constructed the impression of a larger Shakespeare 'brand' that legitimates that new enterprise. After the early, opportunistic collections of plays 'Written by W. SHAKESPEARE' and bound together by printers after his death,[21] the 1623 First Folio was one of the first commercial enterprises to trade on the image of a coherent 'Shakespeare' to endorse numerous plays at once: John Heminges and Henry Condell emphasised that they were uniting for the first time disparate plays they had 'collected' together under the authenticating name of 'Mr William Shakespeare's Comedies, Histories and Tragedies'. While the Folio might benefit from its deliberate similarities with the 'serious'[22] and 'up-scale'[23] packaging of other, classical authors (see also Chapter 5) and of Ben Jonson, Shakespeare's works appear, at the same time, to be self-legitimating. The Folio creates the image, both visually, in the Droeshout portrait, and verbally, in its numerous dedicatory prefaces and poems, of a 'Shakespeare' who presides posthumously over the 'works', and whose absent-presence, like that of an admired but long-dead classical author, is the guarantee of their quality. As Heminges and Condell claim, 'before, you were abused with divers stolen and surreptitious copies, maimed and deformed by the frauds and stealths of injurious impostors that exposed them, even those are now offered to your view cured and perfect of their limbs, and all the rest absolute in their numbers, as he conceived them'.[24] Proximity to Shakespeare's own intentions, symbolised by the repeated presence of his visual image and name, is the signal of their value; and his face and name effectively their 'trademark'.

As a 'trademark', though, the memorable clarity of the Droeshout portrait is challenged by the verbal images that surround it: Ben Jonson's poem evokes a more protean 'Shakespeare' whose image morphs rapidly between the earthly 'Swan of Avon' and the celestial 'constellation' and 'star of poets'.[25] It is, however, precisely this elusiveness that means that 'Shakespeare' is increasingly located by the Folio in the works themselves: 'Read him'. 'Shakespeare' becomes at once brand and product – or, to pick up the ambiguity in early definitions, and in Shakespeare's own uses of the word 'brand', the act of marking ('Brand not my forehead with thy piercing light' (*Rape of Lucrece*)), and the mark itself ('Thence comes it that my name receives a brand' (Sonnet 111)).[26] Hemings and Condell might remind the reader of their considerable efforts to purge textual error from the works (now 'cured and perfect of their limbs'), but they also, more modestly, downplay their intervention in Shakespeare's work ('who only gather his works and give them you'). By doing so, they reinforce the impression that the complete works are at once the product and the symbol of an overarching Shakespeare brand.

This impression of a Shakespeare brand is expanded and confirmed in the early eighteenth century with the sequential production of sharply differentiated Shakespeare editions by the Tonson family, who became 'one of the eighteenth century's most formidable publishing houses', and 'the primary publishers of all of the major editions of Shakespeare produced in the first seven decades of the century',[27] and who, at the height of their monopoly, 'built up a controlling interest in Shakespeare that was eventually to reach about 65 per cent'.[28] Dugas suggests that the early Shakespeare editions were marketed as products of the already desirable Tonson brand: 'the edition of 1709 was specially packaged for the customers the Tonsons knew so well, customers who believed what they were buying was a high-quality product because it carried the Tonson imprint on its title-page'.[29] Dugas very much underplays, however, the significance of a fascinating act of conflation whereby the Tonsons adopted 'Shakespeare's head' as their trademark, merging their own brand with their chief product, to create the impression of a 'Shakespeare' brand that legitimated their work.[30] This 'brand' sanctioned the publication of closely related and, in the case of Alexander Pope and Lewis Theobald, apparently competitive, products, all marketable in the name of reaching ever closer to the emerging standard of 'Shakespeare'.

In 1769, the jubilee celebrations staged by celebrity actor David Garrick in Shakespeare's honour in Stratford-upon-Avon performed that most valuable work of brand extension: detaching a brand name from its primary products in order to permit the development of new ones.[31] Three days of pageantry, songs and poems were held in Shakespeare's honour, but, as critics almost invariably observe, no performances of his plays were staged. Centring on the dedication of the town's new statue of the playwright, the event was built around the celebration of Shakespeare's image and, only to a much lesser extent, his words: unlike the publishing tradition, the jubilee detached the name and person of 'Shakespeare' from its most obvious products. The souvenir medallions and tickets that replicated the image of the statue, and the unfeasibly inexhaustible supply of trinkets supposedly carved from the mulberry tree that he planted at New Place, commemorated Shakespeare's image in new products, in a way that anticipates the tourist souvenirs still retailed in the town. The jubilee confirmed the impression of the 'immortal Shakespeare's' 'transcendence',[32] not just over the rain-soaked and muddy festivities in Stratford that seemed to some commentators to be unworthy of his greatness, but also over his own works.

What all of these early commercial enterprises have in common is the attempt to generate the impression that Shakespeare is above monetary concerns. From the First Folio's claim that the collection is compiled 'without ambition of self-profit or fame, only to keep the memory of so worthy a friend alive as was our Shakespeare',[33] to the 'god of our idolatry' celebrated in Garrick's *Jubilee Ode*, these enterprises appear to lift Shakespeare above the mundanity of their own commercial goals, yet in such a way that makes him ultimately more profitable. Garrick was criticised in the contemporary press for exploiting his jubilee visitors: satirical verses like 'so long as the world's full of nifeys and ninneys,/My mulberry-box will be full of good guineas' suggested that he was only out to make money out of the gullible Shakespeare pilgrims he attracted to Stratford.[34] Yet the very suggestion that Garrick's commercial motives are unworthy of Shakespeare serves to elevate the playwright. Bristol has observed that 'paradoxically it is the belief in Shakespeare's transcendent worth that underwrites his currency in popular culture and secures his commercial value',[35] yet, as these examples suggest, transcendence is created in the market. While it might seem as if Shakespeare was a cultural icon that companies have subsequently commercialised, it is clear that the processes of making Shakespeare an icon and making him appear to be a brand actually happened in tandem. Even if the makers and admirers of *Anonymous* would be all too eager to agree, it is nonetheless true to say that cultural and commercial processes are entwined in the production of Shakespeare's value.

The impression of a Shakespeare brand is effectively 'co-produced' by the commercial and cultural organisations that each deploy his image as if it were their trademark. A term that describes how value is created by the service industries, 'co-production' has been used by marketing analysts to talk, for example, about the way that multiple organisations in a particular town or city work together in the pursuit of 'destination marketing', or the 'branding of places as tourism destinations'. A place is

> comprised of an amalgamation of individual services, such as shopping and sports centres, theatres and museums as well as infrastructural services such as road and rail networks. The place product is therefore co-produced by a multiplicity of autonomous organisations, both public and private.[36]

'Co-production' refers here to the 'amalgamation' of multiple contributions – 'shopping and sports centres, theatres and museums' – to a 'place brand'. It can also helpfully articulate the way in which 'Shakespeare' is constructed by the operation of a range of commercial and cultural organisations. They, not Shakespeare, are brands, but, even as they compete with one another, they help to generate the impression that 'Shakespeare' is an overarching brand that legitimates all their products.

The twenty-first-century 'destination marketing' of Stratford-upon-Avon and its locale provides an excellent example of how the impression of a Shakespeare brand continues to be constructed and deployed to market very different products. The act of 'amalgamation' is exaggerated when 'place marketers ... work together and combine two or more places together in order to provide a more attractive offer'. 'Shakespeare Country' is the trading name for 'South Warwickshire Tourism Ltd', a company whose marketing remit covers not only Stratford-upon-Avon, but also the towns, villages and countryside of the surrounding area:

> Spend time in Shakespeare Country and leave with your own wonderful story to tell. You'll be sure to find something for everyone when you plan your short break or holiday in Shakespeare Country. Visit Stratford-upon-Avon – home of William Shakespeare, historic Warwick and Kenilworth with two of the most magnificent castles in English history and Royal Leamington Spa with its superb shopping in stunning Regency setting. Take time to explore the rolling green countryside of Warwickshire, dotted with an array of historic towns and villages. Journey to the south of Shakespeare Country and explore the Cotswolds with its classic landscape of honey coloured cottages and gentle hills with dry stone walls and grazing sheep.[37]

Shakespeare Country uses 'Shakespeare' to unite as a destination the disparate offerings of Stratford and a number of other Warwickshire towns. While Shakespeare could conceivably have visited the area's 'magnificent castles',[38] his connection to the anachronistic 'superb shopping' and 'stunning Regency setting' of Leamington, and even to the agricultural landscape of the Cotswolds, is more tenuous. Nonetheless, his authorial reputation serves to unite these locations and activities in a coherent, romantic narrative for visitors to take away. This amalgamation is vividly enacted in the simple viral computer game devised for 'Shakespeare Country', in which players help Romeo seek out Juliet in Stratford, passing, in the foreground, Shakespeare's houses, and, in the middle distance, Warwick and Kenilworth castles. 'Shakespeare' is proffered as an umbrella brand that confers value on all the products within a geographical area – much as the National Trust confers value on all the disparate places and activities in the UK that bear its name, while also accruing value from the aesthetic and historical significance of the properties it owns. Partly, 'Shakespeare Country' is an extension of the nostalgic rural aesthetic that has connected Shakespeare to the Stratford countryside since the eighteenth century.[39] But just as adjectival praise like 'magnificent', 'superb', 'stunning' and 'classic' is transferred across from the discourse of Shakespeare's excellence to confer value on a range of anachronistic retail and leisure experiences, so too does 'Shakespeare' accrue from those diverse, up-to-date products a wider range of positive meanings, now associating the theatrical offerings of Stratford-upon-Avon with other enjoyable leisure experiences for those who have never visited the town, or who last did so unwillingly on a long-forgotten school trip to the RSC.

Once elevated above the individual organisations in this way, the 'Shakespeare brand' seems untouched by commercial failure in any one of them. Just as Heminges and Condell distinguished between 'the reputation his, and the faults ours',[40] and the muddy disaster of the 1769 jubilee appeared to fall short of the 'immortal Shakespeare', so commercial failure ironically serves rather to emphasise his elevated, abstract status. When, in 2010, 'Shakespeare Country' went into administration after local-authority funding was withdrawn, its failure was attributed to changing technology and global economic crisis, and not to the weakness of the 'Shakespeare' brand. Likewise, undistinguished productions or film adaptations of Shakespeare's plays – including the allusively titled pornography listed under 'Film Spin-Offs and Citations' in Richard Burt's encyclopedia of Shakespeare in popular culture[41] – are not generally taken to diminish the strength of the 'Shakespeare' under whose name they apparently trade.

The same is true of the numerous, less obviously related UK organisations that bear 'Shakespeare' in their name. Particularly prevalent in Stratford-upon-Avon (Shakespeare Marquees Ltd, Shakespeare Taxis) and in the surrounding area (Shakespeare Coffee Company, Bidford-upon-Avon; Shakespeare Removals, Kinwarton; Shakespeare Beds, Tyseley, Birmingham – which comes with a tagline of 'what dreams are made on' and a claim that 'Like the Bard himself the classic designs will live on for many years'),[42] these titles can be found further afield, too, from Shakespeare Karaoke in Sheffield, to Shakespeare's Landscapes (complete with black letter font and 'Taming of the Shrub' tagline[43]) in Bognor Regis, as well as in the names of numerous pubs across the country. That reviewers have said of the US company Shakespeare Fishing Tackle that 'Thirty years ago Shakespeare may have been number one for producing great tackle, but over the last ten years I can't help but feel they let their position slip'[44] does not, one imagines, reflect negatively on the reputation of the early modern author, nor of other organisations that share his name. It serves these organisations well to treat 'Shakespeare' as a legitimating brand that confers prestige on distinctly unliterary products. At the same time, the name 'Shakespeare' gains from these organisations a cumulative impression of continued currency and cultural centrality.

Shakespeare versus brand

We have seen that culture and the market work hand in hand to produce the impression of a Shakespeare brand, even if some of these commercial combinations sound like rather unlikely destinations for 'Shakespeare'. Other organisations, however, go further still to trade on this very unlikelihood, building their identity around the perception that Shakespeare is the opposite of the market. A 1980s advert for Carling Black Label lager traded very obviously on the perceived high-culture/popular-culture gulf between Shakespearean theatre and football (and, by extension, mass-produced lager) when a performance of Hamlet's speech to Yorick's skull descended into a stage kickabout with that iconic prop.[45] Exploiting this contrast, Shakespearean speech (and reference to high birth, in 'my noble lord Hamlet') was tightly juxtaposed with sporting colloquialism ('over 'ere, son, on me 'ead'), and the advert cut back and forth between Hamlet and Horatio's raucous goal celebrations and the polite shock of the refined inhabitants of the expensive box into which the skull was kicked. Encapsulating this opposition, the final still saw a stony, august bust of Shakespeare wrapped in a football scarf, next to a pint of Carling Black Label: the national poet meets the national sport and, Carling hope, the national drink. The entire advert was constructed out of a palette of clear opposites: football vs theatre, upper- vs working-class, high culture vs mass culture, received pronunciation vs Cockney English, philosophical musings vs plain speaking. The final refrain, common to all adverts in this series, of 'I bet 'e drinks Carling Black Label' admired the Hamlet actor's transgressive ability to break out of these stuffy cultural confines and enjoy a no-nonsense, commercially manufactured drink.

The simplistic opposition between culture and commerce in this 1980s advertisement is, however, difficult to maintain today. To separate the two is to revert to a false division of iconic, high culture and grubby commerce that has recurred at least since the late eighteenth century, but that is not, as John Frow observed in 1995, 'tenable in the twentieth century', as a wider range of modes of cultural production and a new array of groups, niches and interests challenge the stratification of cultural goods by class and status.

High culture is fully absorbed within commodity production. The relation to the market can therefore not be used as a general principle of differentiation between high-cultural and low-cultural products, nor is it any longer possible to employ the traditional value-laden opposition between the disinterested, organic, original, self-governing work of art and the interested, mechanical, formulaic, and commercial mass-cultural text. Works of high culture are now produced in exactly the same serial forms as those of low culture: the paperback book, the record or disk, film, radio, and television (where there now exist specifically high-cultural channels).[46]

According to Frow, the degree of relationship of a cultural good to the market is no longer the determiner of its status as high or low, art or mass-produced commodity. Their modes of production are so entwined as to render this a false distinction. Indeed, recent developments in digital culture suggest that new technologies for cultural goods often aspire to the cachet of earlier forms – the Kindle to the feel and appearance of the book, for example.

Nonetheless, the perceived opposition between 'high culture' and 'commodity production' remains tremendously compelling in the twenty-first century. In a postmodern world where, as branding analysts imagine, 'former barriers fall, sacrosanct boundaries dissolve, irreconcilable opposites are successfully reconciled'[47] this distinction might seem to have less force. But in marketing (which speaks of 'brand culture') as much as in literary and cultural studies (which speaks of the 'Shakespeare brand'), that sense of oxymoronic opposition persists. As Lanier notes, with reference to ironic novelty Shakespeare spin-offs, we should not underestimate the 'recuperative capacity of stratificational schemes and the residual usefulness of connotations of exclusivity, learnedness, and quality long attached to the Shakespeare trademark'.[48] No matter how entwined these realms might be in actuality, the *perceived* gulf between culture and commodity production, cultural icon and brand, remains very potent.

Bridging the perceived gulf between culture and commerce is a particular desire for many commercial brands who seek a 'cultural' status for their work. Recent studies, for example, liken those who work with brands to 'cultural intermediaries', suggest that 'branding is an ancient cultural practice akin to telling stories and forming identity groups', and describe branding as a 'cultural process'.[49] In a more outright declaration of aspiration, an Arts and Business report recently declared that 'The world of business is fast realising that creativity is too valuable to be left to the creatives', and urged that the arts, and their 'ideas', could help businesses to break through 'the sometimes formulaic manner of management thinking' and to be more responsive to 'these globally competitive, fast moving and often disruptive times'.[50] All of these aspirational visions construct 'culture' as a creative, compelling and engaging 'other' to a somehow limited or prosaic realm of commerce.

One can observe very clearly the way in which aspiration reinforces this opposition in Douglas Holt's *How Brands Become Icons*, which asks how certain brands, at certain moments, achieve the resonance more naturally associated with iconic cultural figures. Eschewing older marketing techniques such as 'mind share' and 'emotional' marketing, as well as more recent tools like 'viral' marketing, Holt proposes a new model of 'identity branding' in which successful brands, like icons, manage to address the collective anxieties or identity needs of a group or nation at a certain time in history. This impossible-sounding task comes with such unlikely edicts as

> To become an icon, a brand must not only target the most advantageous contradiction in society, but also perform the right myth, and in the right manner.[51]

Brands are encouraged to engineer for themselves the cultural resonance of icons, whose glittering success he holds just out of reach: 'In terms of myth performances, brands can never compete with films, politicians, or musicians. Even the best sixty-second ad (say, Nike's "Revolution" or Apple's "1984"), can't compete with John Wayne's films, Ronald Reagan's speeches, or Kurt Cobain's songs and concerts'.[52] Holt doesn't allow for the possibility that these and other cultural figures from literature, television and film might be just as carefully produced as brands; nor, conversely, that their resonance with particular cultural moments might be equally hit-and-miss (not least when they are successful precisely *because* they are used in advertisements, as evidenced in the 1991 compilation CD of *Levi's 501 Hits*). With talk of 'breakthrough performances', brand 'authors', and 'stories' people buy, he aspires to the authorial control, affective punch, and perceived cachet that he imagines lie tantalisingly on the other side of the culture/commerce divide. In so doing, he ironically continues to uphold – to strengthen, even – the perceived distinction between culture and the market.

Yet it is precisely the imagined opposition between the realms of culture and commerce that is a source of productive tension, and can be deployed to new creative ends; and it is for this reason that they are still perpetuated in modern culture. Almost thirty years after the Carling Black Label advert aired, one might imagine that its comic opposition of high and low might have lost some of its force, for the reasons Frow outlines above and more. Indeed, a 2010 advert for the energy drink Red Bull seems to blur the categories of culture and commerce: the cartoon figure of Shakespeare paces his study, fulsomely testing out lines that might soon become *Hamlet*, but his facility with words suddenly falters when his can of Red Bull is cleared away by a serving maid. He sighs, 'and the rest is silence, it seems', before glumly signing his name, and ruefully reflecting in a final voiceover as the product shot fills the screen that 'genius does suffer without Red Bull'.[53] Cultural icon and commercial product might be closely entwined rather than, as in Carling, at odds, but for the humour of the advert to work it is essential that Shakespeare seems to be above such mental props: with an iconoclasm only slightly more subtle than Carling's, the advert trades off the imagined irony of Shakespeare's immortal genius being entirely dependent on a mass-produced and anachronistic commercial product, and it hams up Shakespeare's posh voice and florid phrases for comic contrast. For all the blurring of boundaries of 'high' and 'low' culture, advertisers are still creatively exploiting the comic sense of transgression that comes with having a cultural icon implicated in a commercial brand.

To contrast Shakespeare's established cultural status with the 'realities' of the commercial pressures that shaped his work is both a long-running comic trope and a stimulus for creativity. In a *Blackadder*-based sketch for the fundraising comedy show Comic Relief, Shakespeare's crowd-pleasing editor, played by Rowan Atkinson, exhorts him to 'trim some of the dead wood' – the soliloquies – out of *Hamlet* because 'it's boring, Bill', and 'it's the ghost that's selling this show at the moment'. Hugh Laurie's Shakespeare only reluctantly agrees to edit down the original soliloquy he had penned for Hamlet to the over-compressed 'gibberish' of 'To be, or not to be', in order to please 'Joe Public' and get 'bums on seats'.[54] The speech often casually regarded as the epitome of Shakespeare's genius is humorously imagined to be the by-product of heavy cutting for a tough-to-please market, and despised by

Shakespeare himself; Shakespeare, the sketch jokes, is forced like all long-suffering writers to obey the market. Of course, it is only Shakespeare's posthumous reception that placed the working playwright and actor beyond such practical and commercial concerns, elevating him to the status of 'god of our idolatry' and making his dependence on that market seem comically sacrilegious.

The creative exploitation of this perceived transgression has persisted even through the major shake-up of cultural categories attributed to the Internet, and, in particular, to Web 2.0.[55] The capacity of online spaces to allow individuals as well as organisations idiosyncratically to collide and combine 'Shakespeare' with other cultural and commercial symbols seems to some highly liberating, building on the hope expressed in the twentieth century that mass culture might not be a force for homogenisation, but rather a 'rich iconography, a set of symbols, objects and artefacts which can be assembled and reassembled by different groups in a literally limitless number of combinations'.[56] To claim, as some do, that 'cultural commodities are catalyst, not product; a stage in, not the destination of, cultural affairs'[57] is a defiant challenge to the passivity of mass consumption.

New technology – from retweeting companies' messages on social media to personalising commercial products through 3D printing – has reinvigorated a discourse in which people can seize control of brands for their own ends.[58] In such spaces, 'Shakespeare', like other more commercial symbols, can function as raw material for new kinds of creative self-expression and appropriation. Yet some critics have contended that, even in this seemingly free creative space, consumers are still controlled by market forces.[59] Indeed, by encouraging individuals to self-identify with a product, viral marketing lets a company's most active consumers do its marketing work for them, willingly or otherwise; they are even 'put to work in the production of forms of content that can be sold back to them'.[60] Internet companies such as Amazon and Google, social networking sites such as Facebook and Twitter, and supermarket loyalty cards such as the Sainsbury's Nectar card and Tesco Clubcard turn individuals' ready expressions of consumer choice into invaluable and ever more refined data about personal preferences.

In this new branding landscape, the most successful brands are said to be those with 'projectibility': that is, blank and malleable enough to have the priorities of numerous social groups projected on to them. The expressionless cartoon cat 'Hello Kitty' is adopted both by children (in earnest) and by adults (with irony), to astounding global success. Likewise, Red Bull, as Walker notes, is *deliberately* indistinct enough to be variously the province of kiteboarders, computer-gaming teams, extreme sports players and late-night ravers – and, as the Shakespeare advertisement shows, budding writers – and, as a result, leads a $3.7 billion energy-drink industry. The cultural figures wittily imagined to rely on Red Bull, including Shakespeare and Isaac Newton, extend this impression of Red Bull's indispensability into intellectual and creative activity. However, in the advertisement discussed above, it is not so much Shakespeare's adaptability or 'projectibility' as the entirely *familiar*, even clichéd, set of stock associations – inspiration, genius, eloquence, high culture – that provides raw material for the advert's creativity. Rather than embracing its freedom from previously restrictive categories, the advertisement simply riffs in new ways on the contrast between old divisions of high and low, culture and commerce.

For all that the Internet might do to challenge such boundaries, then, this perceived opposition looks set to be a source of creative tension for some time to come. What new technology has in fact transformed is the scale on which these tensions can be exploited – now effectively limitless. Nicelyturned, for example, is a blog-based piece of creative work commissioned for the RSC's 'MyShakepeare' project in celebration of the World Shakespeare Festival. Its designer, Emma Wolukau-Wanambwa, set out to 'collate and re-present quotations, allusions and references to Shakespeare's plays and Shakespeare's characters at work in contemporary culture – primarily within affluent Western societies', and the result is a montage of images of commercial products with Shakespearean names: Coriolanus trinket trays, Ophelia maternity wear, Demetrius lamps and Hamlet shoes.[61] Whether these names are thought to have been emptied of meaning by these acts of commercial appropriation in 'affluent Western societies', or to have accrued new meanings through these commercial combinations, is not overtly stated. The project primarily finds wit and, by sheer repetition, art, in the conflation of lighting, cars and clothing with their high-cultural names, perhaps implicitly comparing its own witty creativity to the more flat-footed appropriations of Shakespeare by these mass producers. Gathered en masse, these appropriations seem endless.

On an even larger scale, *Shakespeare in Love* is an extended exploitation of the perceived incongruity between Shakespeare's iconic status and the commercial 'reality' of his working life: deadlines, writer's block, a vexed professional relationship with Christopher Marlowe, and a less-than-sublime draft of *Romeo and Ethel the Pirate's Daughter*. The film challenges the audience's expectations of an iconic Shakespeare by plunging him into the chaotic state of harassment brought on by these commercial challenges, before ultimately restoring him to the reassuringly inspired figure who voices the opening lines to *Twelfth Night* as the credits roll. Critics suggest that the makers of the film see themselves 'not as iconoclasts or vulgarians, but as conservers or restorers intent on breaking down the cultural encrustations that have made Shakespeare '"highbrow", rarefied, effeminate, and boring'.[62] But for all that it purports to merge these categories, the sense of contrast between high and low is carefully maintained. The film's publicity material trades on the fact, for example, that the writing team brings together the 'high cultural theatrical expertise' of Tom Stoppard with Marc Norman's experience of 'Hollywood blockbusters'.[63] Emma French argues that 'the most successful filmed Shakespeare adaptations are those that effectively blur traditional binaries between high and low, art and commerce, and British heritage and Hollywood popular film in their marketing', in an act of 'hybridisation' that seeks to 'secure the broadest possible audience for the films'.[64] Baz Luhrmann's *William Shakespeare's Romeo + Juliet*, she contends, 'challenges the traditional binary between high and low culture' even in the inclusion of the plus sign in its title. It would be more accurate to observe that, in in their marketing as much as in their content, highly successful film adaptations like *Romeo + Juliet* (whose associated online educational materials say of early modern theatre that 'it was crass, and it was business. It was art, and it was genius') and more recent animated products like *Gnomeo and Juliet* ('Shakespeare's legendary tale ... as you've never seen it before'), deliberately reassert the boundaries of art and commerce, in order creatively to exploit the possibilities of transgression.[65]

Even academic studies of Shakespeare's relationship with commercial culture, then, appear to exploit the shock value of the perceived opposition between culture and commerce. From *Big-Time Shakespeare* and *The Shakespeare Trade* to the more recent *Selling Shakespeare to Hollywood* and *Marketing the Bard* (and even the title of this chapter), their titles are presented as if oxymoronic; Dugas even juxtaposes the florid calligraphy of 'Bard' with a more linear, computer-generated font for 'Marketing' on his cover. While they might not share the severe critique of commercialisation inherent in titles like Herbert Schiller's *Culture, Inc.* (which argues that corporate control of museums, theatres, performing arts centres and public broadcasting represents 'a broad manipulation of consciousness as well as an insidious form of censorship'), or Debora Silverman's *Selling Culture* (which describes commercially sponsored art exhibits as thoughtlessly displayed assemblages without context), these titles share the same provocative polarity. It is an irony of academic studies in this field that, in seeking to overturn the false distinction between culture and commerce, and, particularly, to avoid critiquing the latter,[66] many critics nonetheless build on, and even reinforce, that perceived tension.[67]

Working with the Shakespeare brand

The broad commercial uses of Shakespeare's name described above cast light on those organisations, including the Royal Shakespeare Company and Shakespeare's Globe Theatre, that work more directly with Shakespeare's plays. To speak of a 'Shakespeare brand' can often be to overlook the work that such organisations do to perpetuate the impression of that brand, and the values at stake in that work. Organisations like the RSC and the Globe both benefit from, and confer added value upon, the name of Shakespeare, at once gaining, like many other unrelated organisations, from the sense that 'Shakespeare' authorises their work, while simultaneously creating new value through the production of a rich variety of new interpretations for their audiences. Yet their relationship with the 'Shakespeare' brand is a complex one. Chapter 7 explored the double manoeuvre by which the organisations offered themselves as free sources of Shakespearean value and creativity through their digital presence, but also worked hard to show that their organisation in particular was the physical site of Shakespeare's value. Here, we see how such organisations at once assert themselves as a brand in their own right, and also play down their own commercial success, stressing for their own very particular reasons that it is 'Shakespeare', and not they, who is the brand.

This doubleness is evident in RSC's response to the results of a

UK survey that they conducted in order to collect perceptions of their brand. They were pleased with the results: at least 80% of people were aware of the RSC's name. They were encouraged, too, by the associations the RSC's name triggered: 'high quality', 'successful' and 'entertaining' were the most popular selections from a range of possible responses.[68] One result, though, was greeted more cautiously; 40% of the public deemed the RSC 'upmarket' – a perception that, as Mary Butlin, Head of Market Planning at the RSC noted, most companies would be thrilled by, evoking as it does an aspirational level of quality and desirability. As a publicly funded organisation, though, receiving around £14m of taxpayers' money per year, the RSC has a remit to engage with new, young and minority audiences. Being perceived as 'upmarket', as Butlin explains, risks seeming exclusive rather than accessible, and undermining their espoused role of making 'Shakespeare for all'.

'Upmarket' evokes such expensive brands as Tiffany & Co. and Mercedes, targeted at high-income customers.[69] Brands like the Royal Shakespeare Company and the BBC promote their own kind of high production values, the RSC adding value to audiences' experience of Shakespeare through their investment in rigorous actor training and innovative set design. Yet (also like the BBC) they cannot easily make similar claims to being a luxury good, because their partial reliance on public funding, and the responsibility to reach the widest possible audience, complicates what it means to be a highly successful brand. Even if their inclusion of 'upmarket' in their list of multiple-choice responses suggests that they are to some extent courting this perception as well as rejecting it, the RSC must carefully navigate the poles of desirable brand and valued public service, aspirational luxury good and non-rival public good.[70] As shall be discussed below, however, the RSC's commercial sponsors are far less fazed by the potentially 'upmarket' connotations of the organisation.

The distinction between brand and public service is further complicated by the fact that state and market are not always seen as opposites: it has in recent decades been the state's intervention in the arts – through, for example, the establishment of the Arts Council of Great Britain, and the subsidising of theatre and museums – that has been blamed by some critics for commodifying culture, because of its strong sense of the kinds of value (economic, social or otherwise) that culture should produce. Clive Gray describes the twentieth-century political process that turned the arts into 'commodities that can be judged by the same economic criteria that can be applied to cars, clothes or any other consumer good', by valuing them as 'products of public service',[71] and Robert Hewison blames in particular the 'value for money' edicts of the Thatcher government of the 1980s for creating a climate that encouraged traditional cultural organisations to think of themselves as commercial brands; he greets with horror the 1985 decision of the director of the Victoria and Albert Museum to accept and 'capitalise on what is a more market-oriented society' by merchandising products based on the designs in the gallery, in the hope that 'the V&A could be the Laura Ashley of the 1990s'.[72]

This notion of commercial branding might, for many such critics, be anathema to culture, but Shakespeare's apparently opposite status as a public good can in fact be one of his most lucrative qualities, and his state-supported role in education and theatre makes him profoundly marketable. 'Upmarket' is, as Butlin observed, an association that would delight many other organisations; and the blend of public service and high production values in the RSC's work can attract the attention of very different kinds of organisation keen to associate their work with both of those qualities. The RSC's 'I Cinna' project, written and directed by Tim Crouch as part of the 2012 World Shakespeare Festival, foregrounded an anguished minor character from *Julius Caesar*, and enlisted the help of its young audience to explore the powerful potential of words on the blank sheets of paper provided. To reach beyond its immediate theatre audience, though, it incorporated the work of multiple external organisations:

> On 2nd July 2012, Janet will enable a groundbreaking collaboration between Royal Shakespeare Company, CISCO and Ravensbourne to bring theatre online and live straight to the classroom.[73]

This one-off event, in which the 'I Cinna' performance would be beamed direct to '3000 UK schools', was a collaborative effort between very different kinds of organisation: the Royal Shakespeare Company, the students of Ravensbourne College, Janet (or ja.net; an organisation that provides computer network services to education and research) and CISCO Systems (a multinational corporation that, according to its Google tagline, is 'the worldwide leader in networking that transforms how people connect, communicate and collaborate').

Apart from the practical advantages of helping to broadcast a live event to a very wide audience, this collaboration conferred mutual benefits on all companies involved. Janet added value to the RSC's product, and helped to further the company's educational mission, by co-production: their technology enabled the large-scale broadcast of the production. In return, the RSC project functioned as marketing for Janet's products: 'Our new streaming network works well with our 100 Gbps core fibre network'. The RSC gained financial sponsorship and global profile by its collaboration with the major corporation CISCO; by return, the multinational organisation had the opportunity to see its abstract mission statement of transformative networking and collaboration enacted in an appealing and obviously educationally enriching project, within a high-prestige cultural organisation. This collaboration, and the new models of philanthropic funding it contains, is not so much a value-chain as a complex, mutually beneficial production of new value by commercial and cultural organisations in the name of 'Shakespeare'.

Commercial sponsorship reminds us that, to CISCO and Janet, the RSC is indeed a very desirable and 'upmarket' brand, just as the Globe is to Deutsche Bank and the British Museum is to BP. Being attractive to wealthy commercial sponsors is an enabling condition of these institutions' work. If the notion of the 'Shakespeare brand' has just one use, it is to call attention to the work these specifically Shakespearean organisations do to nurture their own distinctive and attractive 'brand' while seeming to serve in the name of Shakespeare.

In the World Shakespeare Festival – a central part of the Cultural Olympiad that brought together the work of the RSC, the BBC, the British Museum, the Globe, and a host of other arts and cultural organisations in celebration of the playwright's creativity – the name of 'Shakespeare' appears to be a powerful brand. First, 'Shakespeare' is a globally recognisable symbol of English literature, history, culture and nation, and provides an obviously iconic, and usefully politically neutral, figurehead for the 2012 host country of the Olympic Games. Second, Shakespeare is a widely acknowledged and ever-current symbol of 'excellence', a term that, as the Department for Culture, Media and Sport has frequently found to its benefit, can be just as easily applied to the stage as to the track.[74] As such, Shakespeare is called upon to represent the values not only of the United Kingdom but also of the Olympic Games.[75] His high educational status translates into Olympic rigour and challenge and aspiration: in the 'Globe to Globe' festival on Bankside, the feat of attending all of Shakespeare's plays in sequence was presented as an endurance event in which the hardiest 'Yard Olympians' would be rewarded, if not with medals, then with a sliding scale of laurels from free drinks and backstage tours to a copy of the Complete Works signed by all Festival participants.[76] Above all, 'Shakespeare' most resembles a brand at the World Shakespeare Festival because that single name seems to unite all the endeavours of the various organisations taking part in the festival, however disparate their actual contributions and profits. The Olympic-scale event transcends countries, and also transcends the range of organisations that bear or work in Shakespeare's name, as well as a number of corporate and funding bodies including BP and Arts Council England. It gives the powerful impression that they are cooperating in service of a higher goal, namely the 'extraordinary celebration' of Shakespeare.

The celebratory, unifying notion of 'festival' can obscure, however, the important transactions necessarily at work in this festive space. Within the World Shakespeare Festival, Shakespeare's Globe Theatre's 'Globe to Globe' festival, in which thirty-seven of Shakespeare's plays were performed in thirty-seven languages, was made possible by funding from LOCOG (the London Organising Committee of the Olympic and Paralympic Games), with some embassy and airline support to bring companies to London. The participating companies were each given a fee (of varying size), and their travel and accommodation paid for. As the festival director Tom Bird explained, programming choices were 'negotiated' with the companies, and the whole festival attracted valuable first-time audiences from a wide range of London communities.[77] To point out these elements is not cynically to expose the commercial forces at the heart of a cultural festival, but rather to draw attention to the complex combination of public support (via LOCOG), commercial investment (BP), one-off Olympic celebration and the ongoing demands of running the Globe that together shaped the festival. Even bold and politically controversial moves like the invitation of Israel's Habima Theatre, or even of minority groups in the form of Deafinitely Theatre, a professional, deaf-led company, might be read as having not only socio-cultural significance but also marketability, whether directly through the box office, or in terms of attracting funding for inclusiveness.

The notion of the 'Shakespeare brand' is relevant in this festival because, often, Shakespeare's name was all that audiences had to conjure with. The translation of his plays into multiple languages at once stretched the name of 'Shakespeare' to encompass new content, and, for non-speakers of the destination language, removed Shakespeare's language from his plays altogether. Reviewers of the World Shakespeare Festival repeatedly commented that audience comprehension of the new language in which the plays were performed was not a priority; and the Globe chose not to use their surtitles to provide Shakespeare's words, or even back-translate the new versions into English, but rather to summarise each scene.[78] Losses in verbal complexity or nuance were compensated for by the beauty and emotion of the new, unfamiliar language; and the distancing effects for native audiences were, as Laera notes, potentially valuable. What remains of 'Shakespeare' is narrative, or, as the Globe's marketing material expresses it, 'a carnival of stories', in which his plots are elided with the 'inspirational stories' of the theatre companies themselves.[79] The 'Shakespeare' brand, founded in Shakespeare's reputation as a teller of universally recognisable human stories, comes to encompass 'the stories, the characters and the relationships, which are etched into all of us'.

Within this imaginary 'Shakespeare brand', though, are the multiple, and very real, Shakespeare-related brands and organisations that took part in the festival. Organisations like the RSC and the Globe might both benefit from and confer new value on 'Shakespeare', but they are also prestigious brands in their own right, and powerful magnets for actors and audiences. In 2011, the RSC ran an 'Open Stages' festival in which numerous amateur dramatics companies competed for the prestige of being able to perform on the company's stage, suggesting the aspirational pull of the RSC brand for actors and audiences; more recently, it successfully filed trademark invalidity proceedings against an Austrian company that tried to appropriate its name. The Court of Justice of the European Union ruled that 'the CTM ROYAL SHAKESPEARE would take unfair advantage of, or be detrimental to, the distinctive character or the repute of its earlier trade marks, which were well known in the United Kingdom'.[80] The 'CTM RSCROYAL SHAKESPEARE COMPANY had an "exceptional" reputation in the United Kingdom', but not to the point of exclusivity. The Austrian company's appeal that the RSC's theatre products were targeted at a limited audience was rejected by the court, who stated that 'access to theatres was available to all and, in theory, thanks to affordable prices, to the average consumer', and so the trademark would have a strong association in the minds of the wider public, too.

These organisations have considerable symbolic power as brands in their own right, for both actors and audiences. Paula Garfield, director of the Deafinitely Theatre Company, whose 'Globe to Globe' contribution was the first Shakespeare play to be performed entirely in British Sign Language, spoke in interviews of the big break that acting at the Globe Theatre represented for deaf actors; the venue seemed more significant than Shakespeare for its potential to confer prestige and recognition on the participants. Audiences at the festival were also reassured that visiting international companies 'will play the Globe way', with no sets, no recorded music, and completing their performance 'within two and a quarter hours'.[81] 'The Globe way' is a kind of quality control: diverse international visitors are packaged within the known brand of the Globe, reassuringly guaranteeing audiences a certain level of quality, enjoyment – and even authenticity – that legitimates the unusual productions they come to see.

'Shakespeare' can symbolise both England and the world, and the festival rehearses that elaborate dance of local and global that, as Michael Dobson and Barbara Hodgdon have both observed, has been performed in Stratford-upon-Avon since the eighteenth century.[82] Yet, for all its expansiveness, the festival is ultimately a reassertion of ownership, from the closing, patriotic performance of *Henry V* by the Globe's own ensemble of actors, to the declaration in the festival's marketing that 'Shakespeare's coming home',[83] an echo of the musical refrain 'football's coming home', that wistful declaration of supremacy repeated every time the England team engages in international competition. Though the connection between the national sport and the national author is made here once again, it is, crucially, the Globe, rather than England, that is claiming to be the rightful 'home' of Shakespeare. When the Globe declares that it has invited 'artists from all over the globe, to enjoy speaking these plays in their own language, in our Globe', the word 'our' could refer to the nation, but it more likely refers to the commercial organisation, and reminds others of the generosity of their invitation. It must not be forgotten, of course, that competition with other providers in the

World Shakespeare Festival, a project officially led by the RSC, is at work in these claims for ownership. But when viewed cumulatively, from 'our Globe' and 'the Globe way' to the RSC's reminder that the overall festival is 'produced' by them, these assertions make it clear that the authorising figure of the World Shakespeare Festival – the brand, or signature, for the event – is not actually 'Shakespeare'; instead, it is the well-established organisations that bear, add value to and create new value in his name. In the festival, as in twenty-first-century culture more widely, Shakespeare's value is not corrupted by commercial forces, but is continually co-produced by brands and institutions in an increasingly complex dance of the ultimately inseparable forces of culture and the market.

Notes

1 Tim Heberden, managing director of Brand Finance in Australia, quoted in 'Shakespeare's brand worth valued at $600 million – double the combined value of Elvis and Marilyn', *Campaign Brief*, 07.03.12. www.campaignbrief.com/2012/03/version10-starthtml0000000149-176.html (accessed 14.06.13).
2 Brad Berens, 'The Shakespeare Brand and What It Teaches Marketers in 2011: Part II of II', www.youtube.com/watch?v=W_idQtXctDw (accessed 14.06.13).
3 Doug Lanier, 'Shakespeare^{TM}: Myth and Biographical Fiction', in Robert Shaughnessy, ed., *The Cambridge Companion to Shakespeare and Popular Culture* (Cambridge: Cambridge University Press, 2007), pp. 93–113 (p. 93).
4 Barbara Hodgdon, *The Shakespeare Trade: Performances and Appropriations* (Philadelphia: University of Pennsylvania Press, 1998), pp. 232–240.
5 Lanier, 'Shakespeare^{TM}', p. 98.
6 Lanier, 'Shakespeare^{TM}', p. 93.
7 In 'brand, n.', *OED Online*, www.oed.com/view/Entry/22627 (accessed 14.06.13).
8 Philip Kotler, 'Brands', in *Marketing Insights from A to Z: 80 Concepts Every Manager Needs to Know* (Hoboken, NJ: John Wiley & Sons, 2003), p. 90.
9 'Shakespeare's Brand Worth Valued at $600 Million'.
10 Leslie de Chernatony, *From Brand Vision to Brand Evaluation: The Strategic Process of Growing and Strengthening Brands*, 2nd edition (Oxford: Butterworth-Heinemann, 2006), pp. 27–61.
11 http://brandirectory.com (accessed 18.06.12).

12 John Frow, 'Signature and Brand', in Jim Collins, ed., *High-Pop: Making Culture into Popular Entertainment* (Malden, MA: Blackwell Publishers, 2002), pp. 56–74.
13 Lanier, 'Shakespeare™', p. 93.
14 Julie Sanders, *Adaptation and Appropriation* (London and New York: Routledge, 2006), p. 9.
15 Sanders, *Adaptation and Appropriation*, pp. 12–13.
16 Sanders, *Adaptation and Appropriation*, p. 12.
17 Sanders, *Adaptation and Appropriation*, p. 156.
18 Christy Desmet, 'Paying Attention in Shakespeare Parody: From Tom Stoppard to YouTube', *Shakespeare Survey* 61 (2008): 227–238 (p. 227).
19 Sanders, *Adaptation and Appropriation*, p. 25.
20 Brand Finance report quoted in 'Sony gets creative marketing Shakespeare film', *B&T*, 07.03.12, www.bandt.com.au/news/marketing/sony-gets-creative-marketing-shakespeare-film (accessed 14.06.13).
21 See Andrew Murphy, *Shakespeare in Print: A History and Chronology of Shakespeare Publishing* (Cambridge: Cambridge University Press, 2003), pp. 36–41.
22 Murphy, *Shakespeare in Print*, p. 42.
23 Bristol, *Big-Time Shakespeare*, p. 49.
24 John Heminges and Henry Condell, 'To the Great Variety of Readers', *Comedies, Histories and Tragedies* (1623), in Wells and Taylor, eds, *The Complete Works*, p. xlv.
25 Ben Jonson, 'To the memory of my beloved, The AUTHOR, MASTER WILLIAM SHAKESPEARE, AND what he hath left us', *Comedies, Histories, Tragedies* (1623), in Wells and Taylor, eds, *The Complete Works*, p. xlvi.
26 'The mark made by burning with a hot iron.'; 5. 'An iron instrument for making marks by burning' 'brand, n.', *OED Online*. www.oed.com/view/entry/22627 (accessed 14.06.13).
27 Murphy, *Shakespeare in Print*, p. 57.
28 St Clair, *The Reading Nation in the Romantic Period*, p. 154.
29 Don-John Dugas, *Marketing the Bard: Shakespeare in Performance and Print 1660–1740* (Columbia and London: University of Missouri Press, 2006), p. 159.
30 Dugas, *Marketing the Bard*, p. 166.
31 See Frow, 'Signature and Brand', pp. 64–5.
32 Dobson, *The Making of the National Poet*, p. 219. See also Kate Rumbold, 'Shakespeare and the Stratford Jubilee', in Fiona Ritchie and Peter Sabor, eds, *Shakespeare and the Eighteenth Century* (Cambridge: Cambridge University Press, 2012), pp. 254–276.
33 John Heminges, Henry Condell, 'The Epistle Dedicatory', *Comedies, Histories, Tragedies* (1623), in Wells and Taylor, eds, *The Complete Works*, p. xliv.

34 *The London Chronicle*, 15–17 August 1769, quoted in Johannes Stochholm, *Garrick's Folly: The Stratford Jubilee of 1769* (London: Methuen, 1964), p.38.
35 Bristol, *Big-Time Shakespeare*, p.90.
36 Graham Hankinson, 'The Management of Destination Brands: Five Guiding Principles Based on Recent Developments in Corporate Branding Theory', *Journal of Brand Management* 14(3) (2007): 240–254.
37 *Shakespeare Country*, www.shakespeare-country.co.uk (accessed 29.11.10).
38 Katherine Duncan-Jones suggests that 'as a boy of eleven Shakespeare himself probably witnessed some of the spectacular entertainments that took place outside the walls of Kenilworth Castle in the summer of 1575, when Robert Dudley, Earl of Leicester, entertained Elizabeth'. *Shakespeare: Upstart Crow to Sweet Swan, 1592–1623* (London: Arden, 2011), p.205. Helen Hackett notes that Walter Scott's novel *Kenilworth* fuels the persistent myth of Shakespeare and Elizabeth's connection by imagining Shakespeare attending the Kenilworth festivities as an adult. *Shakespeare and Elizabeth: The Meeting of Two Myths* (Princeton, NJ: Princeton University Press, 2009), p.55.
39 See Chapter 6, 'The Original Genius', in Bate, *The Genius of Shakespeare*, pp.157–186.
40 Heminges and Condell, 'The Epistle Dedicatory', p.xlv.
41 Burt, *Shakespeares After Shakespeare*, vol. 1, 'Film Spin-offs and Citations', pp. 132–365.
42 www.shakespearebeds.co.uk (accessed 14.06.13).
43 www.landscapes-shakespeares.co.uk/aboutus.html (accessed 14.06.13).
44 www.worldseafishing.com/reviews/rods/shakespeare-ugly-stik-6lb-class-review.html (accessed 14.06.13).
45 'My Noble Lord Hamlet'. The advertisement is also discussed in Holderness, ed., *The Shakespeare Myth*, pp.67–68.
46 Frow, *Cultural Studies and Cultural Value*, p.27.
47 Stephen Brown, 'Ambi-Brand Culture: On a Wing and a Swear with Ryanair', in Jonathan E. Schroeder and Miriam Salzer-Mörling, eds, *Brand Culture* (London and New York: Frank Cass, 2006), pp.50–66, p.51.
48 Lanier, 'Shakespeare[TM]', p.97.
49 Liz Moor, 'Branding Consultants as Cultural Intermediaries', *Sociological Review* 56(3) (2008): 408–428; Elizabeth C. Hirschman, 'Evolutionary Branding', *Psychology and Marketing* 27(6) (June 2010): 568–583; Jonathan E. Schroeder and Miriam Salzer-Mörling, eds, *Brand Culture* (London and New York: Frank Cass, 2006), Introduction, p.3.
50 Mat Hunter, 'Foreword', 'Beyond Experience: Culture, Consumer and Brand', *Arts and Business* (London: Arts and Business, 2010) http://

www.artsandbusinessni.org.uk/documents/2012-05-16-11-59-29-75-aandb_beyondexperience_exec_summary.pdf (accessed 14.06.13).
51 Douglas Holt, *How Brands Become Icons: The Principles of Cultural Branding* (Boston, MA: Harvard Business School Press, 2004), p.63.
52 Holt, *How Brands Become Icons*, p.60.
53 'Red Bull – Shakespeare', www.tellyads.com/show_movie.php?filename=TA10557 (accessed 30.11.10).
54 'Shakespeare Sketch: A Small Rewrite', www.youtube.com/watch?v=IwbB6B0cQs4 (accessed 14.06.13).
55 See the mixture of digital products that offer access to cultural goods, and invite more creative interaction with them, in John Wyver's '100 Reasons to be Cheerful', www.illuminationsmedia.co.uk/blog/index.cfm?start=1&news_id=872 (accessed 14.06.13).
56 Dick Hebdige, *Hiding in the Light: On Images and Things* (London: Routledge, 1988), quoted in Hewison, *Culture and Consensus*, p.288.
57 Paul Willis, *Common Culture: Symbolic Work at Play in the Everyday Cultures of the Young* (Boulder, CO: Open University, 1990), p.129.
58 See e.g. Leadbetter, *We-Think*.
59 See e.g. Herbert Schiller, *Culture Inc.: The Corporate Takeover of Public Expression* (Oxford: Oxford University Press, 1989). John Guillory, *Cultural Capital*, has argued that this power is not confined to the market, since educational institutions help to maintain the hegemonic control that confirms the social values of the dominant group.
60 Adam Arvidsson, *Brands: Meaning and Value in Media Culture* (London and New York: Routledge, 2006), p.104; Rob Walker, *I'm With The Brand: The Secret Dialogue Between What We Buy and Who We Are* (London: Constable, 2008).
61 http://nicelyturned.tumblr.com, within http://myshakespeare.worldshakespearefestival.org.uk/gallery/nicely-turned-by-emma-wolukau-wanambwa/#more-455 (accessed 14.06.13).
62 Michael Anderegg, 'James Dean Meets the Pirate's Daughter: Passion and Parody in *William Shakespeare's Romeo and Juliet* and *Shakespeare in Love*', in Richard Burt and Lynda E. Boose, eds, *Shakespeare, the Movie, II: Popularizing the Plays on Film, TV, Video, and DVD* (London: Routledge, 2003), pp.56–71 (p.70).
63 Emma French, *Selling Shakespeare to Hollywood: The Marketing of Filmed Shakespeare Adaptations from 1989 into the New Millennium* (Hatfield: University of Hertfordshire Press, 2006), p.138.
64 French, *Selling Shakespeare to Hollywood*, pp.2, 168.
65 A section on 'the Author' on the *R+J* website says of early modern theatre, 'It was crass. It was business. It was art. And it was genius. Shakespeare had the rhymes. Everyone knew it', www.romeoandjuliet.

Branding Shakespeare 239

com. (Quoted in French, *Selling Shakespeare to Hollywood*, who refers to this as another blurring of boundaries, p. 114.)

66 See e.g. French, *Selling Shakespeare to Hollywood*, p. 6: 'This book contends that a process of assimilation into rather than effacement of high culture in American mainstream popular culture is taking place in the marketing of filmed Shakespeare adaptations.'

67 Russell Jackson's Preface to French, *Selling Shakespeare to Hollywood*, reassures readers that 'By focusing so acutely on the "selling" of Shakespeare films, Emma French is not diverting attention from their artistic value, but drawing attention to an important component of it.' (p. x); and the back-cover quotations from Melvyn Bragg and John Carey comment on its consideration of 'high' and 'low' culture.

68 Mary Butlin, 'RSC Brand Values Research Executive Summary', 2010, presented at Chartered Institute of Marketing seminar, Stratford-upon-Avon, April 2010.

69 'Of merchandise, etc.: characteristic of or designed for the more expensive end of the market; superior, expensive, "quality"'. 'up-market, adj. and adv.', *OED Online*. www.oed.com/view/Entry/220019 (accessed 14.06.13).

70 'Q8a Please tell us which of these words or phrases you would use to describe RSC. Please click on as many or as few words as you wish, there are no right or wrong answers, it is just your personal opinion that we are interested in', Mary Butlin, 'RSC Brand Values Research Executive Summary', 2010.

71 Gray, *The Politics of the Arts in Britain*, pp. 6, 15.

72 'Towards a more consumer-oriented V&A', Victoria and Albert Museum press release, 31.10.85, p. 2, quoted in Hewison, *Culture and Consensus*, p. 269.

73 'Janet supports the World Shakespeare Festival production of I, Cinna (the poet)', *JANET News*, 15.05.12, www.ja.net/janetnews/tag/cisco (accessed 01.09.12).

74 'The excellence of our culture, sport and creative industries means that UK skills are in demand around the world': Department for Culture Media and Sport, 'What we do' > 'International', www.culture.gov.uk/what_we_do/international/default.aspx.

75 'Jacques Rogge, President of the International Olympic Committee, said: "As the Olympic torch receives the flame and is held aloft by the first Torchbearer, we are reminded through its light of the Olympic values of excellence, friendship and respect that it carries on its journey."' 'Olympic Flame lit for London 2012', *Department for Culture Media and Sport News*, May 2012, www.culture.gov.uk/news/news_stories/9052.aspx. Shakespeare's role in the Olympics themselves is more ambiguous. Voiced by Kenneth Branagh's Isambard Kingdom

Brunel in Danny Boyle's acclaimed Olympic opening ceremony, just before the 'green and pleasant land' is destroyed by the chimneys of industrialisation, Shakespeare represents both rural nostalgia and the language of progress; voiced by Timothy Spall's Winston Churchill in the closing ceremony, he is comfort against the 'noises' of war. Voiced by Ian McKellen in the Paralympic opening ceremony, Prospero's words take on tones of encouragement to aspiration; absent from its closing ceremony, the ambiguous function of his appearances is resolved into a larger trademark in a triumphal declaration by Sebastian Coe: 'London 2012: made in Britain'.
76 'Tickets', Globe to Globe website http://globetoglobe.shakespearesglobe.com/tickets (accessed 27.06.12).
77 Discussion with Tom Bird, 08.06.12.
78 Margherita Laera, 'In Praise of Translation: On Watching Shakespeare in a Foreign Language', *Year of Shakespeare*, posted 28 May 2012 http://bloggingshakespeare.com/year-of-shakespeare-in-praise-of-translation (accessed 07.06.12).
79 Shakespeare's Globe, *Globe to Globe: 37 Plays, 37 Languages* (London: Shakespeare's Globe, 2012).
80 'Victory for the Royal Shakespeare Company', *Osborne Clarke International Law Firm*, www.osborneclarke.co.uk/publications/services/litigation/insight/2012/victory-for-the-royal-shakespeare-company.aspx (accessed 14.06.13).
81 Shakespeare's Globe, *Globe to Globe*, p. 3.
82 Dobson, *The Making of the National Poet*, Chapter 5, 'Nationalizing the Corpus', pp. 185–222; Hodgdon, *The Shakespeare Trade*, Chapter 6, 'Stratford's Empire of Shakespeare; Or, Fantasies of Origin, Authorship and Authenticity: The Museum and the Souvenir', pp. 191–240.
83 Shakespeare's Globe, *Globe to Globe*, p. 2.

Afterword

The continuity of cultural value

Our account of cultural value in twenty-first-century England began with Tessa Jowell's 2004 personal statement about the 'complex arts'. It ends in the second decade of the new century when the fallout from the credit crunch has placed significant pressure on the capacity of the state to support not only culture but the fundamental services and benefits that have been regarded as their responsibility since the establishment of the welfare state. One view of the changing fiscal situation was vigorously summarised in an op-ed piece in the *Financial Times* in July 2010:

> For the past 13 years (the arts) have been drowning in dosh. In 1997, when a wannabe rock star got to invite a real one to Downing Street, the annual grant to the Arts Council was £186m. By the end of the party, two and a half months ago, it was £445m. In that time, the grant to the National Theatre increased by nearly 80%, the grant to the Royal Shakespeare Company by 89%, to the South Bank Centre by nearly 60%, and to the Serpentine by a whopping 243 per cent. Last year alone, the Tates gobbled up £57m in public funds. In 2001, museums and galleries were thrown open to every Tom, Dick and Gary. At the wave of a hand (and a cost of about £40m a year) they were as free as the air.[1]

Tessa Jowell's high-minded aspiration to manage cultural policy in ways that might address a national 'poverty of aspiration' had been replaced by the *Financial Times* writer's mockery of greedy cultural institutions carelessly squandering public money on 'every Tom, Dick and Gary'.

The tone and the sympathies of the two approaches to cultural value seemed diametrically opposed: a caricature of the different cultural values found at opposite ends of the political spectrum. Behind the muddle of random statistics (x% of what?)

and tendentious value judgements, the 2010 article nevertheless continued to reflect the familiar concerns over how the state was to negotiate the relationship between the costs of funding culture and the value of those who might benefit from it. 'Tom, Dick and Gary' presented another version of the denigrated 'mass' whose tastes Tessa Jowell had excluded from the attention of the state, and the *FT*'s list of greedy institutions overlapped with the high-culture organisations whose right to 'a share of the taxation pot' had been the subject of Jowell's anxious rhetorical questions.

Though the attendance of 'Tom, Dick and Gary' at museums did not apparently justify sustained funding, more deserving beneficiaries apparently did. The *Financial Times* piece went on to regret that private and commercial sponsors would be less likely to support

> the tiny arts organisation at the back of a library which organises poetry readings for pensioners, or the dance project for disaffected teenagers, or replacing the lighting rig at the local theatre.

It concluded with a gloomy list of

> Some £73m of cuts already decided by DCMS, including the cancellation of the £25m Stonehenge visitors centre; the suspension of the £12m libraries modernisation programme; cancelling the £45m contribution for a new BFI film centre; and axing free swimming for the young and the elderly.

The shape of the argument over cultural value revealed the continuities as well as the changes that had taken place since 2004. The rhetorical opposition between costs and value and the conflation of supply and demand continued to inform the discussion but the attention to the 'priceless' content of culture had shifted more firmly to its scope for creative engagement by particular groups of people. The anxiety about how to sustain performances of Shakespeare and Mahler had been replaced by concerns for vulnerable groups ('disaffected teenagers ... the young and the elderly') or the comfort and pleasure of 'visitors' to libraries and heritage sites. The state's responsibility for culture was now to be restricted to ordinary pastimes, located in a visitor centre attached to a historic monument, a modern library or a swimming pool.

The shift, that we identified in Chapter 6, from a view of culture as a special arena of social and intellectual activity to one that dealt with the commonplace, day-to-day leisure activities of the whole population was complete: 'the sacred frontier which makes legitimate culture a separate universe'[2] would no longer be defended; the 'way of life' of competing groups differentiated by ethnicity or class could be replaced by minimal attention to the requirements of what Kuper had called 'unhyphenated citizens'.[3]

The financial logic of diminished state funding had already reduced government responsibility for direct provision of specific cultural goods. As we discussed in Chapters 7 and 8, the established institutions of culture had already taken on the task of insisting on the intrinsic value of their competing products while managing the combination of state and commercial sector funding that would ensure their continued financial viability. The most powerful arts providers, the regularly funded organisations (RFOs), had built up organisational and management capacity during the boom years that would allow them to cope with a shift in funding sources. Writing in *The Guardian* in 2011, Mark Brown described the enormous success of the National Theatre's 2007 adaptation of Michel Morpurgo's 1982 children's novel *War Horse*:

> The £3m-a-year profit from the West End version more or less balanced a loss in grants from Arts Council England. The play is doing well in the US where the NT hopes to generate about £2m a year [Without this funding, the NT] could not have staged its epic production of Ibsen's *Emperor and Galileo* and it might not have put on the revival of Arnold Wesker's *The Kitchen* with its cast of more than 30.[4]

The same story could be told of the RSC 2011 children's show *Matilda*, which turned Roald Dahl's classic children's novel into a new musical that ran successfully in the West End, the regular transmission of Globe Theatre productions to 'Picture House' cinemas nation wide and the circulation of the 2009 RSC *Hamlet* on television and on DVD. The distribution capacity of new theatrical styles as well as new technologies combined with the supply-side organisations' new understanding of the growing market for high-quality cultural experiences had turned out to offer a more viable future for cultural organisations than government efforts to manage the alleged 'poverty of aspiration' of the demand side with limited funds at its disposal.

While continuing to use the high rhetoric of cultural advocacy that insisted on the absolute distinction between cultural value and economic value, creative arts managers have been engaged in negotiating value between 'priceless' works of art and the potential markets of customers with a taste for innovations in design and theatricality. They untangled the value-chain that separates production from distribution, asset value from purchase price, inalienable intellectual property from individual products. New techniques and technologies of market analysis developed by business corporations to understand actual consumer behaviour have been deployed to categorise the public less in terms of pre-existing categories of cultural groups and more in terms of their appetite for engagement with the arts. Like any private sector corporation, the RFOs can be clear about their stakeholders' response to the particular products that they had developed and their scope for increased market share. As Perry Anderson had observed in the closing years of the old millennium,

> The dissolution of frontiers between high and low genres in the culture at large … answered to a different logic. From the start, its direction was unequivocally populist. But it also expressed a new relation to the market – the extent to which this was a culture of accompaniment rather than antagonism, to the economic order.[5]

Reductions in state funding had accelerated the impetus towards the changes that Anderson described. They had been accompanied by a wider distrust of expert authority or any claim to value that did not acknowledge the importance of individual choice. By separating the economic conditions of production from the value of the customer experience, practitioners and managers could sustain the connection between the 'priceless' work of art and the inalienable personal or collective experience that assured its significance. That personal experience would not necessarily be shared by individual spectators. As Kennedy reminds us, every audience will include 'the unwilling spectator, the reluctant spectator, the spectator in a bad mood or feeling poorly, the accidental spectators, the snoring spectator'.[6] It was more the case that the idea of 'experience' had become the new proxy that could act as the authorising marker of cultural value.

Adapting the organisational methods and partnerships of the commercial sector has been critical for the growth and success of the cultural institutions. These supply-side innovations have also significantly altered the products that are included in the new cultural economy. By digging deep into the cultural assets of museums and the material brought to light by academic research in the humanities,[7] the range of material included in culture has been extended well beyond the early twentieth-century canon of the best that has been thought and said. However, by shifting the locus of intrinsic value from the product to the audience, as we described in Chapters 5 and 6, the content of the object or performance needed to be transformed into experiences that would be immediate, arresting and, above all, contemporary. Their appeal might include a connection to history (of Assyrian kings or sucket forks or *Troilus and Cressida*), but that history has to be the history of the present. It can represent a more intense and eloquent version of recognisable social situations ('it's the morning after the night before. Leontes' mind is twisted' as the e-marketing for the new RSC production of *The Winter's Tale* announces[8]) or it can make the link, as the British Museum exhibition of 'Shakespeare's restless world' did, via such abstract conceptualisations of the history of modernity as 'international trade, colonialism and diplomacy'.

Priceless cultural assets from history and from the whole world were the foundations of cultural value but the resources to support the additional work of interpretation and presentation were also put at risk by the changing economic situation. Commenting on the 2012 Royal Academy exhibition on 'Constable, Gainsborough and the Making of Landscape', John Barrell noted that

> It is so evidently a show for the Age of Austerity, a show of our favourite artists intended to raise as much money as possible for as little as possible ... the exhibits are all taken entirely from the collections of the cash-strapped Academy itself, and its explanatory and interpretative resources are very thin – a little pamphlet in lieu of a catalogue, a very few interpretation boards, and a hard to find list of exhibits.[9]

The exhibition's curators had tried to make the most of their limited resources by publicity that connected the best-known paintings directly to the audience, with an invitation to 'fall in love all over again with three giants of British landscape painting'. But as Barrell tartly observed, the publicity 'reflecting no doubt a worry about the possible effects on the gate ... neglects to say that its chief, bold focus is on printed works.'[10] Those printed works were not intrinsically less valuable than the work of the more familiar 'giants' – Barrell's own unrivalled knowledge of landscape prints makes a powerful case for their significance – but their value in the social context of the twenty-first century and for the non-specialist viewer depends, as with all cultural provision, upon the resources that add value in the long and complex process that links the non-rival good to its social existence in time and place.

It was this decline in the resources to transform the non-rival value into contemporary culture that provoked the most controversy over government cuts. In the course of an eloquent critique of the government cuts to higher education, the Cambridge scholar Stephan Collini asserted,

> It is worth insisting that what we call 'the humanities' are a collection of ways of encountering the record of human activity in its greatest richness and diversity. To attempt to deepen our understanding of this or that activity is a purposeful expression of human curiosity and ... an end in itself.[11]

Collini's critique of the fiscally driven decision to raise tuition fees, and thus transfer some of the costs of higher education from the state to the students,[12] reiterated the consensual distinction between economic considerations and the cultural value that was 'an end in itself'. The value of the humanities resided both in its intrinsic characteristics as 'the record of human activity' and its connection to an intrinsically human 'curiosity'. For an established scholar and his students with unrivalled access to 'the record of human activity', there was no gap between those assets and the small-scale, 'human' experience of engaging with culture. For those concerned to sustain those assets through conservation, to ensure their connection to increasing numbers of students through appropriate curricula and to distribute them world wide through new technologies, questions of how best to resource the chain of additional value required inevitably arise. The solution to those questions of management and dissemination had, since the second world war, been a matter of endorsing a sub-set of the record of human activity as highly valued and finding public resources to sustain and distribute them. In the new millennium, the debate over government funding of education and the arts had made the gap between the expanded store of non-rival cultural goods and their distribution on the scale of the whole population both visible and problematic. Analysts of cultural value had addressed this problem head-on; organisational managers had used ingenious financial and management techniques to make their particular organisations sustainable; but rhetorical advocacy for the priceless character of the arts and the essentially human character of their value retained its eloquent and powerful emotional authority.[13]

The complex value-chain that creates the conditions for culture is still seldom explicitly discussed in the public discussion of cultural value. Advocacy on behalf of 'culture' is more inclined to admire its contribution to the economy,[14] using a sum arrived at by the aggregation of indicators such as turnover of cultural organisations and the number of people employed by them. At the same time other advocates of culture continue to deplore its 'commodification' and insist on its non-market value without considering the costs of sustaining all the workers who create, renew, analyse and advocate on its behalf or acknowledging the macro-economic conditions of surplus that have created the fundamental conditions for any social production of culture.

The celebration of cultural value, however, continues to be located outside the market. The transactions that made it possible have already taken place: the cultural object has already been produced, marketed and distributed, or in the case of 'priceless' objects, collected, studied, conserved and reproduced. The moment of consumption may surprise, disappoint, intrigue or sustain the consumer; it may make him or her a fan who will follow that kind of work as it is presented in cultural venues across the globe; it may be used to educate children or structure the consumer's future social life. Establishing its value, however, remains problematic because of the continuing power of the fantasy of 'free' culture.

And Shakespeare?

The continuing difficulty of establishing the value of cultural goods produced, distributed and consumed in complex contemporary markets applies as much to 'Shakespeare' as to other forms. Shakespeare, we have argued, is developed and distributed as a cultural good within a chain of value-added by agents from markets, institutions and technologies of distribution (including books and stages). Though the cultural value of his works increasingly depends upon the added value of performance for their most accessible form, the plays also exist in printed form which allows repeated, revised and adapted forms of the work, with varying degrees of value added. The work of scholars, both historically and in the recent past, serves to establish and dis-establish the status of particular versions of Shakespeare so that any particular performance or edition can be aligned (or not) with an elusive, imagined, authentic and perfect version that provides an impetus for innovation and discursive distinction among them.

Individual experiences of Shakespeare in multiple forms remain impossibly diverse to categorise and quantify: they disappoint and please just as other forms of cultural production do. Advocacy for their value, however, unlike the claims for the value of culture more generally, can return to the ability of an idealised and elusive 'Shakespeare' to represent the significant connection between the actions of human beings and their meaning. The narrative form of the plays and the characters' poetic commentary on the events they experience provide the potential to engage an audience through the management of a structured emotional reaction to its events. Though their setting in early-modern England limits the scope of behaviour and reflection that the plays can represent – they have nothing to say about the experience of living in a technologised, bureaucratically managed democratic consumer society – it is precisely this limited scope that allows them to appear as paradigms of essential human interaction.

In the world of a Shakespeare play, events have consequences and the characters' metaphorical commentary articulates the emotional and the ethical significance of their connection. Because the narratives are structured by conflict and often involve multiple plots, the connection between action and commentary seldom arrives at settled conclusions about 'mourning and melancholy', or 'value' or 'power', so the plays both dramatise uncertainty and provide eloquent poetic statements of quite contradictory ethical positions. Consequently, Shakespeare's plays not only stage debates over value, they also provide an open field in which individual views about the characters behaviour can be given free rein. The discussion of characters' behaviour in a Shakespeare play may fulfil the same social function in face-to-face groups as similar discussions in relation to soap opera or, as we suggested in Chapter 5, *The Sopranos*, but in the case of Shakespeare it comes with the authority of cultural status, reinforced by metaphorical language that extends the scope of its application beyond the day-to-day.

'Shakespeare' thus has the potential to exist in the 'free' space of small-scale face-to-face culture of everyday pastimes – the pub discussion, the fan group or the amateur theatre society – while at the same time providing a resource for the market in cultural goods that ensures the continuity of the idea of 'Shakespeare' in the culture of reproduced 'priceless' artistic treasures. 'Shakespeare' can thus provide a potential to integrate the oppositions that inform the debate over cultural value, resolving the oppositions between excellence and access, acting as spokesperson from the past to the present, a source of complex universal meaning and the occasion for immediate experience, a locus of transcendent value and as an exemplar of the role of effective business practices in managing cultural markets.

Shakespeare, the long dead early-modern maker of plays, of course, does no such thing. It is the 'Shakespeare' constructed by the discourse of value on whose behalf these effects are claimed. The claimed effects hold in place the unstable characteristics of value by the social processes that allow individuals to recognise the potential for value in the non-rival texts, confer added value through the work of interpretation and reproduction, and endorse that value in the consensus of engagement that has come to replace the authority with which value was asserted by cultural leaders. At this point in the twenty-first century, this 'Shakespeare' can appear with a panoply of commentary and annotation in an academic editions or in the full dress of lavishly designed theatrical performance. 'He' can also appear without his language, and even without his narrative, recognisable only in the combination of a moving statue and a sheep, or a bald head, a skull and a book.

These diverse roles of 'Shakespeare' in contemporary culture have been sustained by more than a century of publically funded education and more than half a century of state investment in the arts. Whether and in what form they will continue, as the cohering role of the state is splintered into competing service-delivery brands and the unifying myth of 'the way of life of a particular people living together in one place' is replaced by overlapping groups defined by taste, remains to be seen.

Notes

1 Christina Patterson, 'Is there Room for Art in the Big Society?', *Financial Times*, 21.07.10, pp. 3–4.

2 Bourdieu, *Distinction*, p. 6.
3 Discussed in Chapter 4, p. 90.
4 Mark Brown, 'Ever-Lucrative War Horse Covers the Theatre's Lost Grants', *The Guardian*, 04.10.11, p. 11.
5 Perry Anderson, *The Origins of Postmodernity* (London and New York: Verso, 1998), p. 63.
6 Kennedy, *The Spectator and the Spectacle* (2009), p. 13.
7 For example, television productions routinely feature academic classists such as Mary Beard or social historians such as Amanda Vickery who has brought stories from eighteenth-century court records to both narrative and documentary forms. See Amanda Thorpe, 'Mary Beard, the Classicist with the Common Touch', *The Observer*, 29.04.12, www.guardian.co.uk/theobserver/2012/apr/29/observer-profile-mary-beard (accessed 07.01.13), and 'Men Uncovered in Amanda Vickery's New Radio 4 Series', www.qmul.ac.uk/media/news/items/hss/80296.html (accessed 07.01.13).
8 Email circulation 04.01.13 linked to enews@royalshakespearecompany.org.
9 John Barrell, 'The Virtues of Topography', *London Review of Books* (03.01.13), p. 17.
10 Barrell, 'The Virtues of Topography', p. 18.
11 Stephan Collini, 'Impact on the Humanities', *Times Literary Supplement* (13.11.09).
12 In practice, the transfer was from government funding to a quasi-independent loans company, a technical fix that removed the costs from government fiscal limits while recovering the returns from students over an extended period.
13 The analytical impasse over cultural value is clear from the ongoing debates, consultation and research hosted and funded by the Arts Council. See, for example, http://blogs.culture.gov.uk/main/2012/01/welcome_to_the_priceless_blog.html (accessed 14.06.13).
14 For the most recent example see the *World Cities Culture Report*, published 04.09.12, www.worldcitiesculturereport.com (accessed 06.09.12).

Bibliography

Agnew, Jean Christophe, *Worlds Apart: The Market and the Theatre in Anglo-American Thought, 1550–1750* (Cambridge: Cambridge University Press, 1986).

Anderegg, Michael, 'James Dean Meets the Pirate's Daughter: Passion and Parody in *William Shakespeare's Romeo and Juliet* and *Shakespeare in Love*', in Richard Burt and Lynda E. Boose, eds, *Shakespeare, the Movie, II: Popularizing the Plays on Film, TV, Video, and DVD* (London: Routledge, 2003), pp. 56–71.

Anderson, Perry, *The Origins of Postmodernity* (London and New York: Verso, 1998).

Anderson, Perry, 'A Culture in Contraflow', Part 1, *New Left Review*, 180 (1990): 41–78; Part 2, *New Left Review*, 182 (1990): 85–157.

Appleby, Joyce, *Economic Thought and Ideology in Seventeenth Century England* (Princeton, NJ: Princeton University Press, 1978).

Archer, Ian W., *The Pursuit of Stability: Social Relations in Elizabethan London* (Cambridge: Cambridge University Press, 1991).

Arnold, Matthew, *Culture and Anarchy and Other Writings*, ed. Stefan Collini (Cambridge: Cambridge University Press, 1993).

Arts Council England, *What People Want From the Arts* (London: Arts Council England, 2008).

Arvidsson, Adam, *Brands: Meaning and Value in Media Culture* (London and New York: Routledge, 2006).

Auslander, Philip, *Liveness: Performance in a Mediatised Culture*, 2nd edition (Abingdon: Routledge, 2008).

Barber, Karin, 'Improvisation and the Art of Making Things Stick', in *Creativity and Cultural Improvisation*, ed. Elizabeth Hallam and Tim Ingold. ASA Monographs 44 (Oxford and New York: Berg, 2007), pp. 25–41.

Barber, Karin, *Africa's Hidden Histories: Everyday Literacy and Making the Self* (Bloomington: Indiana University Press, 2006).

Barrell, John, 'The Virtues of Topography', *London Review of Books* (03.01.13): 17–18.

Bate, Jonathan, *Public Value in the Humanities* (London: Bloomsbury Academic, 2011).
Bate, Jonathan, *Soul of the Age: The Life, Mind and World of William Shakespeare* (London: Viking, 2008).
Bate, Jonathan, *The Genius of Shakespeare* (London: Picador, 1997).
Bate, Jonathan, *Shakespearean Constitutions: Politics, Theatre, Criticism 1730–1830* (Oxford: Clarendon Press, 1989).
Beck, Catriona, *The Birmingham Shakespeare Library*, MA thesis in librarianship, University of Sheffield 1974. Unpublished copy held in the Shakespeare collections of the Birmingham Shakespeare Library.
Belfiore, Eleonora, 'Determinants of Impact: Towards a Better Understanding of Encounters with the Arts', *Cultural Trends* 16(3) (2007): 225–275.
Belfiore, Eleonora and Oliver Bennett, *The Social Impact of the Arts: An Intellectual History* (Basingstoke: Palgrave Macmillan, 2008).
Benjamin, Walter *The Work of Art in the Age of Mechanical Reproduction*, trans. J. A. Underwood (London: Penguin, 2008).
Bennett, Susan, *Theatre Audiences: A Theory of Production and Reception* (London: Routledge, 1997).
Berland, Jody and Shelley Hornstein, eds, *Capital Culture: A Reader on Modernist Legacies, State Institutions, and the Value(s) of Art* (Montreal: McGill-Queens University Press, 2000).
Biggart, Nicole Woolsey, *Readings in Economic Sociology* (Oxford: Blackwell, 2002).
Bohm, Steffen and Chris Land, 'No Accounting for Culture? Value in the New Economy' Working Paper No WP 07/08 (University of Essex School of Accounting Finance and Management, November 2007).
Bolter, Jay David and Richard Grusin, *Remediation: Understanding New Media* (Cambridge, MA: The MIT Press, 2000).
Boulton, Jeremy, *Neighbourhood and Society: A London Suburb in the Seventeenth Century* (Cambridge: Cambridge University Press, 1987).
Bourdieu, Pierre, *The Field of Cultural Production: Essays on Arts and Literature*, ed. R. Johnson (Cambridge: Polity Press, 1993).
Bourdieu, Pierre, *Distinction: A Social Critique of the Judgement of Taste*, trans. Richard Nice (London: Routledge, 1979).
Bray, Alan, *The Friend* (London: University of Chicago Press, 2003).
Bristol, Michael, *Big-Time Shakespeare* (London: Routledge, 1996).
Brook, Peter, *The Empty Space* (London: McKibbon and Kee, 1968).
Brown, Stephen, 'Ambi-Brand Culture: On a Wing and a Swear with Ryanair', in Jonathan E. Schroeder and Miriam Salzer-Mörling, eds, *Brand Culture* (London and New York: Frank Cass, 2006, pp. 50–66).
Bunting, Catherine, *Public Value and the Arts in England: Discussion and Conclusions of the Arts Debate* (London: Arts Council England, 2007).
Bunting, Catherine, *The Arts Debate – Arts Council England's First-Ever*

Public Value Inquiry: Overview and Design (London: Arts Council England, 2006).
Burt, Richard, *Shakespeares After Shakespeare: An Encyclopedia of the Bard in Mass and Popular Culture*, 2 vols (Westport, CT: Greenwood Press, 2007).
Burt, Richard, 'To E- or not to E-? Disposing of Schlockspeare in the Age of Digital Media', in Richard Burt, ed., *Shakespeare After Mass Media* (New York: Palgrave, 2002), pp. 1–32.
Burt, Richard and Lynda E. Boose, eds, *Shakespeare, the Movie, II: Popularizing the Plays on Film, TV, Video, and DVD* (London: Routledge, 2003).
Carey, John, *What Good Are the Arts?* (London: Faber and Faber, 2005).
Carey, John, *The Intellectuals and the Masses: Pride and Prejudice among the Literary Intelligentsia 1880–1939* (London: Faber and Faber, 1992).
Chernatony, Leslie de, *From Brand Vision to Brand Evaluation: The Strategic Process of Growing and Strengthening Brands*, 2nd edition (Oxford: Butterworth-Heinemann, 2006).
Clarke, John, *Framing the Arts: The Role of Cultural Institutions* (Birmingham: University of Birmingham, 1975).
Clifford, James, *The Predicament of Culture: Twentieth Century Ethnography, Literature and Art* (Cambridge, MA: Harvard University Press, 1988).
Collini, Stephan, 'Impact on the Humanities', *Times Literary Supplement* (13.11.09).
Collins, Richard, *Public Value and the BBC: A Report Prepared for The Work Foundation's Public Value Consortium* (London: Work Foundation, 2007).
Connor, Steven, *Theory and Cultural Value* (Oxford: Blackwell, 1992).
Cragg Ross Dawson, *The Arts Debate: Research among Stakeholders, Umbrella Groups and Members of the Arts Community* (London: Cragg Ross Dawson, 2007).
Creative Research, *The Arts Debate: Findings of Research among the General Public* (London: Creative Research, 2007).
Cunningham, Stuart, 'Cultural Studies from the Viewpoint of Cultural Policy', in Justin Lewis and Toby Miller, eds, *Critical Cultural Policy Studies: A Reader* (Oxford: Blackwell Publishing, 2003), pp. 13–22.
Denning, Michael, *Culture in the Age of Three Worlds* (London: Verso, 2004).
Department for Culture, Media and Sport, with the Department for Business, Enterprise and Regulatory Reform and the Department for Innovation, Universities and Skills, *Creative Britain: New Talents for the New Economy* (London: Department for Culture, Media and Sport, 2008), www.culture.gov.uk/images/publications/CEPFeb2008.pdf.

Desmet, Christy, 'Paying Attention in Shakespeare Parody: From Tom Stoppard to YouTube', *Shakespeare Survey* 61 (2008): 227–238.
Distiller, Natasha, *Shakespeare and the Coconuts* (Johannesburg: Witswatersrand University Press, 2012).
Dobson, Michael, *Shakespeare and Amateur Performance: A Cultural History* (Cambridge: Cambridge University Press, 2011).
Dobson, Michael, *The Making of the National Poet: Shakespeare, Adaptation, and Authorship, 1660–1769* (Oxford: Clarendon Press, 1992).
Dugas, Don-John, *Marketing the Bard: Shakespeare in Performance and Print 1660–1740* (Columbia and London: University of Missouri Press, 2006).
Duncan-Jones, Katherine, *Shakespeare: Upstart Crow to Sweet Swan, 1592–1623* (London: Arden, 2011).
DuPlessis, Robert S., 'Capital Formations', in Henry S. Turner, *The Culture of Capital* (London: Routledge, 2002), pp. 38–42.
Eagleton, Terry, *After Theory* (London: Penguin Books, 2004).
Eagleton, Terry, 'Capitalism and Form', *New Left Review*, 14 (2002): 123–136.
Eagleton, Terry, 'Afterword', in Graham Holderness, ed., *The Shakespeare Myth* (Manchester: Manchester University Press, 1988), pp. 202–208.
Eisenstein, Elizabeth, *The Printing Press as an Agent of Change* (Cambridge: Cambridge University Press, 1979).
Eliot, T. S., *Notes Towards a Definition of Culture* (London: Faber and Faber, 1948).
Featherstone, Mike, *Consumer Culture and Postmodernism* (London: Sage Publications, 1991).
Febvre, Lucien and H. J. Martin, *The Coming of the Book: The Impact of Printing 1450–1800*, trans. David Gerard (London: New Left Books, 1976).
Fekete, John, 'Introductory Notes for a Postmodern Value Agenda', in John Fekete, ed., *Life after Postmodernism: Essays in Value and Culture* (London: Macmillan, 1988), pp. 1–23.
Fiske, John, 'Popular Discrimination', in James Naremore and Patrick Brantlinger, eds, *Modernity and Mass Culture* (Bloomington and Indianapolis: Indiana University Press, 1991), pp. 103–116.
Flacks, Richard, *Making History: The American Left and the American Mind* (New York: Columbia University Press, 1988).
Franklin, M. B., R. C. Becklen and C. L. Doyle, 'The Influence of Titles on How Paintings Are Seen', *Leonardo* 26(2) (1993): 39–52.
French, Emma, *Selling Shakespeare to Hollywood: The Marketing of Filmed Shakespeare Adaptations from 1989 into the New Millennium* (Hatfield: University of Hertfordshire Press, 2006).

Freytas-Tamura, Kimiko de, 'How Banking Culture Transformed over the Decades', *BBC News* 05.09.12, www.bbc.co.uk/news/business-19463343 (accessed 07.01.13).

Frow, John, 'Signature and Brand', in Jim Collins, ed., *High-Pop: Making Culture into Popular Entertainment* (Malden, MA: Blackwell Publishers, 2002), pp. 56–74.

Frow, John, *Cultural Studies and Cultural Value* (Oxford: Clarendon Press, 1995).

Galloway, S. 'Theory-Based Evaluation and the Social Impact of the Arts', *Cultural Trends* 18(2) (2009): 125–148.

Geertz, Clifford, *After the Fact* (Cambridge, MA: Harvard University Press, 1995).

Geertz, Clifford, *The Interpretation of Cultures* (London: Fontana Press, 1993).

Geertz, Clifford, *Works and Lives: The Anthropologist as Author* (Oxford: Blackwell, Polity Press, 1989).

Gibson, Lisanne, 'In Defence of Instrumentality', *Cultural Trends* 17(4) (2008): 247–257.

Goffman, Erving, *Gender Advertisement* (New York: Harper and Row, 1976).

Gray, Clive, 'Arts Council England and Public Value: A Critical Review', *International Journal of Cultural Policy* 14(2) (2008): 209–214.

Gray, Clive, *The Politics of the Arts in Britain* (Basingstoke: Macmillan, 2000).

Greenblatt, Stephen, *Will in the World* (London: Jonathan Cape, 2004).

Greenblatt, Stephen, *Shakespearean Negotiations: the Circulation of Social Energy in Renaissance England* (Oxford: Clarendon Press, 1988).

Greg, W. W., *The Editorial Problem in Shakespeare* (Oxford: Clarendon Press, 1942).

Guillory, John, *Cultural Capital: The Problem of Literary Canon Formation* (Chicago: University of Chicago Press, 1993).

Hackett, Helen, *Shakespeare and Elizabeth: The Meeting of Two Myths* (Princeton, NJ: Princeton University Press, 2009).

Halpern, Richard, *Shakespeare Among the Moderns* (Ithaca, NY: Cornell University Press, 1997).

Hasitschkaa, Werner, Peter Goldslegera and Tasos Zembylas, 'Cultural Institutions Studies: Investigating the Transformation of Cultural Goods', *The Journal of Arts Management, Law, and Society* 35(2) (2005): 147–158.

Hebdige, Dick, *Hiding in the Light: On Images and Things* (London: Routledge, 1988).

Heminges, John and Henry Condell, 'The Epistle Dedicatory', *Comedies, Histories, Tragedies* (1623), in Stanley Wells and Gary Taylor, eds,

William Shakespeare: The Complete Works (Oxford: Clarendon Press, 1988), pp. xliv–xlv.

Hesmondhalgh, David, *The Cultural Industries*, 2nd edition (London: Sage Publications, 2007; first edition 2002).

Hesmondhalgh, David and Andy C. Pratt, 'Cultural Industries and Cultural Policy', *International Journal of Cultural Policy* 11(1) (2005): 1–14.

Hewison, Robert, *Culture and Consensus: England, Art and Politics since 1940* (London: Methuen, 1995).

Hewison, Robert and John Holden, 'Public Value as a Framework for Analysing the Value of Heritage: The Ideas', in Kate Clark, ed., *Capturing the Public Value of Heritage: The Proceedings of the London Conference, 25–26.01.06* (Swindon: English Heritage, 2006).

Hewison, Robert, John Holden and Samuel Jones, *All Together Now: A Creative Approach to Organisational Change* (London: Demos, 2010).

Hirschman, Elizabeth C., 'Evolutionary Branding', *Psychology and Marketing* 27(6) (June 2010): 568–583.

Hodgdon, Barbara, *The Shakespeare Trade: Performances and Appropriations* (Philadelphia: University of Pennsylvania Press, 1998).

Holden, John, *Democratic Culture: Opening up the Arts to Everyone* (London: Demos, 2008).

Holden, John, *Cultural Value and the Crisis of Legitimacy* (London: Demos, 2006).

Holden, John, *Capturing Cultural Value: How Culture Has Become a Tool of Government Policy* (London: Demos, 2004).

Holderness, Graham, *Cultural Shakespeare: Essays in the Shakespeare Myth* (Hatfield: University of Hertfordshire Press, 2001).

Holt, Douglas, *How Brands Become Icons: The Principles of Cultural Branding* (Boston, MA: Harvard Business School Press, 2004).

Honigmann, E. A. J., *The Texts of 'Othello' and Shakespearian revision* (London: Routledge, 1996).

Hooper-Greenhill, Eilean, Jocelyn Dodd, Lisanne Gibson and Ceri Jones, *Evaluation of the Education and Community Strategy for the Madonna of the Pinks 2004 – 2007* (Leicester: University of Leicester Research Centre for Museums and Galleries, 2007). www2.le.ac.uk/departments/museumstud ies/rcmg/projects/madonna-of-the-pinks/MOTP.pdf (accessed 14.06.13).

Horner, Louise, Rohit Lekhi and Ricardo Blaug, *Deliberative Democracy and the Role of Public Managers: Final Report of The Work Foundation's Public Value Consortium – November 2006* (London: The Work Foundation, 2006).

House of Commons, *First Report – DCMS – National Museums and Galleries: Funding and Free Admission* (London: HMSO, 2002).

Ingram, Martin, *The Church Courts, Sex and Marriage in England 1570–1640* (Cambridge: Cambridge University Press, 1987).
Irish, Tracy, 'World Shakespeare Festival', *Teaching Shakespeare* 1 (2012): 5.
Jameson, Fredric, *Postmodernism, or the Cultural Logic of Late Capitalism* (London: Verso, 1991).
Jameson, Fredric, 'Postmodernism, or the Cultural Logic of late Capitalism', *New Left Review*, 146 (July–August, 1984): 53–93.
Jameson, Fredric, *Marxism and Form* (Princeton, NJ: Princeton University Press, 1971).
Jeffcutt, Paul and Andy C. Pratt, 'Editorial: Managing Creativity in the Cultural Industries', *Creativity and Innovation Management* 11(4) (December 2002): 225–233.
Jowell, Tessa, *Government and the Value of Culture* (London: Department of Culture, Media and Sport, 2004).
Keaney, Emily, *The Arts Debate: Arts Community and Stakeholder Findings* (London: Arts Council England, 2007).
Keaney, Emily, *Public Value and the Arts: Literature Review* (London: Arts Council England, 2006).
Kelly, Gavin, Geoff Mulgan and Stephen Muers, *Creating Public Value: An Analytical Framework for Public Service E-Reform* (London: Cabinet Office, 2002).
Kennedy, Dennis, *The Spectator and the Spectacle: Audiences in Modernity and Postmodernity* (Cambridge: Cambridge University Press, 2009).
Kennedy, Dennis, 'Shakespeare and Cultural Tourism', *Theatre Journal* 50(2) (1998): 175–188.
Kotler, Philip, *Marketing Insights from A to Z: 80 Concepts Every Manager Needs to Know* (Hoboken, NJ: John Wiley & Sons, 2003).
Kroeber, A. L. and Clyde Kluckhorn, *Culture: A Critical Review of Concepts and Definitions*, Papers of the Peabody Museum, vol. 47, no. 1 (Cambridge, MA: Harvard University, 1952).
Kuper, Adam, *Culture: The Anthropologists' Account* (Cambridge, MA: Harvard University Press, 1999).
Laera, Margherita, 'In Praise of Translation: On Watching Shakespeare in a Foreign Language', *Year of Shakespeare*, posted 28.05.12 http://bloggingshakespeare.com/year-of-shakespeare-in-praise-of-translation (accessed 14.06.13).
Lanchester, John, *Whoops: Why Everyone Owes Everyone and No-One Can Pay* (London: Penguin Books, 2010).
Lanier, Douglas, 'Shakespeare™: Myth and Biographical Fiction', in Robert Shaughnessy, ed., *The Cambridge Companion to Shakespeare and Popular Culture* (Cambridge: Cambridge University Press, 2007), pp. 93–113.

Lanier, Douglas, *Shakespeare and Modern Popular Culture* (Oxford: Oxford University Press, 2002).
Leadbetter, Charles, *We-Think: Mass Innovation not Mass Production: The Power of Mass Creativity* (London: Profile Books, 2008).
Lemos, Noah M., *Intrinsic Value: Concept and Warrant* (Cambridge: Cambridge University Press, 1994).
Linnemann, Emily, *The Value of Shakespeare in Twenty-First-Century Publicly-Funded Theatre in England*, PhD thesis, University of Birmingham, 2011.
Lochman, Daniel T., Maritere López and Lorna Hutson, eds, *Discourses and Representations of Friendship in Early Modern Europe, 1500–1700* (Farnham: Ashgate, 2011).
MacDonald, Robert A. and Chuck Thomas, 'Millennial Net Values: Disconnects between Library Culture and Millennial Generation Values', *Educause Quarterly*, 29.04.06.
MacGregor, Neil, *A History of the World in 100 Objects* (London: Viking, 2011).
McLuskie, Kathleen, 'Materiality and the Market: The Lady Elizabeth's Men and the Challenge of Theatre History' in Richard Dutton, ed., *The Oxford Handbook of Early Modern Theatre* (Oxford: Oxford University Press, 2009), pp. 429–440.
McLuskie, Kathleen, 'Figuring the Consumer for Early Modern Drama', in Bryan Reynolds and William N. West, eds, *Rematerializing Shakespeare: Authority and Representation on the Early Modern English Stage* (Basingstoke: Palgrave, 2005), pp. 186–206.
McMaster, Brian, *Supporting Excellence in the Arts: From Measurement to Judgement* (London: Department for Culture, Media and Sport, 2008).
Middleton, Michael R. and Julie M. Lee, 'Cultural Institutions and Web 2.0', Fourth Seminar on Research Applications in Information and Library Studies (RAILS 4) (Melbourne: RMIT University, 2007).
Miles, Andrew and R. Clarke, 'The Arts in Criminal Justice: A Study of Research Feasibility' (University of Manchester: Centre for Research on Socio-Economic Change, 2006).
Miles, Andrew and Alice Sullivan, *Understanding the Relationship between Taste and Value in Culture and Sport* (London: Department of Culture, Media and Sport, 2006).
Moor, Liz, 'Branding Consultants as Cultural Intermediaries', *Sociological Review* 56(3) (2008): 408–428.
Moore, Henrietta L., *Still Life: Hopes, Desires and Satisfactions* (London: Polity Press, 2011).
Moore, Mark, *Creating Public Value: Strategic Management in Government* (Cambridge, MA: Harvard University Press, 1995).

Mousley, Andy, *Re-Humanising Shakespeare: Literary Humanism, Wisdom and Modernity* (Edinburgh: Edinburgh University Press, 2007).
Mulhern, Francis, *Culture/Metaculture* (Abingdon: Routledge, 2000).
Murdoch, James, 'The Absence of Trust', Edinburgh International Television Festival MacTaggart Lecture, 28.08.09, http://image.guardian.co.uk/sys-files/Media/documents/2009/08/28/JamesMurdochMacTaggartLecture.pdf (accessed 14.06.13).
Murphy, Andrew, *Shakespeare for the People: Working-Class Readers, 1800–1900* (Cambridge and New York: Cambridge University Press, 2008).
Murphy, Andrew, *Shakespeare in Print: A History and Chronology of Shakespeare Publishing* (Cambridge: Cambridge University Press, 2003).
Neelands, Jonothan, *Learning through Imagined Experience: The Role of Drama in the National Curriculum* (London: Hodder and Stoughton, 1992).
Newbolt, Sir Henry, *The Teaching of English in England. Being the Report of the Departmental Committee Appointed by the President of the Board of Education to Inquire into the Position of English in the Educational System of England* (London: HMSO, 1921).
Oakley, Kate, 'The Disappearing Arts: Creativity and Innovation after the Creative Industries', *International Journal of Cultural Policy* 15(4) (2009): 403–413.
O'Brien, Dave, *Measuring the Value of Culture: An AHRC Briefing Paper*, in AHRC workshop, 'Valuing Culture: Developing a Toolkit and Evidence to Meet Policy Needs', 2011.
O'Brien, Dave, *Measuring the Value of Culture: A Report to the Department for Culture Media and Sport* (London: Department for Culture, Media and Sport, 2010).
Opinion Leader, *Arts Council England: Public Value Deliberative Research* (London: Opinion Leader, 2007).
Phillipson, Nicholas, *Adam Smith: An Enlightened Life* (London: Allen Lane, 1978).
Pine, B. Joseph, II and James H. Gilmore, *The Experience Economy: Work is Theater and Every Business is a Stage* (Boston, MA: Harvard Business Press, 1999).
Polito, Mary, '"Warriors for the Working Day": Shakespeare's Professionals', *Shakespeare* 2(1) (2006): 1–23.
Pringle, Hamish, 'Creative Britain', in Shelagh Wright, John Newbigin, John Kieffer, John Holden and Tom Bewick, eds, *After The Crunch* (London: British Council, 2009), pp. 56–57.
Proudfoot, Richard, 'New Conservatism and the Theatrical Text: Editing Shakespeare for the Third Millennium', in William R. Elton and John M. Mucciolo, eds, *The Shakespeare International Yearbook, 2: Where*

Are We Now in Shakespeare Studies? (Aldershot: Ashgate, 2002), pp. 127–142.
Purcell, Stephen, *Popular Shakespeare: Simulation and Subversion on the Modern Stage* (Basingstoke: Palgrave Macmillan, 2009).
Quinn, Anthony, *Jack Vettriano* (London: Pavilion Books, 2005).
Raman, Shankar, *Renaissance Literature and Postcolonial Studies* (Edinburgh: Edinburgh University Press, 2011).
Rose, Jonathan, *The Intellectual Life of the British Working Class* (New Haven, CT and London: Yale University Press, 2001).
Rossi, Peter H. and Richard A. Berk, 'Varieties of Normative Consensus', *American Sociological Review*, 50(3) (1985): 333–347.
Roth, Alvin, 'Repugnance as a Constraint on Markets', *Journal of Economic Perspectives* 21(3) (Summer 2007): 37–58.
Rumbold, Kate, 'Shakespeare and the Stratford Jubilee', in Fiona Ritchie and Peter Sabor, eds, *Shakespeare and the Eighteenth Century* (Cambridge: Cambridge University Press, 2012), pp. 254–276.
Sahlins, Marshall, *Culture in Practice* (New York: Zone Books, 2005).
Sahlins, Marshall, *Stone Age Economics* (London: Routledge, 2004).
Sandel, Michael, *What Money Can't Buy* (London: Allen Lane, 2012).
Sanders, Julie, *Adaptation and Appropriation* (London and New York: Routledge, 2006).
Sarton, George, *Six Wings: Men of Science in the Renaissance* (London: Bodley Head, 1958).
Schalkwyk, David, *Hamlet's Dreams: The Robben Island Shakespeare*, Shakespeare Now Series (London: Bloomsbury Academic, 2013).
Scheff, Thomas J., 'Towards a Sociological Model of Consensus', *American Sociological Review* 32(1) (1967): 32–46.
Schiller, Herbert, *Culture Inc.: The Corporate Takeover of Public Expression* (Oxford: Oxford University Press, 1989).
Schlesinger, Philip, 'Creativity: From Discourse to Doctrine?', *Screen* 48(3) (Autumn 2007): 377–387.
Schroeder, Jonathan E. and Miriam Salzer-Mörling, eds, *Brand Culture* (London and New York: Frank Cass, 2006).
Scott, C. 'Exploring the Evidence Base for Museum Value', *Museum Management and Curatorship* 24(3) (2009): 195–212.
Seale, Clive, Giampietro Gobo, Jaber F. Gubrium and David Silverman, 'Introduction: Inside Qualitative Research', in Clive Seale, Giampietro Gobo, Jaber F. Gubrium and David Silverman, eds, *Qualitative Research Practice* (London: SAGE Publications, 2004), pp. 1–11.
Selwood, Sara, 'The Politics of Data Collection', *Cultural Trends* 12(47) (2002): 13–84.
Sennett, Richard, *The Culture of the New Capitalism* (New Haven, CT and London: Yale University Press, 2006).

Shakespeare, William, *King Lear*, ed. R. A. Foakes, The Arden Shakespeare (Walton-on Thames: Thomas Nelson and Sons, 1997).
Shakespeare, William, *Othello*, ed. E. A. J. Honingmann, The Arden Shakespeare (Walton-on-Thames: Thomas Nelson and Sons, 1997).
Shakespeare's Globe, *Globe to Globe: 37 Plays, 37 Languages* (London: Shakespeare's Globe, 2012).
Shaughnessy, Robert, 'Falstaff's Belly: Pathos, Prosthetics and Performance', *Shakespeare Survey* 63 (2010): 63–77.
Shaughnessy, Robert, ed., *The Cambridge Companion to Shakespeare and Popular Culture* (Cambridge: Cambridge University Press, 2007).
Silverman, Debora, *Selling Culture: Bloomingdale's, Diana Vreeland, and the New Aristocracy of Taste in Reagan's America* (New York: Pantheon, 1986).
Skeggs, Beverley, *Class, Self, Culture* (London: Routledge, 2004).
Smith, Adam, *An Enquiry into the Nature and Causes of The Wealth of Nations*, ed. R. H. Campbell and A. S. Skinner (Cambridge: Cambridge University Press, 1978).
Smith, Dorothy E., *The Conceptual Practices of Power: A Feminist Sociology of Knowledge* (Toronto: University of Toronto Press, 1990, repr. 1995).
Somers, Margaret R., 'The Privatisation of Citizenship: How to Unthink a Knowledge Culture', in Victoria E. Bonnell and Lynn Hunt, eds, *Beyond the Cultural Turn* (Berkeley: University of California Press, 1999), pp. 121–164.
St Clair, William, *The Reading Nation in the Romantic Period* (Cambridge: Cambridge University Press, 2004).
Stochholm, Johannes, *Garrick's Folly: The Stratford Jubilee of 1769* (London: Methuen, 1964).
Sundbo, Jon, 'Innovation in the Experience Economy: A Taxonomy of Innovation Organisations', *The Service Industries Journal* 29(4) (2009): 431–455.
Theatre Assessment 2009 (London: Arts Council England, 2009), www.artscouncil.org.uk/media/uploads/publications/theatreassessment.pdf (accessed 04.06.13).
Thorpe, Amanda, 'Mary Beard, the Classicist with the Common Touch', *The Observer*, 29.04.12, www.guardian.co.uk/theobserver/2012/apr/29/observer-profile-mary-beard (accessed 07.01.12).
Throop, C. Jason, 'Articulating Experience', *Anthropological Theory* 3(2) (2003): 219–241.
Turner, Fred, 'The Universal Solvent: Mediations on the Marriage of World Cultures', in *Interculturalism and Performance*, ed. Bonnie Marranca and Gautam Dasgupta (New York: Performing Arts Journal Publications, 1991), pp. 249–265.
Turner, Henry S., 'The Problem of the More-than-One: Friendship,

Calculation, and Political Association in The Merchant of Venice', *Shakespeare Quarterly* 57 (2006): 413–442.
Turner, Henry S., *The Culture of Capital* (London: Routledge, 2002).
Tylor, E. B., *Primitive Culture*, 2 vols (London: John Murray, 1871).
Walker, Rob, *I'm With The Brand: The Secret Dialogue Between What We Buy and Who We Are* (London: Constable, 2008).
Watson, Nicola, *The Literary Tourist* (Basingstoke: Palgrave Macmillan, 2006).
Wells, Stanley, *Shakespeare: A Dramatic Life* (London: Sinclair Stevenson, 1994).
Wells, Stanley and Gary Taylor, eds, *William Shakespeare: The Complete Works* (Oxford: Clarendon Press, 1988).
Williams, Raymond, 'Culture is Ordinary' (1958), in Imre Szeman and Timothy Kaposy, eds, *Cultural Theory: An Anthology* (Chichester: Wiley Blackwell, 2010).
Williams, Raymond, *Marxism and Literature* (Oxford: Oxford University Press, 1977).
Williams, Raymond, *Keywords: A Vocabulary of Culture and Society* (London: Fontana, 1976).
Williams, Raymond, *Resources of Hope: Culture, Democracy, Socialism*, ed. R. Gable (London: Verso, 1989).
Willis, Paul, *Common Culture: Symbolic Work at Play in the Everyday Cultures of the Young* (Milton Keynes: Open University, 1990).
Work Foundation, The, *Public Value in Culture, the Arts and Broadcasting: A Background Presentation* (London: The Work Foundation, 2006).
Worthen, W. B. 'Hyper-Shakespeare', *Performance Research* 7(1) (2002): 7–21.

Index

access 146, 152, 156, 164, 169, 184–7, 189–90, 193–5
Anderson, Perry 244
anthropology 5, 86–90, 107, 154, 187
Arnold, Matthew 183–4
Arts Council England (ACE) 4, 15, 18–19, 20, 23, 119, 144–6, 149, 157–70, 171, 173, 183–5, 188, 197, 232, 243
(as former Arts Council of Great Britain) 229
Arts Debate, The 157, 160–7
Arts and Humanities Research Council (AHRC) 9, 29, 55, 172, 191, 207
audience 6, 12, 14, 19, 21, 29, 54, 76, 99, 119, 122, 128, 129, 137, 151–2, 157, 164, 168, 169, 170, 174, 176, 188–95, 197, 204, 206, 210, 229–30, 232–4, 244–5, 252

Bate, Jonathan 55–7,
Benjamin, Walter 84, 95, 107, 202
Blair, Tony (Prime Minister 1997–2008) 148, 183–6
Bourdieu, Pierre 84, 104–5, 186–7, 190
Boyd Michael (Artistic Director of the RSC, 2003–12) 134–9, 203
Bristol, Michael 218
British Library 96, 174, 188–9, 196, 198, 202–3
British Museum 9–11, 95, 111–12, 117–18, 119–21, 128, 129, 151, 202–3, 205, 231, 245
British Shakespeare Association (BSA) 18, 21–2, 29, 53
Burt, Richard 125, 220

Carey, John 102–4, 157
Connor, Steven 32–5, 37, 44, 51, 92, 106, 155
Council for the Encouragement of Music and the Arts (CEMA) 149
Creativity 6, 114, 146, 154, 166, 170, 176, 187, 189, 193–5, 199, 202, 204–6, 213, 223

Department for Culture, Media and Sport (DCMS) 20, 145, 170–3, 175, 242
digital technology, 195, 197, 200
Doran, Gregory (Artistic Director of the RSC, from 2012) 129, 190, 203

Eagleton, Terry 25, 32, 38, 52
education 9, 25, 30, 33, 36, 51, 93, 98, 105, 119, 124, 130, 139, 145, 148–52, 161, 163, 164, 168, 185, 187, 188, 190, 195, 201, 230–1, 246, 249
higher education 147, 156, 174–5, 206, 246
Eliot, T.S. 83, 85, 156
experience 6, 8, 10–11, 16, 24–6, 30, 106, 126, 134, 136, 137–40, 146–76, 187–8, 191–204, 229, 243–6, 248–9

Featherstone, Mike 6, 14, 43, 96–7, 105–7
Fiske, John 123
Forgan, Liz (Chair, Arts Council England, 2009–13) 15, 17
Frow, John 106, 212, 221–3, 224
funding 2, 4, 7, 10, 12, 15–17, 19–20, 23, 96, 104, 109–10, 125, 144–7, 149, 152, 157, 161, 167–9, 171–4, 188, 198, 205–6, 231–2, 242–4

Geertz, Clifford 88–9, 164
Gibson, Lisanne 144, 149, 186, 206
Goffmann, Erving 121
Greenblatt, Stephen 53–6, 84
Guillory, John 123

Heritage Lottery Fund 4, 97–8, 149, 153, 186
Hewison, Robert 153–6, 162, 163, 230
high and low culture 7, 11, 106, 109, 116, 118, 125, 152, 154, 206, 221–2, 224, 226–7, 244
Holden, John 16–17, 23, 153–6, 162–3, 187
Holderness, Graham 52

Hytner, Nicholas (Director of the National Theatre, 2003–) 184–6

Internet 129, 195–8, 205, 225–6

Jowell, Tessa (Secretary of State for Culture, Media and Sport, 2001–07) 9–14, 146, 148–53, 170–1, 173, 241–2

Kennedy, Dennis 139, 198, 244
Kuper, Adam 86, 90, 244

Lanier, Douglas 133, 210–12, 222
Lemos, Noah 154–5

MacGregor, Neil (Director of the British Museum, 2002–) 9, 10, 111, 151
McMaster, Sir Brian (Director of the Edinburgh Festival 1992–2006) 167–9
Mandela, Nelson 128–130
market 4–7, 37–45, 46–9, 52, 62–4, 71–80, 83, 96–109, 100–2, 112, 116, 120–5, 145, 152, 186–9, 206, 213–14, 218, 221–5, 229–30, 235, 243–4, 247
marketing 42–3, 119, 129, 160, 166, 187, 192, 196, 201–2, 206, 218–19, 222–8, 231, 233, 245
mass culture 19, 107, 195, 221, 225
mass production 13–14, 108–11, 118, 145, 170, 191, 193, 221–2, 224, 226
Miles, Andrew and Clarke, Rebecca 20–1
Miles, Andrew and Sullivan, Alice 16
Moore, Henrietta 92–4
Murdoch, James 100–4

narrative 4–5, 19–30, 42, 52–7, 66–78, 83–5, 89, 93, 100, 124, 126–39, 157, 166, 173, 175, 195, 199, 219, 233, 248–9
National Trust 109, 219
New Public Management 149
new technology 85, 189, 203–4, 225, 226

O'Brien, Dave 172–3, 175–6
Olivier Mythodrama 126–7
Olympic Games, (London 2012) (including 'Cultural Olympiad') 117–20, 176, 231–2
Owen, Diana (Director, Shakespeare Birthplace Trust) 204

popular culture 183, 218, 221, 239
public service reform 149–50

Raphael, 'Madonna of the Pinks' 12–13, 97–100, 104, 106, 156

Royal Shakespeare Company (RSC) 2, 22, 25, 117–18, 119, 129, 132, 137–8, 146, 149–50, 170, 183, 188–92, 194–5, 202–4. 226, 228–31, 233–4, 235, 244

Sahlins, Marshall 86–7, 89, 108
Sandel, Michael 44–48
Shakespeare, William
  Antony and Cleopatra 62–3
  Cardenio 190
  Hamlet 54, 61–6, 119, 185, 203, 221–4, 243
  The Histories 134–6
  Julius Caesar 117, 128–9, 136, 230
  King Lear 66, 67–8, 69, 72–4, 132–3
  Othello 63–5
  The Merchant of Venice 67–72
  The Tempest 127
  Troilus and Cressida 55, 57–61, 245
  Winter's Tale 125, 245
Shakespeare Birthplace Trust (SBT) 129, 188, 192, 199–202, 203–5
Shakespeare's Globe Theatre (Globe) 117, 188, 191, 202–4, 210, 228, 231–5, 243
Smith, Adam 38–40

television 100–2, 134, 136, 176, 200, 203, 222, 223, 243, 250
theatre 3, 8, 18–19, 21–3, 119, 122, 131–9, 170, 176, 183–6, 191, 192, 193–5, 197, 203–4, 218, 221, 227, 228–35
Tylor, E.B., 86, 187

value
  aesthetic 37
  economic 2, 26, 37–8, 41, 44, 163, 170–2, 243
  ethical 47
  exchange 38–42, 46, 48, 61, 67, 112
  intrinsic 32, 38, 39, 45, 51, 52, 56, 62, 112, 138, 145, 150–1, 153–5, 162, 166–7, 189, 190, 202, 203, 243, 245
  institutional 153
  non-rival 5, 77–9, 128, 246
  public 145–7, 149, 153–5, 157–69, 175, 191
  transcendent 2, 5, 34–7, 46, 62, 64, 65, 87, 112, 177, 249
  use-value 38–40, 41, 42, 46, 61, 108
Vettriano, Jack (painter), 'The Singing Butler' 12, 26

Wall, Bruce (Director of the London Shakespeare Workout) 19–20
Williams, Raymond 3, 85, 96, 156, 166
World Shakespeare Festival 138, 176, 202, 226, 230, 231–5